Midget Submarine Commander

*'He was a man whose gallant and distinguished
service to his country will always be remembered'*

Midget Submarine Commander

The Life of Rear Admiral Godfrey
Place VC, CB, CVO, DSC

19 July 1921–27 December 1994

Paul Watkins

Pen & Sword
MARITIME

First published in Great Britain in 2012 by
Pen & Sword Military
an imprint of
Pen & Sword Books Ltd
47 Church Street
Barnsley
South Yorkshire
S70 2AS

ISBN 978-1-84884-800-9

A CIP catalogue record for this book is available from the
British Library.

Typeset in 11pt Ehrhardt by
Mac Style, Beverley, E. Yorkshire

Printed and bound in the UK by CPI Group (UK) Ltd, Croydon,
CRO 4YY

Pen & Sword Books Ltd incorporates the Imprints of Pen & Sword
Aviation, Pen & Sword Family History, Pen & Sword Maritime, Pen &
Sword Military, Pen & Sword Discovery, Wharncliffe Local History,
Wharncliffe True Crime, Wharncliffe Transport, Pen & Sword Select,
Pen & Sword Military Classics, Leo Cooper, The Praetorian Press,
Remember When, Seaforth Publishing and Frontline Publishing.

For a complete list of Pen & Sword titles please contact
PEN & SWORD BOOKS LIMITED
47 Church Street, Barnsley, South Yorkshire, S70 2AS, England
E-mail: enquiries@pen-and-sword.co.uk
Website: www.pen-and-sword.co.uk

Contents

Foreword

Hiding over the horizon from the coast of Nigeria in case the nascent Biafran War exploded and threatened the lives of British nationals, HMS *Albion* sweltered, conserving fuel with an enhanced Marine Commando on board. Having sailed unexpectedly, we midshipmen had to take our planned fleet board in the ship rather than ashore in HMS *Nelson*. I was the senior midshipman of the gunroom and remember with some trepidation entering the Captain's cabin for part of that oral examination. The Commanding Officer was Captain B. C. G. Place VC, DSC and in my eyes and those of his men a god. Many years later when I was a Rear Admiral serving as Naval Secretary, I had the sad duty of phoning his widow within 24 hours of his death to ascertain whether she would like the nation to organize and fund a funeral or a memorial service, an honour extended to winners of the VC or GC. So those were my only personal links with this gallant and complex officer. Little did I think that after further passage of time I would be asked to write a foreword to what is, surprisingly, the first biography of him. At that fleet board he said to me, "Young man if you take life a little more seriously you could go to the very top." I did, and he was right.

Godfrey Place was the son of a barrister who was highly decorated serving in the army in the First World War, winning a DSO and MC. He became a member of the colonial service, and Godfrey's early years were similar to those of so many children of that period whose fathers ran the Empire. He joined Dartmouth and then very quickly the submarine service. With the coming of war he was soon in the thick of things and won a DSC assisting in sinking an Italian submarine when serving in HMS *Unbeaten*. Volunteering for hazardous duty, he became the only long-service officer serving in the X-craft or midget submarine force. He won his VC for the remarkable attack on the *Tirpitz* and became a German prisoner of war. In POW camp he was involved in the 'Albert RN' escape plans. But on return to the UK after the war, a rather insensitive appointer told him he had to go to a submarine backwater in view of all he had missed as a prisoner of war. He turned his back on the submarine service and threw himself into flying, seeing action in the Korean War as a member of the Fleet Air Arm. He was the only officer I ever met who was entitled to Pilot's wings and, in modern parlance, the submariner's dolphins.

Place could at times be headstrong and suffered no self doubt, invariably assuming that what he thought was correct, that he was right and others wrong. He was very harsh on those who did not live up to what he expected of them, and particularly if they let him down. On retirement, amongst many other roles, he became Chairman of the VC and GC Association and showed the kinder and compassionate side of his nature in becoming a friend to all the members.

Paul Watkins has produced a long overdue book which will be of interest both to those who wonder about what makes a man a hero, and to historians who can sift the large amount of detail about the less well known episodes of Place's naval career.

Admiral The Rt Hon. The Lord West of Spithead GCB, DSC, PC
First Sea Lord 2002–2006

Preface

In the early months of 1966 England was preparing to host the World Cup, and there was much speculation as to whether the host nation would be able to win the Jules Rimet trophy. As a young boy, still at primary school, I was always keen to follow the news, including football, by reading my father's copy of the *Daily Telegraph*. It was in February 1966 that I read about Captain Godfrey Place, VC, who had recently assumed command of the commando carrier HMS *Albion* in the Far East. His picture appeared in the paper, along with a very short summary of his career in the Royal Navy. Over the following years I have pursued an interest in both naval history and the Victoria Cross, and have been fortunate to read many of the excellent biographies written about men who have been awarded the country's highest award for gallantry.

Almost forty years after seeing the picture of Godfrey Place I decided that, with a little more time on my hands, I should read his biography; I was aware that he had died in 1994 and was certain that someone would have written his biography in the intervening years. I was wrong. I started to research his naval career and was immediately struck by the extent of his service in the Royal Navy. Not only had he been awarded the Victoria Cross for his part in the midget submarine attack on the German battleship *Tirpitz*, an operation described by Winston Churchill as 'an audacious and heroic attack', but he had learnt to fly and became a Fleet Air Arm pilot, flying from the aircraft carrier HMS *Glory* in the Korean War. But there was more: he had been a prisoner of war, and his early service in the Second World War involved appointments to both HMS *Newcastle* and to submarines based at Malta. Later in his career there were few, if any, conflict areas around the world where Godfrey Place did not serve his nation.

At the time of his retirement in 1970 Godfrey Place was the only serving member of the Royal Navy holding the Victoria Cross; since that day in April 1970 no one else has held it. His devotion to duty did not stop at retirement and led him to serve as Chairman of the Victoria Cross and George Cross Association for over twenty years, during which time he was very much the spokesman for the most exclusive club in the world.

But what of the man himself? I have tried to learn and understand more about him: his upbringing, the tragedies that affected his family whilst he was still young and his response to them. And what of his background? Was he from a family with a strong naval tradition? For a man who saw so many friends and colleagues die in the Second World War, why was he always in the 'thick of it' over the ensuing twenty-five years. And although he reached flag rank in the Royal Navy, why did he not reach the highest positions in the service, as had been predicted by at least one of his Commanding Officers?

In writing this book, I have tried to answer some of these questions. Wherever possible, I have tried to tell the story of his life using his own words; I have made use of accounts published in books as well as a sound recording that he made for the Imperial War Museum in 1988. However, I have also been privileged to have been able to explore a significant archive of unpublished material, courtesy of Godfrey Place's family, who have allowed me unfettered access to this, and to whom I am exceptionally grateful.

As to whether I have succeeded in answering the many questions that I posed myself, that is a matter for the reader to decide. I hope however, that in writing this book I have been able to detail the life of a man who I believe was a true hero, in the established sense of the word. His determination and gallantry in the face of the enemy has allowed me, and many others of my generation, to enjoy a freedom which might not have been possible if it had not been for the courage and commitment of Godfrey Place and those who served with him.

Paul Watkins
Somerset, 2011

Acknowledgements

I have been most fortunate to have received so much help and assistance from so many people in researching and writing this book. Without them it would not have come to fruition, and all have been very kind in assisting me.

I must firstly express my thanks to Godfrey Place's family, Mrs Althea Place, Charles Place, Andrea Gray and Melanie Place. They, and their respective families, have all have been exceptionally helpful, and I am especially grateful for being allowed access to the archive of material held by them. It was a remarkable and humbling privilege to read the contents of the archive, especially the letters between Godfrey Place and Althea both before and after their marriage. Thank you.

Tony Kenber has helped in providing insights into other aspects of family life, and I would also like to thank Valerie and Alan Bramwell for providing information about the Hawkins family.

Mrs Didy Grahame has been most helpful in providing information about that most exclusive and deserving collection of gallant men and women, the Victoria Cross and George Cross Association.

It has been a privilege and honour to have been able to talk with three men who took part in 'Operation Source', and I wish to thank John Lorimer, Robert Aitken, and Roland Hindmarsh for taking time to talk to me, and to acknowledge their remarkable bravery in what was a most audacious, brilliant and daring operation.

I wish to thank staff at Pen & Sword involved with the production of this book; Henry Wilson who so kindly offered me a contract for the book, based on my very early writings, Jon Wilkinson for the design of the jacket, George Chamier for his editorial review and input and the many others who have contributed to the completion of this book.

A number of individuals have provided information about Godfrey Place, by granting me interviews, sending photographs or responding to letters and emails. Wherever possible I have used the information provided by them, and I am grateful to: Simon Houfe, Tom Cadwallader, Andrew Sewell, Arthur Gillan, Bill Clarke, Geoffrey Higgs, Admiral Sir John Treacher, Rear Admiral Mike Stacey, Harry 'Dusty' Miller, Patrick Bruce-Gardyne, Terry

Parker, Eric Carter, Christine Warren, Paul Seward, Anne Yates, Cathy Pugh, Diane Coleman, Admiral Sir William O'Brien, Denis Askham, Vice Admiral Sir James Weatherall, Annie Macaulay, Andrew Mackay, the late Captain G.E. Hunt, Admiral of the Fleet Sir Benjamin Bathurst, Dr Jane Harrold, Vice Admiral Sir Edward Anson, Derek Redman, Jack Harrall, Philip Harrall, David van Lennep, David Evans, Diana Mason, Paula Volkes, Rear Admiral Robin Hogg, Dr Basil Morson, Captain Eric Brown, Field Marshall the Lord Bramall, Rodney Agar, Philip Gibbons, Tim Ayers, Nigel Kelland and the late Peter Cornish, George Malcolmson, Captain Richard McCandless, Bill and Anne Lavender, Dr Alan Borg, Dick Husk, Admiral Sir Raymond Lygo, Geoffrey Barwell, 'Windy' Gale, David Hamilton, William Pakenham, Jim Worlding, John Lefaucheur, Pete Wilson, David Hunt, Tony Bailey, Clive Lambird, Clive Matthews, Colin Davies, Bob Beacock, David Evans, Douglas Cramp, Dennis Rigley, Gavin Read, Stan Laurie, Mike McAllister, Michael Page, Colin Jenkins, Cerwyl Jones, Robin Shercliff, Brian Davies, Jack Casemore, Jonathan Brett-Young, Allan Ward, Derek Redman, Carole Carter, Dennis Cooper, Colin MacGregor, Graham Owens, Robert Winkworth, Rachel Wells, Alan Mawbey, Don Currell, Rob Murray, Jack Halliday, Bill Grice, Keith Watson and Alan Burgess.

Much of the material used in the book has been obtained from libraries and museums, and I would like to thank the staff of the following: the Imperial War Museum, the British Library (including staff at the Newspaper Library at Colindale and at the Document Supply Centre at Boston Spa), the National Archives, the National Army Museum, the Fleet Air Arm Museum (especially Barbara Gilbert), the Bute Museum (especially Jean MacMillan), the Royal Naval Museum, Rothesay Library, the Gloucester County Archives, the Worcester County Archives, the Devon Record Office, Cambridge University Library, particularly those responsible for the collection of the Royal Commonwealth Society, Glasgow University Library and Archives, the Royal College of Veterinary Surgeons' Library, North Somerset Libraries, the Folkestone Library, the Torquay Library, the Law Society Library, the Liddell Hart Centre for Military Archives, King's College, London and the Derbyshire Family History Society.

I would also like to thank the archivists at: Trinity College Cambridge, Queens' College Cambridge, Pembroke College, Cambridge, Trinity College, Dublin, St Columba's College, Rathfarnam and the Slade School of Art, University College, London.

It would be wrong not to record the special contribution made by the following: Peter Bevan, who so kindly talked with me about his late brother David, and allowed me access to David's photograph album covering his and Godfrey Place's time at Dartmouth; Charles Brazier, who provided a great deal of information about the history of Kemerton; Mrs Pat McCarthy, who provided me with a most extensive summary of the Tickler family; Michael Olizar, who has helped me with my examination of the archives at the Polish Institute and Sikorski Museum and has provided me with further information about Borys Karnicki and the Polish navy; Charles Coles, who so kindly told me so much about life in Marlag; Rear Admiral Richard Hill, whose contacts with HMS *Cardigan Bay* allowed me to gain a far clearer insight into the ship's role in the Mediterranean; Derek Bamford, who provided a superb first-hand account of his time in HMS *Albion* in 1967; Captain Alan Leahy, who so kindly and carefully took me through the basics of naval aviation; the late Admiral of the Fleet Sir Julian Oswald, who was a great source of information about life on board HMS *Theseus*, serving as he did under two very different men who had each received the Victoria Cross.

Surgeon Rear Admiral Mike Farquharson-Roberts has kindly given me access to his extensive knowledge of life in the Royal Navy, especially of the Royal Naval College, Dartmouth in the inter-war years, and has also been a great sounding board for 'all things navy' as I tried to put my thoughts and findings into an acceptable form.

My great friend Hamish Batten, who so kindly drew the maps showing the attack on the *Tirpitz*, has proved once again that retirement is no barrier to both enjoyment and achievement.

My friends Ian Fraser, Paul Houghton, Stephen Lisney, Ashley Brown, Geoff Pearson, Adrian Hayday, Mike Hansen and Carole Gentry, have all helped me in this project, in one way or another.

Mike Hinton has been a great soul mate, whose attention to detail is second to none, and whose helpful suggestions and continuous support have been most helpful.

And finally my thanks go to Frances Hughes, whose unwavering support, guidance, focus and overall tolerance and understanding has made this book possible. Thank you indeed.

Chapter 1

Under Attack: War in the Mediterranean

As the storm clouds of war gathered over Europe in 1938, politicians and military planners were predicting that naval control of the Mediterranean would be critical to the survival of Britain and its allies. After the declaration of war, the Royal Navy rose to the challenge from both German and Italian forces in the region, with a number of significant naval encounters in 1940, not least the successful attack by the Fleet Air Arm on the Italian navy at Taranto. During 1941, however, the Royal Navy suffered a series of setbacks in the Mediterranean. In November HMS *Ark Royal* was lost at Gibraltar following a torpedo attack from a U-boat, and later that month the battleship HMS *Barham* was attacked off the coast of North Africa by U-331 and sunk with the loss of over 850 men. *Barham* had been patrolling in the company of HMS *Valiant* and HMS *Queen Elizabeth*, the flagship of Admiral Sir Andrew Cunningham GCB, DSO**, Commander-in-Chief, Mediterranean Fleet. Following the loss of *Barham*, *Queen Elizabeth* and *Valiant* returned safely to Alexandria harbour, a supposedly secure and protected anchorage and home to the Mediterranean Fleet. Events in the coming month would reveal how secure the anchorage really was.

Once the fleet had returned to Alexandria harbour, Admiral Cunningham sent a signal in the morning of 18 December warning the fleet that 'attacks on Alexandria harbour by air, boat or human torpedo might be expected in calm weather.' (1) Later that evening, the Italian submarine *Scire* surfaced just outside Alexandria harbour and three human torpedoes were hauled from their transport containers and carefully launched. The human torpedo, also called a *Maiale* (pig), was just over 7 metres long and had a 300kg detachable warhead at the bow. (2) It was manned by two men, who sat astride, and had a speed of up to four and a half knots and a range up to fifteen miles. Just after midnight, the boom across the entrance to Alexandria harbour opened to allow ships of the Royal Navy's 7th Cruiser Squadron to enter the harbour; this provided the perfect opportunity for the Italian frogmen on their torpedoes to sweep through into the harbour, unnoticed by sentries. (3) They placed their explosive charges on the hulls of *Queen*

Elizabeth and *Valiant,* and at 03.05 two frogmen were seen holding on to the forward mooring buoy of *Valiant.* They were apprehended, questioned and removed from the ship. Just before 06.00 the *Valiant's* tannoy sounded 'all hands on deck.' (4) Arriving on deck, men were shaken by a huge explosion under the ship, and soon her quarterdeck was at an angle of five degrees. Less than ten minutes later there was a tremendous explosion amidships of *Queen Elizabeth.* The attack had caused significant damage to both ships; *Queen Elizabeth,* the pride of the fleet, soon listed to starboard as her bow settled gracefully on the floor of the harbour. At 08.00 that morning a Royal Marine guard and band paraded on her quarterdeck, and the white ensign was hoisted as usual to give the pretence that the ship was going about its normal routine. (5) However, this could not mask the seriousness of these attacks, and both ships required extensive repairs in American and South African dockyards before they could serve with the fleet again. Admiral Cunningham wrote to the First Sea Lord and summarised the position:

> We are having shock after shock out here. The damage to the battleships at this time is a disaster. (6)

The loss of the capital ships caused considerable consternation to Winston Churchill, who on 19 January 1942 wrote to the Prime Minister of Australia (John Curtin) to advise him, in confidence, of his 'deadly secret':

> I have already told you of the *Barham* being sunk. I must now inform you that the *Queen Elizabeth* and *Valiant* have both sustained underwater damage from a human torpedo, which put them out of action, one for three and the other for six months. As the enemy do not yet know about these three last-mentioned ships, you will see that we have no need to enlighten them, and I must ask you to keep this last deadly secret to yourself alone.

A day earlier Churchill had written to his Chief of Staff, General Ismay, seeking answers:

> Please report what is being done to emulate the exploits of the Italians in Alexandria harbour and similar methods of this kind ... Is there any reason why we should be incapable of the same kind of scientific aggressive action that the Italians have shown? One would have thought we should have been in the lead. (7)

Over the coming months and years considerable effort would be exerted to emulate the exploits of the Italians, and a crucial figure in this operation would be Sub Lieutenant B.C.G. Place, who at the time of the attack at Alexandria was a young officer serving in HMS *Urge*, a submarine attached to the 10th Submarine Flotilla operating from Malta. He had joined the Royal Navy as a cadet in 1935 and was promoted to Midshipman just prior to the outbreak of war. Over the coming years, his courage, endurance and utter contempt for danger in the face of the enemy, in an operation that was described as 'one of the most courageous acts of all time', would lead to his being awarded the nation's highest award for gallantry, the Victoria Cross. By the autumn of 1942 he would be posted to a secret submarine flotilla created to deploy midget submarines (X-craft) against enemy targets, including the pride of the German navy, the battleship *Tirpitz*. In September 1943 he, in the company of many other brave young submariners, would dine on board HMS *Titania*, the night before they left for 'Operation Source' (the attack on the *Tirpitz*). The dinner was hosted by Rear Admiral C.B. Barry DSO, the former Captain of *Queen Elizabeth*, who as Flag Officer Submarines had ultimate responsibility for the forthcoming mission. Some of the men would not return; others, including Lieutenant Place, would, but only after nearly two years of captivity. On his release in May 1945, Place would continue to serve in the Royal Navy for a further twenty-five years, during which he would be involved in numerous conflicts on and above the waves. He would have the distinction of being the last serving member of the Royal Navy to hold the Victoria Cross, and his career would be testimony to his unending sense of duty to the Royal Navy and to his country.

Chapter 2

A Nomad for the Navy

Basil Charles Godfrey Place was born on 19 July 1921 at Wintercott, Little Malvern, a village over fifty miles from the nearest coast, into a family with few, if any, recent connections to the Royal Navy. He was the first and only son of Major and Mrs Godfrey Place. At the time of his birth, his father was some 4,000 miles away in Africa, and his mother and sister were living in rented accommodation. It was a somewhat inauspicious start in life for a boy who would later be awarded his country's highest award for gallantry.

His father, Charles Godfrey Morris Place, known professionally as Godfrey, was the only child of Mr and Mrs George William Place, and was born on 2 November 1886, at Ranchi in Bengal, some 400 miles from the Indian capital, Calcutta. George Place was an Irishman, born in 1852 in Dublin, who later studied law at Trinity College Dublin. He successfully passed the entrance examination for the Indian Colonial Service in 1873, and arrived in Assam in November 1875 to start work as an assistant commissioner. After leaving Assam he served in Bengal until 1900 when he retired from the service and returned to Dublin. He was married to Henrietta (neé Usher), who was also born in Dublin. Later in life Charles Place acquired the nickname of Pat, and this is used in this book, rather than Godfrey, so as to minimise possible confusion with his own son (who changed his name from Basil to Godfrey, following the death of his father.)

Pat was a true character, a fun-loving out-going person but one who also had an obvious and strong sense of duty, both to his family and his work. Despite being born in India, Pat was described by his own son as being 'intensely Irish'. Pat was educated at St Columba's College, Rathfarnam, a Protestant school south of Dublin, joining the school in 1899 at the age of thirteen. After leaving school he followed in his father's footsteps to Trinity College Dublin to read History and Law, graduating BA and LLB in 1908. At Trinity he was known as 'Dobbie' Place, a nickname that he soon lost after graduation. Pat was considered one of the most brilliant and versatile Trinity men of his day and there was 'nothing he did not do well, whether as a scholar or an athlete.' He won a gold medal in legal and political sciences, and was an oarsman of some repute as well as an accomplished golfer. His interest and skill in golf would remain with him throughout his life and may have caused Basil to later write that his father did 'nothing but play golf when at university.' Pat had a number of other talents: he was a pianist and a singer of great ability, but was also noted as a 'kind and modest man.' Many of these traits would also be apparent in his son. After graduating from Trinity College, Pat was called to the Irish Bar in 1909 and in the succeeding years he worked for the Land Registry in Dublin. During this time he lived comfortably at 9 Ailesbury Road, Dublin with his parents.

With the outbreak of the First World War in August 1914, Pat commenced training with the Dublin University Graduation Corp. (1) The following month, on 14 September 1914, he joined the 7th (Service) Battalion, Royal Dublin Fusiliers, with the rank of private, but was immediately discharged in order to apply for a commission in the East Surrey Regiment. Temporary 2nd Lieutenant C.G.M. Place was posted to the 8th (Service) Battalion, and by September 1914 the regiment was billeted at Purfleet. After completing their training, the battalion left England, from Folkestone, in July 1915, and within a month the men were serving in the trenches of northern France. An early example of Pat's character and leadership was shown in January 1916. On a dark night, Pat (now Acting Captain) complained that there was nothing to do and went for a walk in 'No Man's Land', taking two men with him. After walking for some time he said 'We'll get back home.' The party climbed over barbed wire and dropped into a trench. 'Go to Company Headquarters and say we're back,' he instructed one of the men. At that moment an unarmed man, sporting a beard, walked around the corner of the trench. Pat flattened himself and his men against the side of the trench. The bearded man said '*Gute Nacht*' to which Pat replied '*Gute Nacht*'. The man looked at them and walked on, round another corner. Immediately Pat whispered to his men, 'Off like hell, we're in the *Boche* trenches,' but as soon as the man rounded the corner he alarmed a sentry, who shot one of Pat's companions. Commotion broke out in the trench, and Pat, with his remaining colleague, shinned up over the parapet and out of the trench. Pat got through the wire, but his colleague lost his sense of direction and ran three hundred yards along the German wire, being shot at all the way, but eventually reached safety. (2) The 'Place' lack of fear when encountering the enemy and taking them by surprise would later become apparent in his son's naval career.

In March 1916 Pat was admitted to No. 3 General Hospital at Le Treport suffering from jaundice and within a few days was evacuated to the Endsleigh Palace Hospital in London. Just prior to his admission to the hospital a notice of his forthcoming marriage appeared in *The Times* (3):

Captain C.G.M. Place and Miss Stuart-William
A marriage will take place shortly, about May, between Charles
Godfrey Morris Place, Captain, East Surrey Regiment (Barrister at
Law) son of Mr G.W. Place (late ICS) and Anna Margaret Stuart-
William, daughter of the late Mr W.A. Stuart-William (RICE,
Cooper's Hill) and Mrs Stuart-William of 101 Kedleston Road, Derby.

Anna Margaret Stuart-William (known as Peggy) was born on 23 December
1894 in Delhi, the daughter of Mr and Mrs Wilfred Arthur William. Her
father was born in India in 1865 and entered the Royal Indian College of
Engineering at Cooper's Hill in England in 1885. Most graduates from the
college were recruited into the Indian Civil Service, but for some reason he
was not. Despite this, he made his way to India and gained employment as a
civil engineer with the Assam-Bengal Railway Company. In September 1893
he married Mabel Hawkins at Silchar in Assam. She was born in 1867, the
daughter of Benjamin Lawrence Hawkins, a surgeon living and practising in
Woburn, Bedfordshire, and Anna Hawkins (neé Green), also from Woburn.
Mabel's grandfather was Benjamin Waterhouse Hawkins, a sculptor and
zoologist who had been responsible for creating the concrete dinosaurs for
the Great Exhibition in 1851. (4) Her mother's family, the Greens, had
strong links with the clergy, the law and the world of art. Mabel Hawkins
studied at the Slade School of Art in London, from 1886 to 1889, gaining
several prizes as well as meeting the illustrator Randolph Caldecott, before
travelling to India in 1890. Following Peggy's birth, a brother, Wilfrid
Lawrence Stuart, was born in August 1896 when the family were living in
Mussoorie. Later, a second brother, Victor Philip Stuart, was born in
September 1898, when the family were residing in Nahan, Umballa.

The family left India at the end of the century and by 1901 they had
returned to England and had adopted the surname of Stuart-William. Peggy,
at the age of five, had been sent to the High School for Girls, Lichfield. Over
the following years tragedy struck the family; Peggy's brother Victor died in
March 1906 in Calcutta from cerebral malaria, and six months later in the
same city her father died of dysentery. After school in Lichfield Peggy
attended Friargate School, a private school in Derby run by her aunt, Mary
Hawkins; at the same time her mother and brother moved to Derby. After
leaving school, Peggy moved to London on her own, at what was considered
a relatively young age, in search of employment, much to the concern of her
mother.

Pat and Peggy had met through mutual friends, the Queketts, who lived
in Maida Vale. Arthur Quekett (later Sir Arthur) had been a contemporary of

Pat's at Trinity College Dublin. In April 1915 Pat and Peggy spent time at Berrystead (the home of Peggy's great-aunt, Miss Mary Hamilton Green) in Eversholt, Bedfordshire. In May 1915 Pat took Peggy to Dublin to introduce her to his parents, and it was around this time that they became engaged to be married.

Having been evacuated to London, Pat spent a short time in hospital in March 1916, and in mid-April was granted two months' sick leave. Away from the rigours of life in northern France, he took the opportunity to marry his fiancée on 26 April 1916 at St Michael's Church, Derby. Pat and Peggy enjoyed a two-week honeymoon at Dovedale in the Peak District, followed by nearly a month in Ireland, touring the country and hosting parties at his home in Dublin. Family stories retold in 1943 by their son gave the impression that relations with both sides of the family were somewhat awkward, and that his parents' marriage had not been foreseen:

> When my mother was at school she was always told 'No one will ever marry you – they couldn't bear your relations,' and at the same time in Trinity College Dublin my father was being told the same thing.

Pat rejoined his regiment at Dover in June 1916 and in August was assessed as medically fit and ordered to return to France, subsequently rejoining his battalion in October 1916. In January 1917 the *London Gazette* announced the award of the Military Cross to Captain C.G.M. Place. At this time Peggy was living at Woodside, Aspley Guise, near Woburn, in a house owned by a relative. She gave birth to their first child, Barbara Hamilton Place, on 5 February 1917. However, tragedy struck and on 28 February little Barbara died. The death certificate identified the cause of death as 'congenital debility, acute inanition and diarrhoea'. Later Basil would say that his sister had died as a result of 'being scalded by a hot water bottle that had been incorrectly placed in her cot by a district nurse.' When he had children of his own he remained concerned about the use of hot water bottles, and was very keen that there was appropriate heating in the house to avoid the need for them. Battalion records indicate that Pat did not return from France (5), and it appears that he never saw his daughter. It was left for his young wife to cope alone with the tragic loss of their first child.

August 1917 was marked by a major offensive at Ypres involving the 8th Battalion, East Surrey Regiment, and Pat was promoted to the rank of Acting Major, serving as second-in-command of the battalion. The first battle of Passchendale commenced on 10 October, and the battalion diaries for that night recorded:

Major Place, commanding B Company, led a night advance at Poelcappell. It was dogged by problems, with the men losing their way. Three hours after the start of the advance, Major Place returned wounded, having suffered a bullet wound to his left upper arm, to the battalion headquarters and reported that many men had been wounded.

Despite his injuries, Pat continued to organise fresh attacks before returning to headquarters. The Commanding Officer, Lieutenant Colonel Irwin, would later write: 'The gallantry displayed by Major C.G.M. Place both before and during the action was of a very high order and was acknowledged by the award of the DSO.'

Some fifteen years later, Basil wrote that his father had suffered the effects of poisonous gas at this battle, and that this affected his health throughout his post-war life. There is, however, no record of Pat receiving any medical attention for gas, nor is it identified on his medical record at the time of discharge from the Army. Pat had, however, sustained a gunshot wound to his left arm and was evacuated to hospital in London. Following recuperation he joined a reserve battalion in Dover, but was then posted to Cambridge, serving with No. 2 Officer Cadet Battalion at Pembroke College until 1919. In December 1917 he was awarded the Distinguished Service Order for his actions. (6) Later, Basil would reflect that his father's military service was one of 'tolerable distinction'.

Peggy gave birth to their second child in 1919, when she and Pat were living in Aspley Guise. Helen Margaret Place, who acquired the nickname 'Bunty', was born on 12 February. Soon after this Pat was released from the Army, but subsequently joined the Army reserve, allowing him to retain the rank of Major. The family moved to Dublin to allow Pat to resume his legal career. They lived in the town of Killiney, near Dublin, and Pat became an Examiner in Titles in the Land Registry.

Dublin was a very different city to the one Pat had left in 1914. The drive for independence had been marked by many violent episodes, not least the Easter Rising of 1916. By 1919 there was an on-going war for independence, between nationalists and the British forces. Family life appears to have started well for the Place family, but before long they were made unwelcome due to religious hatred. Their life was abruptly altered when shots were fired at Helen's pram; fortunately she was not injured, but they were forced to leave Ireland in 1920 under duress from Sinn Fein. Pat was a committed Protestant, having declared that he was 'Church of England' on his Army application forms in 1914; he was also a member of the Army reserve. Knowledge of this incident may have contributed to Basil's later admission of his 'loathing of religious fanatics.' Fortunately, with the help of the Reverend William 'Fred' Green (Peggy's great-uncle) Pat was able to secure a position with the Colonial Office as a magistrate in Uganda. The appointment took effect from March 1921, and before long Pat was heading to Africa, arriving in April. His wife and daughter remained in England since Peggy was expecting another child. Basil Charles Godfrey Place was born on 19 July 1921, at Wintercott, Little Malvern, Worcestershire, and on 21 July *The Times* carried the announcement of his birth:

> Place. On the 19th July at Wintercott, Little Malvern, the wife of Major Godfrey Place, DSO, MC, District Magistrate Uganda, of a son.

Basil was baptised on 22 August 1921 by the Reverend Cyril Holmes at Little Malvern Church, just across the road from Wintercott. Peggy and her two children left London for Mombasa at the end of November in order to join her husband. They sailed via the Suez Canal to Aden (a port that Basil would visit many times over the next fifty years), before arriving at Mombasa three weeks later. They then travelled by train to Kisumu, on the eastern shores of Lake Victoria, before embarking on a steamer for the final leg of the journey to Entebbe. It is likely that the whole journey from London to Entebbe took almost a month. Their arrival was the first opportunity for Pat to meet his son, and it would be a feature of much of Basil's life that he would spend a great deal of time away from his father. Despite this, he would be remembered by Basil as a 'wholly lovable character and immensely popular', a father with whom Basil and his sister would have great fun.

Uganda was a country full of challenges for Europeans. In 1908 Sir Frederick Treves travelled to Uganda on holiday and wrote that 'it is not a white man's country, that is to say it is not a country where a European with his way to make can settle for life and hope to bring up a family.' (7) There was a significant threat from diseases, including sleeping sickness, malaria, typhoid, plague and tick fever. Other threats included indigenous animals; there were often reports of man-eating lions in the towns and villages. Entebbe was the administrative capital of Uganda, home to the Governor. Treves wrote that Entebbe gave an impression of being a 'summer lake resort' and that it was 'almost a garden with a few homes in it.' At that time, Kampala, some twenty-six miles from Entebbe, was the main site for commercial and legal activities.

Basil and his family lived in Entebbe, and from there Pat travelled to different areas of the protectorate to carry out his duties as a District Magistrate and Judge. The challenges facing the judiciary were many and varied, and during 1922 there were prosecutions for cannibalism, as well as public executions of murderers. In the same year Pat, having experience in land registration, took on extra responsibilities, becoming conveyancer to the land office; he also passed the government examination in Luganda, the native language of Uganda. In January 1923 he acquired further responsibility as the Registrar of Titles.

The family enjoyed a high standard of living, having free housing with Pat's appointment, and employed several house servants. Pat pursued his enjoyment of golf, being a member of the Royal Entebbe Golf Club, a course described as 'the best in East Africa'. Pat was also a very able stage performer, and Basil recalled how he would 'tell stupid stories,' as well as write lyrics for songs. He was popular amongst other officers in the colonial service, often performing in plays or other shows, acting and singing as well as playing the keyboard. Sometimes Peggy would act alongside him, but reviews indicate that she was not such a gifted performer as her husband.

In June 1923 the family returned to England on leave. Pat's departure was recorded in the *Uganda Herald* as 'a number of well known figures left on the last boat, including the popular Entebbe entertainer Major Place.' The family stayed with Peggy's relatives in Bedfordshire, and it was decided that Helen and Basil should remain in England rather than return to Uganda. They were to spend the next two years living with the Allen family in the farming village of Kemerton in north Gloucestershire. Mrs Mary Allen was a widow (her husband had been a schoolmaster) who lived at Wayside, a large house in the centre of the village which was to become Basil's home for the next two years. Mrs Allen had five daughters, of whom three were spinsters, including Mary Cooke Allen, aged forty, and Gertrude Victoria Allen, aged thirty-four, who lived with their mother; they became known to Basil as 'Aunt Maisie' and 'Aunt Queenie', respectively. Aunt Maisie had been at school in Lichfield with Peggy some twenty years earlier, and had offered to look after Peggy's children. Some years later Aunt Maisie wrote that Basil 'was <u>such</u> a baby when he first came to me at two and a half.' The sisters were responsible for looking after the children, and Basil retained a lifelong respect and affection for Aunt Maisie, who died in 1982 at the age of ninety-nine. She was a formidable character, a devout Christian who was keen to help others and would challenge things she believed to be wrong; both these traits were also part of Basil's character. Good manners and courtesy were to be thought of as normal and bad behaviour was not acceptable. Right and wrong were clear; there were few, if any, grey areas.

Kemerton is a small village on the edge of the Cotswolds, between Tewkesbury and Evesham. Living in Kemerton allowed Basil to pursue an active outdoor life, climbing nearby Bredon Hill and playing in the Iron Age fort at the summit, as well as watching the abundant wildlife. There were events that made him laugh, and on one occasion he and Helen came across a woman by the back door of Wayside making a desperate attempt to pin up her underwear which had come down in the road. Basil later recalled that the first time the woman had realised the problem was 'when her knickers were around her ankles and restricted her stride so much that she fell flat on her face.' Such enjoyment of others' misfortunes would have been frowned upon by the Allens, who were always keen to demonstrate their Christian values. To that end, Basil and Helen would have attended St Nicholas Church in the village regularly.

Aunt Maisie remained a lifelong friend of Basil, and many years later, when he was married, she would visit and stay with the family. Even when aged seventy she would drive herself to Dorset and spend a week or so with them. Here she made her mark with Basil's children; his son Charles recalled how she would quickly and firmly correct any poor or incorrect English that the children used.

Pat extended his leave until just after Christmas 1923, but then he and Peggy said goodbye to Helen and Basil and sailed to Mombasa, arriving in Uganda on 1 February 1924. Later that year Pat was promoted to Senior Magistrate and in December was appointed Assistant to the Attorney General, a position he held for the next two years. In this role he often appeared for the Crown in the High Court before the Chief Justice, with varying degrees of success. Amongst the highlights of life in Uganda in 1925 was a Royal visit. The Duke and Duchess of York undertook a safari holiday to East Africa in 1925, starting in Kenya. They arrived in Uganda to much excitement on 13 February and over the next few days attended a number of official engagements in Entebbe, with a garden party and dinner being held at Government House. Pat and Peggy would have attended these functions, meeting the future Queen Elizabeth, who would herself in coming years meet their son on many occasions.

Social life in Uganda continued as before, and Pat contributed to concerts and shows. In October 1924 a concert was held in aid of All Saints Church, Kampala and the *Uganda Herald* reported:

> Comic relief was provided by Major Place … [who] has a wonderful repertory of the best comic songs and plays his own accompaniment with most effective mastery of the keyboard … an artist of no mean order having a cultivated and unusually sympathetic voice of a charming quality.

Pat also continued to make his mark on the golf course; in October 1925 the Royal Entebbe Golf Club hosted the East African Golf Championship in which Pat reached the final. Basil was later to write that his father 'would undoubtedly have been in the first rank of amateur golfers but for a war wound.'

Pat and Peggy returned on leave in June 1926 and arrived in London the following month. Any plans to return to Uganda were altered by Pat's appointment, in October 1926, to the position of Assistant Attorney General in Northern Rhodesia. His experience in land law and registration appears to have helped his application. His service in Uganda was recognised by the Governor who wrote that he was 'a very promising officer of the Judicial Department with good ability and outstanding social qualities.' The autumn was spent at Folkestone where Pat's parents, who had left Dublin, were now living in the Holderness Hotel, a private hotel with commanding views of the Channel. Basil attended school for the first time at the Conamur School, Sandgate for just one term; his school report at Christmas 1926 recorded:

> Basil has made a very good beginning at school. He is very intelligent and always does his best. He has been a very good little boy in every way and we are extremely sorry to lose him so soon.

The family sailed from London to Cape Town in December 1926. Basil was nearly five and a half years old, and departed on a journey that took him to Livingstone in Northern Rhodesia, which would be his home for two and a half years. Christmas was celebrated on board, and both children attended a fancy dress party, Helen dressed as a nurse and Basil a gondolier. After disembarking at Cape Town, the family travelled by train on the Rhodesia Express, passing through Kimberley and Mafeking to Bulawayo in Southern Rhodesia, then on to Livingstone on the Zambezi Express. The journey took two days, and their gateway to Northern Rhodesia was the railway bridge across the River Zambezi. They arrived in Livingstone in early January 1927 and stayed as guests of the Governor, His Excellency Sir Herbert Stanley KCMG, at Government House. Basil made an early impression by being sick on the veranda following what he described as 'eating a surfeit of mangos.' No sooner had Pat started work than he was promoted; his boss, Mr G.D. Clough, the Attorney General, had died from typhoid, and Pat acted in his place. Before long, the Governor noted that 'Major Place could not carry on without a replacement,' and requested the appointment of a judge or barrister. Mr Frederic Gordon-Smith (Pat's predecessor as Assistant Attorney General) was appointed Attorney General in April. Later that year,

Pat was appointed a visiting Justice to all prisons in the country, and acted as Attorney General for almost six months when Gordon-Smith was on leave. In 1928 Pat was appointed to the position of Solicitor General, but at times also had to undertake the duties of Attorney General.

For Basil, growing up in Livingstone was fun. Despite having demanding work commitments, Pat would organise picnics for the family which often lasted three days and involved camping out in the bush. Later, Basil would consider a typical English picnic of a stroll and some sandwiches as 'rather tame.' Helen and Basil would be taken swimming by their father in lakes or rivers. Recognising the potential risk from crocodiles, Pat would take a double-barrelled shotgun with them; on reaching the bank he would fire one cartridge into the water and tell his children that they had ten minutes to swim safely. Basil later recalled his father's unconventional habits:

> I always remember him the night he was cleaning the gramophone in his bath, more interested in how it worked than in the Governor and his wife who were drinking more than was good for them in the drawing room waiting for dinner.

Basil also demonstrated an interest in mechanics and later in life he savoured the challenge of taking an engine apart and rebuilding it, or building model ships in bottles. The family became involved with the scouting movement, Peggy with the Girl Guides (being District Commissioner), and Basil became a cub scout. In August 1929 the family returned to England in order for Basil to start preparatory school. He left with fond memories of Northern Rhodesia as well as an open reference from the Honorary Secretary of Livingstone Local Association of the Northern Rhodesia Boy Scouts Association, which read:

> To Any Old Wolf
>
> That you may know that Basil Place, who bears this is a Two Star Cub and has been Sixer of the yellow Six of the 1st Livingstone Pack for some time past.
>
> Basil leaves us to go home to England and is prepared to do his best in whatever pack he may join.

Basil started school at The Grange, Folkestone in September 1929. A 'private school for young gentlemen', it had been founded by the Reverend Arthur Hussey in about 1870 and moved to purpose-built premises in 1896. These comprised the main building called 'The Grange', along with 'Little Grange' (the Masters' house) and the Sanatorium; in addition there was a gymnasium and a chapel with seating for 100 people. To the rear of the buildings lay nearly seven acres of grounds, stretching as far as the railway line, containing playing fields, tennis lawns, a cricket pavilion and stables. Basil's headmaster was Mr C.H. Wodeman (known as Woody), who had graduated from Queens' College Cambridge in 1902, having read History. He arrived at The Grange in 1909 and bought the school, in partnership with Mr H.W. Roach, at the end of the First World War. Two years later his father, the Reverend Henry Wodeman, was appointed as Chaplain. The school brochure of the 1930s described how the school was run along the lines of a 'junior public school'. Despite this, the school had had its heyday and was struggling to attract pupils; in 1929 there were only forty-five boys.

Woody had a significant and long-lasting influence on Basil. He was a keen Francophile; boys had to speak French in the school's dining room, and he organised school trips from Folkestone to France. Woody had a keen interest in Gilbert and Sullivan operas, allowing the local Operatic Society to use the school gymnasium for rehearsals as well as introducing Gilbert and Sullivan songs into school concerts. David van Lennep attended The Grange at the same time as Basil. Some eighty years later he remembered it as an austere school, in which all the staircases and stairways were stone, and that the building had been constructed with fire prevention as a priority, making it very uncomfortable. The Grange had a reputation for preparing boys for the Royal Naval College, Dartmouth, although in the period 1914-34 only six boys from the school appear to have joined as cadets. David van Lennep remembers Basil as someone who was 'very much his own person' and who did not talk about himself. Basil was very bright, and excelled both at academic subjects and sports, being captain of the cricket team. David van Lennep remembers overhearing some parents walking down to watch a cricket match and saying, 'That Place boy is far too clever to go into the navy.' Basil remembered his time at The Grange with affection, and recalled how 'tuck' was not allowed at the school. On one occasion all the boys at the school entered a competition to win free chocolate bars, all were successful and the winnings had to be delivered to the school in a small van. Later in life, Basil regretted not going back to visit his former headmaster, who died in 1962 at the age of eighty-one. Basil's grandparents were living close to his school, and this provided some family contact whilst his parents were overseas. It was a short distance from the Holderness Hotel to The Grange, and Basil's grandparents would walk down to the school to watch him play sport. This caused him considerable embarrassment, not least because his grandmother came wearing shabby old clothes, usually adorned with a battered old fur coat.

With Basil settled at school, his parents returned to Livingstone in March 1930. On their return Pat again took on the additional responsibilities of Attorney General and was appointed to the Legislative Council, where he often relieved the tedium of debates by his witty speeches. In September 1931, Pat and Peggy returned on leave (planned to total four months) in order to seek medical attention for a disorder of his throat. On arrival they stayed at the Wampach Hotel in Folkestone before Pat was admitted to St Mary's Hospital, London. Towards the end of November he underwent an operation for laryngitis, but developed bronchopneumonia and died on 12 December 1931, at the age of forty-five. His death was reported in *The Times*, (8) and there was a full obituary in the *Livingstone Mail* on 16 December 1931. It described how he had 'come to England on sick leave in order to consult specialists in regard to an affection of the throat, from which he had suffered from over the last two years.' In describing Pat's contribution to life in Livingstone the author recorded how both he and Peggy endeared themselves to all sections of the community from their moment of arrival. Pat had been closely involved in a production of 'Make Believe', in which he had taken a leading role, and the show was hailed as one of the most successful stage efforts ever produced in Livingstone. It was at that time that the first problems with his throat became apparent and he lost his voice, which never fully recovered. The respect and affection felt for Pat was evident from the large congregation at a memorial service held on Sunday, 20 December at St Andrews Church, Livingstone. Amongst the large congregation was the Governor, His Excellency Sir James Crawford Maxwell KCMG.

Just like his mother, Basil had lost his father at a young age; this loss was to have a significant impact on Basil, and he would adopt his father's name of Godfrey. Later in his life he wrote down his thoughts on growing up without a father, in which he outlined his and Helen's upbringing after Pat's death:

My father died when I was ten. He had been gassed and wounded in the Passchendale offensive in the Autumn of 1917, but as he lived for more than ten years my mother was not entitled to a widow's pension; she took a residential job. My sister and I lived with my grandmother [Mabel Stuart-William], who had been widowed nineteen years before I was born. Her income was just under two pounds a week but I do not doubt my mother contributed to our keep: we were poor, but not as desperately poor as many. Many of my contemporaries had widowed mothers and were as poor or poorer than we were. Living in the country was very different from town life and we had few contemporary friends within walking distance. Entertainment at home consisted of reading in turn – the free library came round once a week. We acted playlets (improvising costumes from any cast offs we could find) and recited monologues. We played card games. There was no television and it was only latterly that we had a wireless. We went to the cinema (by bus) once a week if funds allowed. My grandmother thought we should go to those which provoked thought but I remember few had any violence and none specific sex. We took very little notice of advertisements and were aware that we had fewer toys and possessions than some other children. Occasionally, if something I wanted desperately was refused due to lack of cash, the frustration seldom lasted over night. We were not a particularly religious family, but went to church on Sundays as a matter of course. We were brought up that our father had all the virtues and was an example to be followed.

Basil had wanted to join the Royal Navy from a young age – four, according to his mother. Since 1903 there had been a system for boys to join as cadets at the age of thirteen, when they would attend two Royal Naval Colleges. Five terms were spent at the Royal Naval College, Osborne, on the Isle of Wight, followed by six terms at the Royal Naval College, Dartmouth. The latter had been built in 1905, designed by Sir Aston Webb, and was described as 'a masterpiece of Edwardian architecture'. In 1921 the college at Osborne closed as a result of financial cuts imposed by the 'Geddes Axe', and from then on all cadet training took place at Dartmouth.

Towards the end of 1934 Basil sat the entry examinations for Dartmouth. All applicants were to be 'of pure European descent and the sons of natural born or naturalised British subjects.' (9) Applicants had to be between the age of thirteen years and four months and thirteen years and eight months in the month before they intended to join the college (i.e. on 1 December, April or August). Each boy was interviewed by a committee, following which recommendations were made to the First Lord of the Admiralty. Those applying were advised that the interview was 'an informal affair and holds no terror for the average youth.' This appears to have been taken quite literally by Basil when he attended on 30 October 1934. On the following day, the secretary to the committee wrote to his headmaster. Referring to Basil as a 'star-turn', he described how one of his answers would go down in history as a classic. On being asked what he was usually called at school – monitor or prefect or whatever it might be – Basil replied, 'Well Sir, I'm generally called Fishface.' This was followed by the entire disintegration of the committee. It was pointed out, however, that the reply had done 'no harm at all to Basil's chances.'

Woody wrote to Peggy on 15 November that they were 'delighted that Basil had passed the interview and had not expected any other result.' After the interview, acceptance to the college was dependent on passing the written examination. This was held at the Russell Hotel, London, and the officers' outfitters, Gieves, provided a light lunch for the applicants as well as taking the opportunity to measure boys for their cadet uniform. The advice for this part was that 'it is a great mistake to try and cram a boy for these examinations.' The examination was deemed to be harder than Common Entrance at the time, and had a strong emphasis on mathematics. (10) In his letter to Peggy, Woody predicted that 'Basil would pass the written examination with flying colours, unless anything untoward occurs.' In the same letter he summed up Basil's time at the school and wrote that 'we shall miss Basil next term. He has been such a dependable fellow and his influence as a Prefect and Captain has always been sound.' He finished by writing, 'you ought to be jolly proud of your son – as I know that you are.'

On 22 December 1934 *The Times* published a list of those boys who had passed the qualifying examination for entry into the Royal Naval College, Dartmouth. This included 'Place B.C.G', and on 1 January 1935 he arrived at Kingswear by train, crossed the River Dart by ferry and, along with the other new cadets, was marched up the hill to the College and joined Hood term. This was to be his home for next three and a half years.

By 1935 the Royal Navy was recovering from years of austerity, following the end of the First World War. In 1932 government spending on the Royal Navy was less than a quarter of that in 1914, and in 1931 there had been unrest in the Fleet at the Invergordon Mutiny. Finally, in 1932, in response to world events, including the Japanese invasion of Manchuria and the growing threat from mainland Europe, spending on the Royal Navy started to increase. Plans for expansion were constrained as it was soon recognised that much of the necessary expertise in shipbuilding in Britain had been lost over the last decade. The Royal Navy started to increase its manpower, and in October 1934 the Admiralty announced that the number of cadets to be admitted to Dartmouth each term would increase from thirty-three to forty. In fact, the first entry after this announcement, in January 1935, had fifty-one cadets.

Conditions at Dartmouth were demanding, although for each boy their opinion was, of course, influenced by previous experiences. Boys were advised that, 'For ninety-nine per cent of cadets who pass through the college's portals, the period spent at Dartmouth remains for all time the happiest of memories.' (11)

Gerard Mansfield, who joined the college on the same day as Godfrey Place, and became a lifelong friend, recalled that Dartmouth was 'heaven' compared with his own preparatory school, which had been exceptionally spartan. (12) At Dartmouth, members of a term slept in one dormitory and boys had to move everywhere at the double. There was enormous deference to anyone senior; boys were not allowed to talk with other boys in a different term without permission (even if they were brothers). There was a rigorous and rather pernickety disciplinary code, with a system of 'ticks' for misdemeanours, whereby three 'ticks' led to a boy being caned by either a senior cadet or a naval officer. Charles Fetherston-Dilke, who also joined Hood term in January 1935, recalled being thrashed for having a button undone. In charge of each term was a Term Officer, who was a serving naval officer. Cadets were charged fifty pounds per term, but there could be reduction for the sons of officers of the Army, Royal Navy or Air Force. It is not clear if Godfrey Place received such a reduction, but his mother, who was working for the Duke of Portland, struggled to pay his fees.

Dartmouth had two categories of staff: the naval staff, responsible for discipline and teaching naval subjects, under the command of a Captain, and the professional staff, who taught the cadets in the classroom under the direction of the Headmaster. In 1935 Captain R.V. Holt DSO, MVO, was Captain and the Headmaster was Mr E.W.E. 'Eric' Kempson, sometimes referred to as 'Daddy'. He was a graduate of Trinity College, Cambridge, having studied mechanical sciences before joining the Royal Navy in 1903 as an Instructor. After serving in HMS *Albion* for two years he became a master at Dartmouth in 1907-11. He subsequently served with the Royal Engineers in Palestine in the First World War and won the Military Cross. After demobilisation he returned to teaching and in October 1927 was appointed Headmaster of Dartmouth. Kempson was a big man and had a commanding presence, although also had a sense of fun. One cadet wrote that he was a 'huge figure of a man with jowls like a bulldog, his robed presence struck dread with the cadets.' He wore a monocle at his left eye, and if that dropped it was a signal that 'thunder was imminent'. (13) David van Lennep followed Godfrey Place to Dartmouth, joining Rodney term in April 1935, and later recalled that Eric Kempson was 'widely respected, although on the surface had a gruff personality, but under that he was actually a very nice person.' Overall, the cadets considered the masters to be very good and tolerant towards the boys, and to be men who led by example.

The aim of the course was to educate cadets rather than give them a professional training. This was reflected in the syllabus, which covered Mathematics, Science, Engineering, French, English, History, Geography, Scripture, Seamanship, Navigation and Drill and Physical Training. There was no opportunity for discussion or debate in any subject. Engineering was taught in the engineering workshops, and although the boys were taught mechanical drawing and the use of lathes, there was no instruction on engine room machinery despite cadets, in the future, being required to send orders to the engine room. Cadets were taught English naval history, and re-enacted the Battle of Trafalgar with model ships, but there was no planned teaching or discussion of any later events. The teaching of French was considered poor by the cadets, who were required to read works by rather obscure French authors rather than develop their skills in French conversation. There was no teaching of Latin or Greek.

Not all future naval officers entered as cadets at Dartmouth; there was an alternative route of direct entry from school (so called special entry) at the age of eighteen. This had led to questioning of the relevance of the Dartmouth education, leading to the captain of one ship which was taking cadets to write:

> 'The Dartmouth system tends to create officers of the deserving, unimaginative type who may take matters as they find them, the late entry on the other hand produces officers who lead their men and are more inclined to strike out on a line of their own.'

By contrast the Captain of HMS *Valiant* wrote: 'I think there is very little wrong with the modern naval cadet as he leaves Dartmouth.' (14)

Very soon after arriving at Dartmouth, Godfrey Place became best friends with David Bevan; both boys stood out as being physically much smaller than their peers and they would serve together until June 1941. Cadet D.R.L. Bevan came from a naval family; his father Captain R.H. Bevan, had served at the Battle of Jutland and from 1936 to 1938 was the naval attaché in Rome. Godfrey Place never talked about his time at Dartmouth to his family, but there is no doubt he was an exceptionally capable cadet. Gerard Mansfield, another member of Hood term, recalled that Godfrey Place 'had a very good sense of humour and a very keen perception of anything pretentious or pompous.' With regard to his academic performance, Gerard Mansfield recalled:

> Godfrey was extremely intelligent, without making any apparent effort he was invariably second in the term order of merit at Dartmouth.

> Most of us felt he could easily be first if he wanted to. As it was his best
> friend [David Bevan], who appeared to make an effort, was always top,
> I think Godfrey may have felt it would have been discourteous to
> displace him! (15)

Godfrey Place's term reports show that initially he did very well, being
second in the class. Comments made by staff included, 'developing into a
useful cadet.' In 1936 he slipped down the class list to fifth, prompting his
tutor to write, 'he can do much better than this.' Staff also noted that at times
he was untidy and that this was 'a serious handicap to his maths and science.'
More general comments which, in hindsight, appear rather pertinent were:
'rather lacking in self confidence and [he] must learn to assert himself more
when taking charge.' In April 1937 Godfrey Place was again second in the
term order and selected for the 'Alpha' class. This was a system that had been
introduced by Eric Kempson with the aim of providing a less rigorous
academic curriculum for the most able cadets, who were given more time for
private study, as well as facilities to pursue other subjects. 'Alpha' cadets were
exempted from part of the passing out examinations, except for Navigation,
Engineering and Seamanship. Thirteen other cadets were in the 'Alpha'
class, including David Bevan.

During 1937 there were also changes to the 'term' system, which was
replaced by a 'house' system on the instruction of the Second Sea Lord.
There were to be six houses, each named after a distinguished admiral,
namely Blake, Exmouth, Grenville, Hawke, St Vincent and Drake, the latter
for the new entrants. Godfrey Place was assigned to Exmouth House.
Despite these changes, cadets were still taught in term groups, but these were
now identified by a number. In their last terms, three cadets from each were
selected to be Cadet Captains (equivalent to prefects), having been
recommended by their Term Officers. They would take charge of a more
junior term in their gun room and dormitory and be able to impose corporal
punishment. In 1937 Godfrey Place's report stated that 'he was of excellent
character and set a good example and should be a useful Cadet Captain.' It
was no surprise that he was selected and assigned to Drake House, whose
new entrants included John Harvey-Jones who later worked in naval
intelligence in the early years of the Cold War and later still became
Chairman of ICI.

Speaking in 2003, Charles Fetherston-Dilke recalled, perhaps with more
than a little hindsight, that if anyone in Hood term was going to win the
Victoria Cross it would have been Godfrey Place. He described him as 'a
small chap, very dogged with a dry sense of humour, who kept a low profile
and was very clever academically.'

During his time at Dartmouth Godfrey Place witnessed a number of different occasions. In July 1935 Eric Kempson's daughter Rachel was married in the chapel at Dartmouth. The bridegroom was the actor Michael Redgrave (later Sir Michael), and a number of cadets were invited to sing at the wedding. (16) In December 1936 Captain Holt was succeeded by Captain F.H.G. Dalyrymple-Hamilton. Before the change of command there was an inspection of the college by members of the Board of the Admiralty. The team, led by Sir Samuel Hoare (First Lord of the Admiralty) included the Second Sea Lord, Admiral Sir Martin Dunbar-Nasmith VC, KCB, who had been awarded the Victoria Cross in 1915 when commanding the submarine HMS *E-11* in the Dardanelles. At the visit, in October 1936, all 450 cadets were inspected by the visiting party; this is likely to have been the first time that Godfrey Place had encountered a member of the Royal Navy who had been awarded the Victoria Cross.

The early months of 1937 were a busy time for the cadets of Hood term. In April there was a trip to France, with visits to Notre Dame and other famous sites in Paris. Next month, Godfrey Place was one of 300 cadets who attended the Coronation Review. HMS *Iron Duke* had been the flagship of the Grand Fleet at the Battle of Jutland, but in 1931 was converted into a gunnery firing ship, most of her armament being removed under the terms of the Treaty of London. Under the command of Captain C.E. Douglas-Pennant DSC, she arrived in Torbay on 17 May to embark the cadets (17). The ship arrived at Spithead early the next morning and anchored in her allotted position for the review, between the battle cruiser HMS *Hood* and the battleship HMS *Revenge*. From there the cadets saw the impressive ranks of the Royal Navy, along with many visiting warships. Amongst those nearby were the battleships HMS *Queen Elizabeth, Barham,* and *Repulse,* as well as the aircraft carriers HMS *Glorious* and *Hermes.* On Thursday, 20 May the King, in the company of the Queen and Princess Elizabeth, inspected the fleet from the Royal Yacht *Victoria and Albert.* On a misty day, with occasional pale sunshine, the yacht sailed almost six miles past eight lines of ships, which included some 135 ships of the Royal Navy. At 15.30, as the King passed *Iron Duke,* a royal salute was fired. Later that evening Godfrey Place witnessed the illumination of the fleet at anchor. Ceremonial parades continued the following morning when the King inspected the ships of the Home and Mediterranean Fleets, and at 12.00 the order was given to 'Splice the Mainbrace'. Later that evening *Iron Duke* sailed to Torbay, and on 22 May the cadets left the ship to return to Dartmouth. Godfrey Place had witnessed the Royal Navy at its finest, and had seen many foreign ships, including the German pocket battleship *Admiral Graf Spee*; in less than three years time his encounters with the German navy would not be ceremonial but in battle.

There were often visits to Dartmouth by ships from the Royal Navy and foreign navies. In March 1938 the submarines HMS *Spearfish* and *Sturgeon* visited and provided an opportunity for instruction of cadets. Later that year, an exercise involving all three services took place in the Dartmouth area. Elements of the Ninth Infantry Brigade, under the command of Brigadier B.L. Montgomery DSO, landed at Torcross and Slapton Sands in the early hours of 6 July in order to 'capture' the port of Dartmouth. They caught the defenders by surprise, and the exercise was described as a 'brilliant attack' by a reporter from *The Times*. Montgomery initially had his headquarters in the cruiser HMS *Southampton* but soon came ashore. Despite the success of the operation, stormy weather developed and the Brigade was unable to re-embark, so some 1300 men, all soaked by the rain, were fed and housed overnight at the College.

A feature of life at Dartmouth was the speech days held at passing-out parades. Godfrey Place listened to a number of distinguished guests talking about the challenges that faced cadets as they progressed to serving as naval officers. In August 1937 Lord Lloyd spoke of the issues facing the Royal Navy as it entered a period of expansion, and foresaw challenges in the Mediterranean. He questioned the notion that the key to the Mediterranean lay in the Suez Canal, believing instead that it lay at Portsmouth and Dartmouth. Perhaps most interesting, in the light of Godfrey Place's later career, was a speech in July 1935 by Vice Admiral Sir Reginald Plunkett-Ernle-Erle-Drax KCB, DSO, Commander-in-Chief, Plymouth. Taking as his theme 'courage', he spoke of its importance at sea and of how 'courage and trust in providence would pull cadets through.' He advised cadets not to pay undue attention to the maxim 'safety first'; safety first was all right when travelling on the road, but it never made their Empire nor would it maintain one. Cadets must not be afraid to live dangerously and to take risks, whenever duty or honour demanded. He reminded his audience that 'fortune loves a daring suitor,' and great results could only be achieved by those who had the courage when necessary to take heavy risks. (18)

By the end of 1937 many cadets were of the opinion that war was inevitable. David Bevan had personally witnessed the build up to war when visiting his parents in Italy in May 1938, when he saw Hitler's visit to Rome, coming as it did just a few months after the German invasion of Austria. In the summer of 1938 members of Hood term sat their passing-out examinations, which involved a combination of oral, written and practical examination, held over a period of a week; the results were published in August 1938. Top of the First Class list was D.R.L. Bevan, who was awarded the King's medal, a gold medal awarded to the cadet winning the 'highest aggregate marks in the passing-out term.' Second was B.C.G. Place, who won prizes in Science and Engineering. Both gained four months' seniority as a result of their performances. The following day, *The Times* announced the appointment of all the successful cadets to the training cruiser HMS *Vindictive*, from 12 September 1938.

Chapter 3

Going to War

Cadet B.C.G. Place was posted to the training cruiser HMS *Vindictive* (9,100 tons), a ship that had had a varied career in the Royal Navy. She was launched as HMS *Cavendish* in January 1918, but was renamed later that year. She was initially designed as an aircraft carrier but in 1924 was reconfigured as a six-inch cruiser. Further changes were completed in 1937, when most of her armament was removed in order for her to serve as a training ship. The previous HMS *Vindictive* was a cruiser of considerable distinction; she had been lost in the raid on the Belgian port of Zeebrugge in April 1918, during which her Commanding Officer, Captain Alfred Carpenter, was one of eight men to be awarded the Victoria Cross for his gallantry in the action.

In 1938 *Vindictive* accommodated some 200 cadets who worked the ship under the direction of officers, allowing them to experience the life of a sailor. Throughout the tour the cadets attended instructional classes in the morning and afternoon on most days, except Sundays. Life for cadets was tough; they would be expected to start each day at 06.00 by scrubbing the wooden decks. During their time on board they were expected to gain an understanding of life at sea as well as developing self-reliance. (1) On Monday, 12 September Godfrey Place was one of fifty cadets from Dartmouth who joined *Vindictive*, Commanding Officer, Captain E.J. Spooner DSO, at Chatham. Eighty-eight special entry cadets from HMS *Erebus* (who had joined the Royal Navy at the age of eighteen) also joined the ship that day. Four days later *Vindictive* departed to the Scilly Isles, arriving on 18 September and spending a week there before sailing to Plymouth. (2)

HMS *Vindictive*'s cruise to the Mediterranean had been disrupted by Hitler's plans for the Sudetenland, part of Czechoslovakia. Although he had made secret preparations to attack his neighbour in June 1937, it was in February 1938 that Hitler made clear to the world his intentions to claim the territory inhabited by ethnic Germans. In the summer of 1938 there were several attempts to resolve the issue peacefully, but on 12 September Hitler made a speech further inflaming the situation. War was seen by many to be fast approaching, and on 28 September the First Lord of the Admiralty sent a signal to mobilise the fleet. At the same time, the Prime Minister, Neville Chamberlain, met Hitler in Munich and signed an agreement with him, Mussolini and Daladier (the Prime Minister of France) allowing the ceding of Sudetenland to Germany. Chamberlain returned home, holding a copy of the Munich agreement, and pronounced there was 'peace in our time.'

The political machinations at Munich meant that *Vindictive* remained moored in Plymouth Sound for over six weeks, before finally sailing on 4 November to Malta. The ship arrived at Grand Harbour on 11 November, where she stayed for five days, during which time thirty-six cadets went to the airfield at Hal Far for flying exercises. Her next destination was Algiers, and then Gibraltar, arriving on 23 November. During the next week the senior cadets, who had joined in May 1938, took their final examinations, and *Vindictive* headed to Chatham, arriving on 6 December. Three days later all the cadets departed on Christmas leave.

After Christmas, Godfrey Place rejoined HMS *Vindictive*, by which time Captain H.R. Bovell had assumed command of the ship. Instructional classes commenced a few days later, and on 19 January the ship sailed to Portland, spending a week there during which some cadets were able to go to sea in submarines. Departure from Chatham had been delayed for a week due to problems with the ship's condensers, and the Captain was subsequently to record his concern at having 260 cadets on board when the ship was in the dockyard, circumstances that made living conditions on board 'very difficult'. The weather in England was wet and dull in early January 1939, but towards the end of the month the southwest of the country was hit by heavy snowfalls. *Vindictive* sailed west to Barbados but spent the first four days battling gales and high seas, before the storms abated and the crew started to enjoy finer weather. The ship arrived on 6 February, and over the next two weeks visited Curacao, Antigua and Tortola, before sailing to San Juan in Puerto Rico in early March, where cadets met American women for the first time. During this period Godfrey Place and all the other 'second cruise' cadets obtained some flying experience. However, the tour of the Caribbean came to an end, and *Vindictive* returned to Plymouth, arriving on 24 March. The following week, Godfrey Place and his peers sat their final examinations as cadets. The subjects examined included 'Officer-like qualities', 'Seamanship', 'Navigation and Pilotage', 'Gunnery', 'Torpedo' and' Engineering'. Amongst the many questions asked were, 'Why does a mine explode when a horn is struck?' and 'How can you tell if a mine is safe to handle or not' (both from the Torpedo examination paper and highly pertinent in the light of Godfrey Place's later experiences when being towed across the North Sea in a midget submarine.) The seamanship examination included a very obvious spelling mistake, where candidates were asked to comment on 'the enemies [sic] position'. In the light of Godfrey Place's later attention to detail of the written word, he was probably quite irritated by such poor English. (3)

The results of the examinations were released on 2 April 1939, and only one ex-Dartmouth cadet achieved a First Class certificate, namely D.R.L. Bevan. The next highest mark for this group was achieved by Godfrey Place, who was awarded a Second Class certificate, missing out on a First Class by less than one per cent. Soon after, Captain Bovell wrote on 5 April lamenting the 'poor results achieved by the Dartmouth cadets' and pointing out that these were 'a matter of deep concern.' He intended to discuss the results with the Captain of Dartmouth in the following month, but was of the opinion that 'the cadets were expected to absorb too much knowledge in the short time that they were on board the ship.' Godfrey Place and the other cadets left the ship in April; theirs was the last training cruise for *Vindictive*. In the summer of 1939 she was converted to a fleet repair ship and saw service in a number of theatres of war.

As a result of his performance in examinations at Dartmouth and *Vindictive*, Godfrey Place was awarded a total of four and a half months' seniority. He was promoted to Midshipman, effective 1 May 1939, and on the same day Midshipman B.C.G. Place and Midshipman D.R.L. Bevan reported for duty in HMS *Newcastle* at Portland. Commanded by Captain R. Vivian, she was a 'Southampton' class cruiser, built at Jarrow on the Tyne and launched in January 1936. She had a displacement of 9,000 tons and was classed as a light cruiser. Her armament consisted of twelve six-inch and eight four-inch guns. The ship also carried two Supermarine Walrus seaplanes. Earlier in 1939 it had been planned for her to join the Eastern Fleet, but with war looming she was retained in the Home Fleet. On 6 May 1939, when attached to the 2nd Cruiser Squadron, *Newcastle* sailed into the English Channel for exercises in the company of HMS *Repulse, Ark Royal* and *Glasgow*. At 17.30 the ships passed SS *Empress of Australia*, which was flying the Royal Standard as she sailed west. On board were the King and Queen, who were starting a two-month tour of Canada and the United States. The crews saluted the ship, gave three cheers for their Majesties and fired a twenty-one gun salute. (4)

During the following months *Newcastle* was based at Portland, carrying out exercises with a number of other warships of the Royal Navy. Despite the storm clouds of war gathering over Europe, the ship opened to visitors at Portland on several occasions during May and June. There was also a visit by the First Lord of the Admiralty and the Commander-in-Chief, Home Fleet.

In July *Newcastle* sailed to Plymouth, and entered dry dock for a short refit. At the same time Captain J. Figgins assumed command. He was an unusual officer, having joined the Royal Navy as Acting Mate in 1912 and gained a commission in 1915. Godfrey Place had made an impression on his predecessor, and Captain Vivian wrote of him, 'A zealous and hardworking officer who shows much promise.' The refit was completed at the end of August, and on 1 September the ship's crew were preparing for war. Two days later, Captain Figgins recorded in the log, '11.00: State of hostility now existent between Great Britain and Germany.' Godfrey Place, now aged eighteen, was a member of the Royal Navy at war. (5)

A week after the outbreak of war three destroyers from the Polish navy arrived at Plymouth, having fled from the Baltic port of Gydnia on the eve of the German invasion. On 12 September *Newcastle* sailed north to Scapa Flow and en route, just south of the Isle of Man, a suspicious object was seen floating in the water. As Britain was at war, the captain ordered depth charges to be dropped. *Newcastle* arrived at Scapa Flow on 14 September and joined the 18th Cruiser Squadron. All crew members were issued with two pairs of anti-gas goggles and one tin of bleach ointment in preparation against a possible attack with mustard gas. Over the ensuing days *Newcastle* worked up alongside a number of ships of the Home Fleet, including HMS *Hood, Nelson, Renown* and *Ark Royal. Newcastle* later sailed with elements of the Home Fleet to provide cover for the returning submarine HMS *Spearfish*, which had been damaged off the coast of Jutland and was unable to dive.

In her next patrol, HMS *Newcastle* left Scapa Flow on 1 October and sailed to the north-east of Scotland, where she intercepted two Norwegian ships, placing an armed boarding party on each and ordering them to make to Kirkwall. On 8 and 9 October she searched, unsuccessfully, with the battleships HMS *Nelson* and *Rodney* and the aircraft carrier HMS *Furious*, for the German battleship *Gneisenau*, which had been reported in the North Sea. On returning to Scapa Flow on 11 October, she speedily took on stores in order to sail in the company of HMS *Glasgow*. Both ships proceeded to the South West approaches and escorted a convoy of over fifteen oil tankers making their way to England. Fortuitously, *Newcastle* had left two days before the battleship HMS *Royal Oak* was sunk at anchor in Scapa Flow. During the passage south she challenged a number of merchant vessels, before arriving at Plymouth on 26 October, where leave was granted. After taking on stores, *Newcastle* sailed east to Spithead and from there to Scotland.

November was a busy month for *Newcastle* and her crew, since they encountered the enemy. On 12 November, whilst patrolling in the Denmark

Strait between Iceland and Greenland, a ship was sighted at 16.10, and *Newcastle* altered course to close her, identifying the vessel as the German merchant ship SS *Parana*. *Newcastle* fired warning shots across the bow, and the German crew responded by attempting to set fire to the vessel and scuttle her. Over the ensuing two hours, the crew abandoned ship into lifeboats, and whalers were launched from *Newcastle* and sent across. By 19.00 the *Parana's* crew had been brought on board and *Newcastle* opened fire with six-inch shells to sink her. This was the first time Godfrey Place had come face to face with the enemy. *Newcastle* sailed to Kirkwall to discharge the prisoners and then on to Loch Ewe, on the west coast of Scotland to take on stores, before rejoining the northern patrol on 21 November.

On 23 November, *Newcastle* was patrolling with the Armed Merchantman *Rawalpindi*, Commanding Officer, Captain C.E. Kennedy, between the Faroe Islands and Iceland. The *Rawalpindi* was a P&O liner that had been requisitioned at the outbreak of the war, and had been armed with eight outdated six-inch guns. Her crew comprised both civilians and Royal Naval officers, but despite these changes she was not a warship. Her high freeboard and towering superstructure made her an excellent target for the enemy, and her armament was no match for a battleship. In the late afternoon, as dusk approached, the *Rawalpindi* sent a signal that she was 'under attack from the *Deutschland*.' At 15.53 *Newcastle* altered course to close her at full speed. In fact the *Rawalpindi* was under attack from two German battleships, *Scharnhorst* and *Gneisenau*, and the ensuing engagement lasted just fifteen minutes. The *Rawalpindi* engaged the enemy as best she could, and at least one six-inch shell hit the *Scharnhorst* but did not breach the deck. However, the *Rawalpindi* was no match for the overwhelming German firepower and she was sunk. In the darkness, *Scharnhorst* attempted to pick up the survivors (some 27 from a crew of 300) from lifeboats. However, before this could be completed she was ordered to leave the area. There had been a sighting of another ship, *Newcastle*, but due to the darkness, poor weather and a range of 11,000 yards, the Germans were unsure as to its type and size. Reports from the *Scharnhorst* revealed that she had had *Newcastle* under observation for some time, but the captain felt that there was little to be gained by opening fire at that range, and he was worried that by doing so his own position would be revealed. *Newcastle* sighted the two darkened German ships, but the log recorded that both were steaming away from her. With poor weather and visibility, and without radar, *Newcastle* lost contact with the enemy and made her way back towards the wreckage of the *Rawalpindi* to take on survivors. In retrospect, the crew of *Newcastle* were fortunate that the German battleships had not pursued them, since there was little assistance nearby from Royal Naval ships of a similar calibre to the German raiders. (6) (7)

Over the following months *Newcastle* continued to serve in northern patrols, based at Scapa Flow. Christmas and New Year were spent at anchor, but patrols recommenced on 2 January 1940. During January a further two Norwegian vessels were intercepted, boarded and then taken to Kirkwall. By this time there was, however, an ever increasing list of faults with the ship, not least an ongoing issue with the condensers which prevented her from reaching speeds above 25 knots. In March *Newcastle* sailed to Palmer's Yard at Hepburn, near Jarrow, where she entered dry dock for refitting. By early June repairs were complete and *Newcastle* sailed to Rosyth and then to Scapa Flow. Her first sortie involved escorting the battlecruisers HMS *Renown* and *Repulse* during a fruitless search for *Scharnhorst* and *Gneisenau* between Iceland and the Faroe Islands. Before long *Newcastle* sailed south, through the Channel and arriving on 15 July in Plymouth Sound, where she would be based for the next two months. Whilst there the crew witnessed the start of the German bombing campaign against the town, and the ship's four-inch guns made a significant contribution to the town's defences against aerial attack, a fact that would be remembered for many years by the people of Plymouth. The crew also took part in fire-watching duties in and around the docks, and at this time David Bevan fell down a bomb crater, sustaining injuries to his legs and head. At Plymouth there was a change of command, Captain E.A. Aylmer DSC relieving Captain Figgins. The latter, in his report on Godfrey Place wrote:

> Not afraid of responsibility, he is inclined to be intolerant of accepting the advice and greater experience of others. As 2nd officer of the Armed Guard on Northern Patrol he carried out his duties with courage, zeal and ability. A likeable officer with a pleasant personality, character and a sense of humour.

The next six weeks were spent undertaking anti-invasion patrols in the English Channel, and then in October *Newcastle* was involved in several sorties against the enemy. She sailed with HMS *Revenge* and a number of destroyers, including three from the Polish navy, to undertake 'Operation Medium', an attack on Cherbourg, now occupied by the Germans. Here *Newcastle* fired six-inch star shells as a decoy whilst *Revenge* pounded the town with fifteen-inch high explosive shells. One week later, whilst on patrol south of the Scilly Isles, *Newcastle* was attacked by torpedoes launched from German aircraft, but they missed their target. In company with the cruiser

HMS *Emerald* and destroyers of the Fifth Flotilla, commanded by Captain Lord Louis Mountbatten, *Newcastle* intercepted four German vessels off Brest. On sighting the ships, *Newcastle* hoisted flags ordering 'General Chase' and during the next two hours she emptied her forward magazines as she fired relentlessly at the enemy. The chase was called off when the squadron was level with Ushant and the enemy destroyers had escaped back into harbour at Brest. *Newcastle's* forward guns had been damaged by the action, and she returned to Plymouth to make repairs.

In November *Newcastle* sailed to Malta carrying 200 RAF personnel and supplies, including 40 Hurricane engines and 15,000 gallons of aviation fuel. At this time, Malta was under attack from the Italian airforce, although her own air defences of aged Gloster Sea Gladiators had recently been reinforced by the arrival of twelve Hurricanes. *Newcastle* departed from Plymouth on 13 November, sailing alone, and arrived at Gibraltar three days later. The next day she sailed in a gale and, when passing the island of Pantellaria, was attacked by a submarine, but no damage was sustained, and *Newcastle* arrived at Grand Harbour on 19 November under tow from tugs, her condensers and boilers again having caused problems. Following urgent repairs, *Newcastle* embarked Fleet Air Arm personnel and aircraft and sailed on 26 November for Gibraltar, in company with HMS *Malaya, Ajax* and *Orion*, as part of Force D. On the following day *Newcastle* was ordered to join Force H, commanded by Flag Officer H (FOH), Vice Admiral Sir James Somerville KCB, DSO, flying his flag in HMS *Renown*.

Force H comprised a number of capital ships and was tasked with protecting a convoy making its way to Alexandria, under the codename 'Operation Collar'. At 08.52 an aircraft flying from HMS *Ark Royal* spotted elements of the Italian fleet south of Cape Spartivento (the southern tip of Sardinia). Over the following two hours it became apparent that the enemy forces included two battleships, the *Vittorio Venetio* and *Giulio Cesare*. The Italian fleet were keen to seek revenge for the recent attack on their base at Taranto, carried out by the Fleet Air Arm. In *Newcastle* 'action stations' were sounded at 12.06, and at 12.20 the enemy opened fire. Force H engaged the enemy at 12.23 and over the next thirty minutes *Newcastle* opened fire alongside the cruisers *Manchester* and *Berwick*; during this time *Newcastle* claimed to have hit an Italian cruiser, but this was not confirmed. (8) Despite *Newcastle* struggling to maintain her position, due to persistent boiler faults, action on board was intense. A-turret was rendered out of action after the gun jammed, and a fire started on the deck near to X-turret. Action was broken off at 13.15 by Admiral Somerville as the enemy was, by then, out of range. He would later be criticised for his decision, but pointed out that he had no idea of the state of enemy fleet and that by pursuing them he could easily have failed in his objective of ensuring safe passage of the convoy to Alexandria. Although his encounter with the Italian navy had been brief, Godfrey Place would within a year be back in the Mediterranean pursuing the enemy, including the battleship *Vittorio Venetio*.

HMS *Newcastle* sailed to Gibraltar in the company of *Renown*, *Ramillies*, *Ark Royal*, *Sheffield* and *Berwick*, entering harbour at 14.30 on 29 November. They received almost a heroes' welcome, being cheered by the ships' crews and their bands. In the afternoon of Sunday, 1 December five midshipmen left *Newcastle* at Gibraltar to sail to Glasgow in HMT *Franconia*. (9) The group included Godfrey Place, who had now completed his training as a Midshipman, and in the Certificate of Examination in Seamanship for the rank of Lieutenant was awarded a First Class Certificate, having achieved a mark of eighty-six per cent. Whilst on board *Franconia*, Godfrey Place received a signal; 'To Mid Place, from FOH. I congratulate you on your first class in seamanship examinations.' The signal from Admiral Somerville came just two days after Somerville had been informed that a Board of Enquiry was to be held at Gibraltar to 'enquire as to the action by Force H on 27 November and the breaking off of the attack.' This decision, initiated by Winston Churchill, caused Admiral Somerville serious irritation and he wrote that he was, 'amazed and, I may add, indignant that my conduct and that of my officers serving should be called to account before any information could have been received on which to base a considered opinion on our actions.' (10)

After Christmas leave, Acting Sub Lieutenant B.C.G. Place reported to HMS *Excellent* at Portsmouth in January 1941 to attend courses for promotion to Lieutenant. Over the following months he also undertook courses at HMS *Vernon*, *Mercury* and *Dryad*. He again showed his aptitude and intelligence by gaining First Class certificates in Signals, Pilotage, Gunnery and Torpedoes. During this time, Portsmouth was bombed by the Luftwaffe and Godfrey Place and his colleagues helped around the city, rescuing people from collapsed buildings and putting out fires. They were often up all night, and many then fell asleep in lectures during the day. HMS *Vernon* was evacuated to the girls' school Roedean, near Brighton. Officers slept in the now empty dormitories which produced much amusement, especially when they saw signs advising 'If you want a Mistress, please ring.'

Having completed the courses at Portsmouth, Godfrey Place was promoted to Sub Lieutenant in May 1941 and at the end of June was appointed to HMS *Elfin* at Blyth, Northumberland to train for service in submarines. The course lasted six weeks, and on its completion Godfrey Place, now twenty years old and already having seen action against the enemy, was appointed to the 10th Submarine Flotilla at Malta.

Chapter 4

The Fighting Tenth: Service in Malta

The island of Malta played a crucial role in the war due to its geographical position, just 60 miles from Sicily and 180 miles from Tunisia. In 1941 the advance of German and Italian troops in North Africa was dependent upon materiel transported across the Mediterranean from Europe, and Malta was of vital importance for the Allies as a naval base for operations against the Italian Navy. From the middle of 1941 the Axis powers attacked Malta by sea and air, in an attempt to destroy the military bases and occupy the island. The people of Malta were increasingly isolated, the nearest British naval bases in the Mediterranean being Alexandria nearly 1,000 miles to the east, and Gibraltar almost 1,200 miles to the west. Winston Churchill recognised Malta's role when he wrote: 'Since the days of Nelson, Malta has stood a faithful British sentinel guarding the narrow and vital sea corridor through the Mediterranean. Its strategic importance was never higher than in this latest war year.' (1)

Godfrey Place's first posting at Malta was as liaison officer to the Polish submarine *ORP*[1] *Sokol* (Polish for Falcon). The *Sokol* was a U–class (Utility) submarine, 191 feet long with a displacement of 750 tons. The crew comprised four officers and up to thirty-six ratings. The boat had a speed of 10 knots surfaced and up to 8 knots submerged, with a safe diving depth of 250 feet. Her armament consisted of six twenty-one-inch torpedoes and a twelve-pounder gun. She was the former HMS *Urchin*, given to the Polish Navy by the British government in January 1941 as a replacement for the submarine *ORP Orzel*. The *Orzel* had made a dramatic escape at the outbreak of the Second World War, sailing from Gydnia without charts for three weeks and finally reaching Rosyth in Scotland with barely any drinking water left on board. She later served with the Royal Navy, but was lost on 8 June 1940 in the North Sea. HMS *Urchin* was laid down on 9 December 1939 at Vickers Armstrong in Barrow, and launched on 30 September 1940. A naming service for the *Sokol* took place in January 1941, attended by, amongst others, General Sikorksi. (2) The Commanding Officer of *Sokol* was the redoubtable Lieutenant Commander Borys Karnicki, who was second in

1. *Okręt Rzeczypospolitej Polskiej* or 'Vessel of the Republic of Poland'.

command of the submarine *ORP Wilk*, which had also escaped from Poland in September 1939.

Sokol sailed from Fort Blockhouse, Portsmouth on 8 August 1941 to Dartmouth, arriving the following day. She departed from Dartmouth on 12 August, with orders to sail to a patrol area in the Bay of Biscay, and 'to carry twenty-one days of provisions'; an important instruction in the light of later activities. (3) The patrol was to last two weeks and aimed to locate German U-boats off the west coast of France, after which she returned to Fort Blockhouse. On 7 September *Sokol* departed for passage to Malta, via Gibraltar. *Sokol*'s service had not gone unnoticed, and on 1 December 1941 Flag Officer Submarines, Admiral Sir Max Horton KCB, DSO**, wrote: 'While in England *Sokol* proved herself to be an efficient submarine and there is no doubt as to the keenness and pensive spirit of her commanding officer.' (4)

Sokol reached Gibraltar on 15 September 1941, and four days later departed for Malta, arriving on 1 October, having covered the complete journey from Gibraltar on the surface; her arrival was greeted by Captain G.W.G. 'Shrimp' Simpson, the Commanding Officer of the 10th Submarine Flotilla. At this time, the situation in the eastern Mediterranean was challenging for the Allies. The Italian Navy was a considerable force, and the Mediterranean Fleet, commanded by Admiral Sir Andrew Cunningham, was constantly menaced from the air. On land the Africa Korps was consolidating its gains, and vital supplies were still entering Libyan ports. The survival of Malta lay with the submarines of the Royal Navy which undertook offensive patrols as well transporting materiel from Alexandria, with many vital stores reaching the island this way. In August 1941 two submarines (*P32* and *P33*) were lost to enemy action, and on 1 September the 10th Flotilla consisted of just eight U-class boats. In the same month Admiral Cunningham sent a succinct signal to the Admiralty seeking more submarines and highlighting that 'every submarine that can be spared is worth its weight in gold.' (5)

Following the arrival of *Sokol* at Malta, Captain Simpson noted how the boat and her crew brought 'comradeship, variety and an irrepressible sense of humour to our isolation.' (6) Borys Karnicki and his officers wasted no time in getting to know Malta and its people, and they were described as a 'wild and utterly charming bunch.' Suzanne Layton[2] recalled that Borys Karnicki would often invite her out to lunch and always placed a posy of pink rose buds on her plate. He was a charmer with the ladies and described as 'devastatingly sexy and attractive.' (7)

2. Daughter of Admiral Sir Geoffrey Layton KCB, DSO, Second in Command, Mediterranean Fleet.

Godfrey Place joined *Sokol* soon after her arrival at Malta and discovered that not all the crew were submariners. Some had come from surface ships, while others had been brought up in France and been in the Polish Brigade in the French army, finally escaping to England after the fall of France in 1940. He also observed that, 'Borys [Karnicki] was determined that his boat should be considered just like any other British boat and that no one in Malta, Alexandria or London should consider a soft option for him.' (8)

There was, however, a problem with *Sokol's* arrival; Poland was not at war with Italy. Karnicki recalled how this was overcome with the assistance of his second in command, Jurek Koziolkowski, a man described as a 'great dreamer.' Whilst on patrol near Naples, Karnicki announced to the whole crew that the Poles and Italians were officially at war, and ensured that all the crew repeated what he had said. He was then passed the 'official' declaration which had been drawn up by Jurek Koziolkowski, which he duly signed. The declaration read:

War Manifesto

To His Majesty Victor Emmanuel II of Savoy, King of Italy, Eritrea, Ethiopia, Libya and island territories.
Hail!!!

Due to the disgraceful support offered by His Majesty's Government to the barbaric invader Hitler, as well as the support of his world-shattering ideas, against the best interests of amity between the Polish and Italian nations and in the name of the fighting independent Polish Republic.

I, Borys, son of Aleksander, from the Zmudz clan of Karnicki, with the heraldic names of Ilgo–Hadbank, descendant of Prometheus, do hereby declare war on Your Majesty's government and commence military actions against the armed forces of Italy, Libya and other conquered territories along the shores of the Adriatic, and I call upon the brave Italian nation to renounce the fascist dictatorship and join the just cause of the allied nations!

Captain of the victorious and invincible submarine ORP 'Sokol'.

It was delivered to the Italians inside a shell, emptied of explosive, on which was written *Non pericoloso* (Not dangerous). The *Sokol* sailed close to a small island and a crew member standing on the bows hurled the shell on to land. (9)

Sokol's first patrol, from 4 to 6 October 1941, was undertaken at short notice in an area close to the Tunisian coast, with instructions to search for the crew of a missing Blenheim aircraft. On 9 October *Sokol* sailed with HMS *Upholder* and *Unique* to the waters off Sicily, returning three days later to Malta after an uneventful patrol. *Sokol* next departed on 23 October 1941, sailing to the Gulf of Naples. Patrolling off Ischia, *Sokol* attacked an Italian convoy consisting of a small liner, four cargo ships and two destroyers, and sank the armed merchant vessel *Citta di Palermo* (5,413 tons). Godfrey Place described the action: 'the first success was an escorted cargo vessel, the *Citta di Palermo*, followed by a couple of hours' counter-attack, noisily nowhere near.' The rest of the patrol was uneventful, and the boat was about to return to Malta when word was received that a convoy might be heading her way, and she was ordered to extend her patrol. But there was a problem; the Poles had nearly finished their rations. Place explained how this had arisen: 'When submarines left their base they normally took three weeks' provisions with a further three weeks' emergency provisions. This was more than enough for most patrols. But *Sokol*'s company had instituted an eight-meals-a-day routine.'

On her way back, *Sokol* failed to encounter the promised convoy, and by this time emergency rations were running very low. On 1 November, north of Palermo, an unescorted merchant ship was sighted and attacked with torpedoes, but they missed. However, the crew of the merchant vessel abandoned ship on seeing the wake of the approaching torpedoes, and the vessel was then sunk by gunfire, the *Sokol* using all her ammunition in the attack. By the end of the patrol, Place recalled, 'the Wardroom had been dicing for the largest piece of biscuit and there was no tinned meat left of any sort.' Finally, on their way home and south of Sicily, the crew of *Sokol* sighted an Italian U-boat on the surface, at a range of 2,000 yards. 'We could do no more than just watch her go by,' Borys Karnicki remarked. 'If I had even a loaf of bread I'd have chucked it at her.' (10)

Sokol returned to Malta on 3 November 1941. She arrived just before mid-day, flying the Jolly Roger with two chevrons, and was greeted by General Sikorski and Captain Simpson. Sikorski was a friend of the Karnicki family and was undertaking an unannounced tour of the region, having already visited Gibraltar. On the dockside General Sikorski presented the *Krzyz Walecznych* (Polish Cross of Valour) to three members of the Royal Navy serving in *Sokol*, including Godfrey Place. The award led to some interesting correspondence between the Admiralty and the Polish government in London. On 22 January 1942 the Polish Naval Attaché in London wrote to the Permanent Secretary of the Admiralty:

On the recommendation of the Commanding Officer of the Submarine (Sokol) General Sikorski personally decorated the British Liaison Officer and the two British members of the crew with the Polish Cross of Gallantry in recognition of their outstanding efficiency and brave conduct during recent patrols of the submarine.

The three recipients were Sub Lieutenant B.C.G. Place, Petty Officer Telegraphist W.H. Chisholme and Leading Signalman W.G. Seddon. The Head of Honours and Awards appeared somewhat unimpressed by the apparent circumvention of procedure, and on 28 January 1942 he wrote:

Except that Foreign Governments are generally expected to consult the Admiralty before making awards to Officers or Men of the Royal Navy, no objection is seen to these awards, and it is thought that the occasion of the presentation justifies the irregularity in procedure.(11)

The awards were subsequently announced in the *London Gazette* on 6 February 1942:

His Majesty has also been graciously pleased to grant unrestricted permission for the following Officer and men of the Royal Navy to wear the Krzyz Walecznych (Cross of Valour).

Back in Malta, on 4 November 1941, the day after Godfrey Place received his award, a ceremony was held in the submarine base which was attended solely by the Polish submariners. At this time General Sikorski removed his *Virtuti Militaria* (VM) medal and pinned it on Borys Karnicki's chest.

The successes of the *Sokol* were noted by Captain Simpson, who wrote: 'this very successful patrol which resulted in the torpedoing of a 5,400 ton vessel and the sinking of a home-bound laden 3,000 ton merchant ship was carried out with great determination by *Sokol* and also with excellent judgement and submarine sense.' In commenting on how the crew fitted in with the rest of the flotilla, Godfrey Place recalled that 'the Polish Commanding Officer was a much respected and popular officer in the wardroom at Lazaretto, and the company of his junior officers was also greatly enjoyed.' He went on: 'But very few of the ratings spoke enough English to be able to mix with other crews and, although none of them showed signs of self-pity, their lot was particularly difficult.' (12)

After a rest period, *Sokol* departed from Malta on 13 November to patrol close to the Navarino area off Greece. By 18 November, at the entrance to the Gulf of Corinth, she had received reports that a small convoy of ships had taken refuge in Navarino Bay to the south. Godfrey Place described how *Sokol* was ordered to enter the bay and launch an attack, having been told that there were no nets or booms. Karnicki made a cautious investigation and decided the attack might be possible. He summoned the crew and had barely finished speaking when wires could be heard grating on the hull. The mine-warning lamps flashed red and two or three small explosions were heard. *Sokol* was stuck in a net, and Borys Karnicki remarked: 'It is a bad thing for any submarine to be caught in any net, but it is a pity for a Polish submarine to be caught in an Italian net before Poland has declared war on Italy.' In taking avoiding action, *Sokol* surfaced and, going full-astern with a huge bow-down angle, experienced ungainly dips and jumps, with depths varying widely between 50 and 150 feet. However, Karnicki was finally able to regain control. Godfrey Place recalled:

> It was cheeky, perhaps, to return later and fire the torpedoes set shallow to pass over the net. The range was extreme and, although explosions were heard, the result could not be seen. Following the incident, despite a flooded periscope, *Sokol* stayed on patrol and carried out three further attacks, but the hits she claimed were not confirmed. (13)

In fact, the torpedoes had hit the Italian destroyer *Aviere*, and two days later *Sokol* attacked and damaged the Italian tanker *Berbera*. She returned to Malta on 27 November, when Place left the boat.

In December 1941 Captain Simpson reported on the *Sokol*, that:

> This patrol again proved the efficiency and fearless determination with which Lieutenant Commander Karnicki commands *Sokol* and resulted in the certain sinking of a large Italian destroyer and the probable sinking of a medium sized supply ship bound for Benghazi. *Sokol* has proved to be a unit of the Tenth flotilla with an experienced and efficient crew and an outstandingly able commander. (14)

Further recognition of *Sokol's* service was recorded in January 1942 when Captain Simpson wrote to Admiral Cunningham: '*Sokol* under Lieutenant Commander Karnicki's able command though not at war with *Il Duce* is proving a very considerable thorn in his side.' The exploits of *Sokol* became more widely known when they were reported in *The Times* on 20 January 1942:

> In October and November she made two hits with torpedoes on a large enemy destroyer, which was almost certainly sunk, one hit an armed

merchant cruiser of over 5,000 tons which was escorting a convoy, she torpedoed two enemy supply ships which were under escort, and one similar ship of medium tonnage was sunk by gunfire. In the course of this service the *Sokol* was many times counter-attacked with depth charges by enemy escort craft, but skilful handling avoided damage.

In late 1941 submariners lived ashore on Malta when not on patrol. They were based in HMS *Talbot*, the submarine base at Lazaretto on Manoel Island, occupying buildings which had formerly served as both a leper hospital and a brothel; former residents included Lord Byron, who had been held in quarantine there. An overview of life at HMS *Talbot* was provided by Lieutenant Peter Allen, when writing to his parents in December 1941:

> This is a magnificent spot – large, airy and cool, with a high balcony from the mess overlooking the side of the harbour. Everybody is very cheerful and pleased with life – no rules, orders or regulations; one just does what one likes. This is easily the most popular station for us. (15)

However, food was in short supply due to enemy action disrupting convoys. In order to supplement their diet, several submariners kept pigs and rabbits ashore in a farm, and leading this venture was Lieutenant Commander M.D. 'David' Wanklyn DSO, Commanding Officer of *Upholder*. Once the pigs were reared to an appropriate size, Borys Karnicki was able to turn them into a variety of succulent Polish-flavoured seasonal dishes. (16)

Lazaretto's situation on Manoel Island made it rather isolated from the rest of Malta, as Godfrey Place found out. One evening when in Valetta and needing to return to Lazaretto, on the opposite side of Sliema harbour, he decided to save time by swimming back. He was stark naked, with his clothes in a neat bundle on the top of his head, when he was arrested by a Maltese sentry, who was quite sure he had captured an Italian frogman and was making very free with his fixed bayonet. 'You feel extremely unprotected in such circumstances,' Place recalled. (17)

HMS *Urge* was commissioned in December 1940 and arrived at Malta in April 1941. She was commanded by Lieutenant Commander E.P. 'Tommo' Tomkinson DSO*, who was six feet and two inches tall, powerfully built and sported an impressive black beard. Simpson recognised he was a born leader and summarised his attributes as 'qualities of concentration, a strong will and tenacity.' Tomkinson was a great friend of David Wanklyn, who in December 1941 became the first submariner to be awarded the Victoria Cross in the Second World War. He hated war, but had a particular loathing for the regimes that caused it and regarded the enemy with contempt. (18)

Godfrey Place joined HMS *Urge* on 10 December 1941, by which time she had completed eleven patrols in the Mediterranean. Despite the crew's experience, the strains of war were starting to become apparent, and in September 1941 Captain Simpson recognised this in his flotilla summary:

> The Commanding Officer has not referred to an incident in his Patrol Report, which shows the strain experienced by the crew during the first close attack subsequent to being forced to the surface. For some time after evading this attack one Leading Stoker, a normal man of submarine experience, was walking up and down the Engine room reciting the Lord's Prayer. (19)

Such strain was not unique to *Urge*; when *Upholder* was under attack by depth charges a signalman tried to get out of the submarine when it was submerged at 150 feet. As a result, Captain Simpson informed all commanding officers to withdraw if the strain imposed by any specific incident temporarily affected a submarine's efficiency.

Urge slipped from her berth at 14.05 on 10 December to start her twelfth patrol in an area south of the Straits of Messina (between Sicily and mainland Italy). It was apparent that there had been operational problems with some of *Urge*'s crew since, during her previous patrol, an error had led to torpedoes being fired at twelve-second intervals instead of twenty-four seconds, as intended by Tomkinson. This was attributed to an inexperienced Torpedo gunner's mate, a man who joined *Urge* in August 1941 and, despite trying his hardest, was described by Captain Simpson as 'not quick at learning.' The response by Tomkinson was to place an officer in the torpedo compartment during an attack to supervise the crew. At 08.43 on 14 December, two 'Cavour' class battleships, *Vittorio Venetio* and *Littorio*, with four accompanying destroyers, were sighted thirteen miles from Cape dell'Armi, heading north through the Straits of Messina. Three minutes later four torpedoes were fired in a dispersed salvo, with three hits resulting in significant damage to the *Vittorio Venetio*, putting her out of action for the next few months. Less than twenty minutes later the enemy commenced a counter-attack, and forty depth charges were dropped in the ensuing twenty minutes. The rest of the patrol was uneventful, and *Urge* returned to Malta during the morning of 20 December. On the following day Tomkinson recommended Godfrey Place for promotion:

21 December 1941
HMS *Urge*

This is to certify that
Sub Lieutenant Basil Charles Godfrey Place Royal Navy
Is competent to take charge at sea as Lieutenant to perform efficiently
the duties of that rank
Is recommended as in all respects fit for promotion to the rank of
Lieutenant.

E.P. Tomkinson

By late December 1941 the 10th Flotilla comprised ten U-class boats, and all
were at Malta for Christmas. Just before Christmas, news arrived of the
award of the Victoria Cross to Lieutenant Commander Wanklyn for action on
24 May 1941, when *Upholder* sank an Italian troopship, after which the
submarine was heavily attacked by depth charges. Official notification of the
award was made in the *London Gazette* of 16 December 1941. At that time
Wanklyn was on patrol and returned to Malta on 23 December. No one said
anything about the award to him, but Captain Simpson arranged for the
Victoria Cross ribbon to be sewn on Wanklyn's shirt overnight. The next day
he put his shirt on but did not notice the new ribbon until lunchtime.[3]
    At Christmas, Tomkinson wrote to his mother:

The little boat is working very well, and all the sailors are in great
heart. We gave them all a bottle of beer on Christmas day and had a
few minutes talking with them. They are so good and have to work so
very hard – but keep the boat looking like a new pin at all times. It really
is quite cold out here and we have a wood fire in our cabin in the
evenings, it makes things much more cheerful. There's no coal to be
had here, so we have to go scrounging for old boxes which we break up.
We feed like fighting cocks all the time – in fact far better than we did
at home. The only nuisance is from the sky – there are far too many
bombs falling. (20)

Godfrey Place was appointed to HMS *Una* from 28 January 1942, for a
month. *Una* was a recent addition to the 10th Flotilla, having arrived at

---

3. This is at slight odds with the description in the *Times of Malta* (24 December 1941)
   in which Wanklyn recalled being woken at 6 am, expecting to be ordered to sea but
   instead was informed of the award.

Malta on 4 January 1942, under the command of Lieutenant D.S.R. Martin. She had left for her first Mediterranean patrol, to the Gulf of Taranto, on 11 January. Despite a number of enemy sightings, she was unable to press home an attack, and returned to Malta on 23 January. The next patrol, commencing 9 February, resulted in controversy, both in the Mediterranean and London. By 12 February, *Una, Upright* and *Tempest* had all sailed to form a patrol line across the Gulf of Taranto, with the intention of catching any enemy ships entering or leaving Taranto. Sailing orders contained the Admiralty signal:

> The Italian tanker *Lucania* will sail from Taranto on 11 February on passage to the Atlantic. She will not be zig-zagging, will not be escorted and will be marked on both sides amidships with the Italian flag. *Lucania* has been promised safe passage by the British government and is not to be molested. (21)

Lucania had been afforded immunity from attack in order for her to provide fuel for the passenger liner *Vulcania* which was to sail, via Gibraltar and the Cape of Good Hope, to Mombasa, where she would embark Italian non-combatants and families from an internment camp for repatriation. This was not *Lucania's* first errand of this sort, and previously both the Royal Navy and the RAF had received orders to let her pass, but had both complained of inadequate and dirty markings on the ship. At 10.10 on 12 February *Upright* spotted the tanker and let her pass. However, two hours later *Una* spotted a vessel with a monoplane overhead, which was taken to be an escort, and fired three torpedoes at a range of some 2,000 yards. One hit the ship, which sank after some hours. Looking through the periscope, just minutes after the impact, Lieutenant Martin saw that the vessel was in fact the *Lucania* with correct, though very indistinct, markings. On the evening of 12 February a signal was sent to Captain Simpson from the Admiralty, enquiring if the *Lucania* had been attacked. This was passed to *Una*, and it was confirmed that they had indeed sunk an escorted tanker that morning; Captain Simpson ordered *Una* to return to Malta. When entering the harbour, she was commanded by Lieutenant L.F.L. 'Rocky' Hill, the first lieutenant, since Lieutenant Martin was unwell in his bunk. Simpson went aboard the boat and interviewed Martin, who reported that he had sunk the *Lucania* without, in Simpson's view, 'a shadow of an excuse', leaving Simpson considering that he had been 'deliberately insulted and disobeyed.' (22)

Following the incident, *Una's* third officer, Sub Lieutenant R.L. Jay, recalled that he had presented the Admiralty signal to Lieutenant Martin in the usual way before sailing. Martin declined to read it, saying that 'he had already studied the latest signals in the Staff Office in the base, before coming on board,' a procedure which was not uncommon. Signalman Thomas, another member of the crew, expressed the view that the general feeling in the *Una* was that 'we had been involved in an "accident of war".' (23) The skipper was, in Thomas' words, 'an honourable and highly professional submarine commander.' In response to the loss of the *Lucania*, the Italian torpedo boat *Circe* attacked *Tempest*, Commanding Officer, Lieutenant Commander W.A.K.N. Cavaye, on 13 February; the damage inflicted forced her to surface, and her crew were captured

Lieutenant Martin was sent by plane to England in order to explain to the Admiralty why he had sunk the *Lucania*. In London, the issue of the *Lucania* was raised at the War Cabinet on 23 February 1942. The Foreign Secretary had noted that there were 'extenuating circumstances' behind this incident. Nevertheless, he felt that the Cabinet should express its regrets, but the idea of compensation was ruled out. It was, however, suggested that the Government might provide a quantity of fuel oil equivalent to that which had been carried by the stricken tanker. The Cabinet nominated the Foreign Secretary and the First Lord of the Admiralty to draw the matter to a close, although it was recorded that 'the sinking of the tanker should not bring to an end the scheme for repatriation of Italian civilians from Italian East Africa.' (24)

Back in Malta, Lieutenant C.P. Norman was appointed as Commanding Officer of *Una*. He had previously been in temporary command of *Upholder* when, returning to Malta on the surface, she was attacked by Me109s and hit by both cannon and bullet fire. Lieutenant Norman was wounded but managed to close the hatch of the conning tower and bring the boat safely into harbour.

The middle of December 1941 had marked a turning point for the war at Malta, with a significant increase in the boldness and number of enemy air raids. The result was damage and destruction of submarines and shore establishments, and loss of personnel. During January and February 1942 air attacks increased in ferocity and led Captain Simpson to introduce a new policy to reduce the risk of damage. From early March 1942 submarines were to be submerged throughout daylight hours at deep water berths in the harbour, except for one boat which occupied the mooring alongside HMS *Talbot*, and all repair staff were to concentrate on her. It was recognised that keeping submarines submerged by day would not allow their crews to rest, so they were manned by half a crew, with either the first lieutenant or the third officer in charge. Often an officer with less than one year's experience was expected to take a submarine to a buoy and submerge it. The effect on the crews may be judged from the recollections of telegraphist Fred Buckingham:

Life was far from pleasant. After fourteen days on patrol where we saw
no daylight, we spent the day on the bottom of a creek when on duty
and most of the time in the shelter when not on duty. Very often we
took a chance and had a run a shore. Half the crew were in The Olde
Dun Cow one day when the Ju88s came over and bombed the creeks.
Jose the landlord dived for the shelter at the first bleep of the siren,
leaving us to help ourselves. Strange as it may seem we paid for what
we took. (25)

The Luftwaffe's attack on Malta was unrelenting, and on 27 February 1942
1,000lb bombs caused the destruction of two-thirds of the officers' quarters.
The now homeless submarine officers were placed on lodging allowance and
many took rooms in Sliema. More destruction followed when in March
bombs fell on the farm run by members of the flotilla, killing their pigs and
rabbits.

Godfrey Place was promoted to Lieutenant on 16 February 1942 and five
days later joined HMS *Unbeaten* as Third Officer; he was remembered by the
crew as a quiet officer who was respected and liked, and as being very happy
to talk to the lower deck. *Unbeaten* had arrived in Malta in May 1941. She
was commanded by Lieutenant Commander E.A. 'Teddy' Woodward, a man
of exceptional physical stamina, who was believed by Simpson to probably
be 'the best middle distance swimmer in the Navy.' He also had the
distinction of having taken his dog, 'Mr Pimm', to a depth of 200 feet in a
submarine. Simpson noted that Woodward had a 'particularly good eye for a
periscope attack, while his theory and mathematical ability put him in the top
flight.' Woodward played the game of war 'in reverse'; he arrived in Lazaretto
from the rigours of holiday in Malta and 'watering resorts', looking pale and
in need of a complete rest. He would climb to the conning tower, say, 'Let go
everything. Slow ahead port' and leave Malta for the refuge of a wartime
submarine patrol. Once clear of the harbour, his first lieutenant, Lieutenant
A.D. Piper, DSC, RNVR would take over and direct *Unbeaten* to her patrol
position. By the time the submarine arrived there, Woodward was as fresh as
a daisy. Piper, who had served in *Unbeaten* since June 1941, described
Woodward as 'an extremely brilliant submarine officer,' and he became the
most decorated Commanding Officer in the 10th Flotilla to return to Great
Britain. (26)

On 21 February *Unbeaten* sailed under the command of Lieutenant
J.D. Martin, who had replaced Woodward in command for the patrol. On
1 March *Unbeaten* attacked a convoy off Monastir in Tunisia, sank the Vichy
French tanker *PLM20*, 3,415 tons, and was counter-attacked by fifteen depth
charges. Woodward resumed command for the next patrol, departing from

Malta on 12 March to an area off Taranto. On 16 March in the early evening a convoy of three destroyers and the Italian troopship *Pisani*, 6,339 tons, were attacked with four torpedoes. The *Pisani* was damaged, but not sunk, and the enemy destroyers responded by dropping depth charges for the next ninety minutes. Early on the following day, when it was still dark, a U-boat was sighted on the surface. Four torpedoes were fired, and less than two minutes later an explosion was recorded followed by the noise of the U-boat breaking up. They had hit the Italian submarine, the *Gugliemotti*. About thirty minutes later *Unbeaten* attempted to surface to pick up survivors, thought to number about twelve. However, the presence of fighter aircraft overhead, along with E-boats, forced Woodward to dive. The enemy dropped depth charges but did not inflict damage, and *Unbeaten* returned to Malta on 26 March. Godfrey Place's service in *Unbeaten* during this patrol would be recognised by the award of the Distinguished Service Cross. (27)

Once back at Malta, *Unbeaten* followed Captain Simpson's orders and spent the days submerged to reduce the risk of damage from air attacks. By this time Lieutenant Piper had left the boat and returned to Britain to join the submarine commander's course, and Godfrey Place assumed the role of first lieutenant. *Unbeaten* unloaded her torpedoes and early the following morning, 1 April 1942, a skeleton crew of about six men commanded by Godfrey Place took her to Sliema creek where she dived to 50 feet. Jack Casemore, the coxswain, remembered how, after settling on the bottom, they ate breakfast and then settled down to sleep. At about 10.00 bombs were heard to fall, but the crew, apparently unfazed, went back to sleep. About forty minutes later the crew heard another bomb fall, but this one hit the boat and suddenly there were red, white and green lights throughout the compartments and water pouring into the torpedo-tube space. Water leaked from the forehatch and the lights were extinguished. Jack Casemore, in the forward compartment, called through to the control room using the voice pipe. Godfrey Place replied that they were unharmed in the aft compartments, and they started to try to surface. This took several attempts and required air to be pumped into the forward tube space, but finally they reached the surface, although the bow remained partly flooded. (28) *Unbeaten* then sailed to Grand Harbour, where the damage was inspected; it was found that the torpedo tubes were useless although the boat remained seaworthy. Despite this, *Unbeaten* could be considered to be lucky; nearby HMS *Pandora*, Commanding Officer, Lieutenant R.L. Alexander, which had recently arrived, was 'cut in two' by bombs with the loss of twenty-six men. On the same day attacks on Sliema destroyed three blocks of flats which had been home to officers from *Unbeaten*, *Urge* and *Sokol* and further undermined Simpson's ability to provide suitable accommodation for crews between patrols. Borys Karnicki went to the bomb site and there, glinting in the sun on top of ten feet of rubble, was his *Virtuti Militaria* which General Sikorski had personally presented to him. Less fortunate was the cat which had been rescued by *Sokol's* crew from the Italian schooner *Guiseppina*[4] and was now lying dead under the billiard table.

Following the damage sustained in the air attack, *Unbeaten* was ordered to return to England for repairs. She departed for Gibraltar on 8 April but en route she was to rendezvous with *Upholder,* which had departed from Malta two days earlier to the Gulf of Sousse. On board *Upholder* were Captain R.A. 'Tug' Wilson and Lance Corporal Charles Parker, who were experienced in canoe (or folbot) landings from submarines and who were to help land two Arab agents. Having landed the agents, *Upholder* was to rendezvous with *Unbeaten* on 10 April near the islet of Lampione to allow Tug Wilson to transfer to *Unbeaten*. The rendezvous took place at night, but with the winds rising and an increasingly rough sea David Wanklyn suggested that Tug Wilson might reconsider the transfer and return to Malta on *Upholder*. He refused the offer, and transferred to *Unbeaten* in the early hours of 11 April by folbot, taking with him a spare battery and other equipment for *Unbeaten*. On reaching *Unbeaten,* he was greeted in humorous tones with, 'Piss off Tug, we've got two feet of water in the fore-ends and the batteries are gassing. You'll never make it to Gib!'.[5] Despite this he joined *Unbeaten*, and it was Godfrey Place who helped to bring his folbot on board. The rendezvous was the last time *Upholder* was seen; she was reported overdue, presumed lost, on 20 April 1942. *Upholder* had been one of the most successful of the submarines of the 10th Flotilla, and her Commanding Officer had been awarded the Victoria Cross and the Distinguished Service Order and two bars. (29)

Unbeaten arrived at Gibraltar on 21 April 1942 for repairs, having spent the last day of her journey surfaced because of the damage to her bows. On 29 April the Admiral Superintendent at Gibraltar reported that a survey of the pressure hull showed that she was unfit for patrol until after permanent repairs had been effected, and it was not until 26 May 1942 that she departed Gibraltar. On 8 June 1942 both *Unbeaten* and HMS *Torbay*, also returning from the Mediterranean, met off Start Point, on the south coast of Devon,

---

4. *Sokol* had sunk the *Guiseppina* on 8 February 1942.
5. The 'gassing' batteries were the result of damage that occurred during bombing in harbour at Malta. The day after they left, Woodward had detected chlorine, a smell associated with leaking batteries. Norman Drury, a telegraphist on board *Unbeaten*, described how this was treated by short circuiting the cells with 'cutting out strips' and that they picked up some more strips from *Upholder* at the rendezvous.

and proceeded up the English channel together to arrive at Portsmouth. The Commanding Officer of *Torbay* was Commander A.C.C. Miers VC, DSO*, who had won the Victoria Cross in March 1942 for his successful raid on shipping in an enemy harbour.[6] Showing deference to rank, *Unbeaten* followed *Torbay* into Portsmouth, where they were greeted by bands and by the Captain of HMS *Dolphin*. On 18 June *Unbeaten* departed from Portsmouth to Chatham for refit, which lasted until the middle of September.

Godfrey Place left *Unbeaten* on 8 July 1942, and had made an impression with his Commanding Officer, who reported:

> An excellent Navigating Officer and Third Hand, most efficient and enthusiastic – but he must cure himself of his untidiness. Place has contributed greatly to *Unbeaten*'s success in the Mediterranean and is a most capable and promising young officer. He is highly recommended as 1st Lieutenant of a Submarine.

In 1942 *Unbeaten* had been adopted by the town of Hove, Sussex. In March, Hove Borough Council organised 'Warship Week' commencing 14 March, a campaign to raise funds for their adopted submarine. The First Lord of the Admiralty officially opened a week of events which included parades, dances, a church service and a ball. The target of £425,000 was reached within a week and the total raised was £521,000, an amount equivalent to £10 per head of population in the town. Shortly after their return to England, Lieutenant Commander Woodward, accompanied by some of the officers and ratings from *Unbeaten*, were entertained to lunch at Hove by the Mayor, Councillor A.H. Clarke. Godfrey Place attended this lunch, sitting next to his Commanding Officer in the official photograph. The Jolly Roger from *Unbeaten* was presented to the Mayor on this occasion; unfortunately it was later lost when Hove Town Hall was bombed during an air raid.

Following *Unbeaten*'s refit, there were numerous changes to the crew. Godfrey Place was appointed to HMS *Varbel* for training with midget submarines, and Woodward took command of the submarine attack teacher course, initially at *HMS Dolphin*. Lieutenant D.E.O. Watson DSC was

---

6. In November 1941, commandos had landed by folbot on the coast of Libya on a mission to destroy enemy installations, including Rommel's headquarters. *Torbay* had been under the command of Commander Miers and on board was Lieutenant Colonel Geoffrey Keyes MC, who led the detachment assigned to attack Rommel's base. On the night of 17/18 November 1941 Keyes was killed leading the raid, and was awarded the Victoria Cross, posthumously.

appointed as Commanding Officer of *Unbeaten*, and the boat left Chatham on 17 September 1942, en route to Portsmouth and Plymouth. On 6 November she was ordered to patrol in the Bay of Biscay, subsequently being ordered to return from patrol on 8 November. On 11 November *Unbeaten* was asked to report her position, course and speed, but nothing was heard from her. She failed to arrive at a predetermined rendezvous, south of Bishop's Rock. It is believed that *Unbeaten* was attacked on 11 November, in error, by an RAF Wellington of No 172 Squadron, leading to her loss with all hands.

There were mixed fortunes for the other boats of the 10th Flotilla. *Sokol* sustained significant damage from air attacks at Malta in March and April 1942. In early April it became apparent that the Luftwaffe had targeted her and were doing their best to destroy her. On 17 April following repairs, and despite having only one propeller working, *Sokol* departed before dawn for Gibraltar. Borys Karnicki was in the conning tower as she prepared to leave when Captain Simpson hailed: 'You must let me know, Borys, when you are west of Sardinia, then I shall be able to stop worrying about you, but make your signal short'. He added, 'I shall be seeing you soon, Borys, but if I should miss you in England, what will your address be in Poland?'

'My address in Poland? Ah let me think now, Captain, when you come to Poland after the war just ask for the office of the Commissar for the Socialisation of Women and walk right in.'[7] (30)

Sokol departed from Gibraltar on 21 June and arrived at Dundee on 22 July 1942, where she was taken into refit. Borys Karnicki was later made an Honorary Member of the Distinguished Service Order.

By April, Simpson was only too aware of the extreme difficulties faced by Malta and in May 1942 reported:

> The loss of four submarines by air attack while in harbour, and the difficulty of giving crews of boats back from patrol any proper rest, eventually caused the Tenth Submarine flotilla to be temporarily withdrawn to Alexandria. On 4 May Captain Simpson and his staff left by air, leaving a care and maintenance party under Lieutenant Commander Marsham in charge of the depot at Malta. (31)

---

7. Borys Karnicki did not return to Poland after the war but remained in Britain. Towards the end of the war he became a father; his wife Jadwiga (neé Micklewicz) gave birth to a daughter Maria Anna on 31 March 1945 in London. He wrote of his time in the navy in 'A Duffle Bag of Memories', and died in Blackheath, London on 15 February 1985. His ashes were interred at Gydnia, Poland in May 1985 with full military honours.

At the end of April there were five deployable submarines at Malta, *P31, P34, P35, Una* and *Urge*; all were ordered to sail for Alexandria. *Urge* departed on 29 April, but by 6 May 1942 she was forty-eight hours overdue and no contact had been made. She was presumed missing. The news of her loss was withheld for several months pending enemy claims of her destruction, but by June none were forthcoming. It seems probable that *Urge*, which was not fitted with mine detector units, struck a mine in the first forty miles of her passage from Malta. She had undertaken eighteen patrols since leaving the United Kingdom in April 1941, and had been responsible for, amongst other things, the sinking of a large liner, the Italian cruiser *Bande Nere* and damaging the battleship *Vittorio Venetio*. She had also undertaken four special missions, landing commandos by folbot. Captain Simpson wrote, '*Urge's* loss is a bitter blow which will nevertheless in no way affect the morale of the 10th Submarine Flotilla.' He then proceeded to describe the qualities of some of the crew:

> Lieutenant Commander Tomkinson was an outstandingly able leader, whose strict disciplinary methods were mellowed by a great sense of humour, charm and understanding. The chief difference between Tomkinson and Wanklyn was that the former suffered fools less gladly. The determination, forethought and excellent eye of both officers produced results of an equally high merit.

The original recommendation for the award of the Distinguished Service Cross to Godfrey Place was completed by Lieutenant Commander Woodward and Captain Simpson before *Unbeaten* left Malta in April 1942. However, by December 1942 the papers had not been received by the Admiralty and Simpson realised there was a problem. The recommendations had been lost when he transferred his headquarters from Malta to Alexandria. The recommendations were resubmitted in December 1942, and the citation read:

> Lieutenant PLACE has served in 'Unbeaten' for the last 15 patrols[8] in capacity of Navigating Officer and latterly as Armament Officer. His coolness in the face of the enemy and keenness for offensive action together with alert efficiency have largely contributed to these successes. (32)

8. This is an error in the account submitted by Captain Simpson, since Godfrey Place served four patrols in HMS *Unbeaten* and not fifteen.

On 4 May 1943, the award was announced in the *London Gazette*, and Godfrey Place received a letter:

> On the advice of the First Lord, the King has been graciously pleased to award you the Distinguished Service Cross for skill, coolness and determination in His Majesty's Submarine UNBEATEN on her patrols in the Mediterranean in March 1942, in which a U-boat and a heavily escorted Enemy merchantman were destroyed.

The role of the Royal Navy in disrupting the supply lines to Rommel's forces in North Africa was recognised by Winston Churchill in 1942, in his wartime diaries: 'British submarines operating from Malta played a leading part, and the scale of their activities and successes mounted steadily.' Godfrey Place was one of many in the submarine service who contributed to the success at Malta, and soon he was to be appointed to a very different type of submarine operation. The experiences he had gained would go with him, and without doubt what he had learnt from working with a number of commanding officers, each with their own characteristics, would influence him in the years to come. After the war he spoke warmly of the Polish submariners who had served with him.

As for Malta, recognition was forthcoming from the King. The George Cross was awarded to the island; this was not announced in the normal manner through the *London Gazette*; King George VI sent a hand-written letter, dated 15 April 1942, to the Governor, Lieutenant General Sir William Dobbie, which contained the following citation:

> To honour the people I award the George Cross to the Island Fortress of Malta to bear witness of a heroism and devotion that will long be famous in history.

Dobbie left Malta on 8 May 1942, and was replaced as Governor by Field Marshall Viscount Gort VC, who brought with him the George Cross and presented it to the Chief Justice, Sir George Borg, at a ceremony in Valetta. Just over a year later King George VI visited Malta at a time when the focus of conflict had shifted from North Africa to Southern Europe. The visit would, in a small way, impact on Godfrey Place back in England.

Chapter 5

The Prize is Waiting: Preparation for Operation Source

The *Admiral von Tirpitz* was the largest battleship to have been built in Europe. The simple mention of her name irritated Winston Churchill, who expressed his annoyance when writing to the First Sea Lord in January 1942:

> Is it really necessary to describe the TIRPITZ as the ADMIRAL VON TIRPITZ in every signal. This must cause a considerable waste of time for the signalmen, cipher staff and typists. Surely TIRPITZ is good enough for the beast? (1)

With a displacement of 45,000 tons, *Tirpitz* was slightly larger than her sister ship, *Bismarck*. She was laid down at Wilhelmshaven on 24 October 1936, launched on 1 April 1939 and completed in November 1940. With a complement of 2,000 officers and men, she was commissioned in February 1941 and spent the rest of the year undertaking trials in the Baltic. Her main armament comprised eight fifteen-inch guns with a range of over twenty miles, and these, combined with a speed of 30 knots, made her immensely powerful. Even before *Tirpitz* or *Bismarck* had been commissioned, their threat was recognised by Churchill, who wrote that they were 'targets of supreme consequence.'

In May 1941 the *Bismarck* was sunk by ships of the Royal Navy in the Atlantic, and this allowed Churchill's focus to shift to the *Tirpitz*. Germany declared war on Russia in June 1941, and the presence of the *Tirpitz* in the Baltic ensured German naval superiority in the area. However, the threat of her heading west to the Atlantic caused Churchill to write that *Tirpitz* 'exercises a vague and general fear.' With the entry of Russia into the war, Britain started supply convoys to Northern Russia. Responding to this, Hitler and Admiral Raeder, Head of the German navy, agreed to move *Tirpitz* to a base in Norway in December 1941. Doing so had three benefits: it strengthened German defences in Norway (Hitler remained concerned that the British would mount an attack there), tied up British naval forces and provided a base for the German navy to attack convoys. In January 1942 *Tirpitz* sailed from Gydnia to Trondheim. Churchill's frustration became evident in a letter dated 18 January to General Ismay, reminding him of the effect that small submersible weapons had already had, to Britain's cost, and seeking an update on the development of similar weapons by the British:

> Please report what is being done to emulate the exploits of the Italians in Alexandria harbour and similar methods of this kind. At the beginning of the war Colonel Jeffries[1] [sic] had a number of bright ideas on this subject, which received very little encouragement. Is there any reason why we should be incapable of the same kind of scientific aggressive action that the Italians have shown? One would have thought we should have been in the lead. (2)

On hearing of *Tirpitz's* arrival in Norway, Churchill wrote again to General Ismay:

1. The presence of *Tirpitz* at Trondheim has now been known for three days. The destruction or even the crippling of this ship is the greatest event at sea at the present time. No other target is comparable to it. She cannot have ack-ack protection comparable to Brest or the German home ports. If she were even only crippled, it would be difficult to take her back to Germany. No doubt it is better to wait for a night attack, but moonlight attacks are not comparable with day attacks. The entire naval situation throughout the world would be altered, and the naval command in the Pacific would be regained.
2. The whole strategy of the war turns at this period on this ship, which is holding four times the number of British capital ships paralysed, to say nothing of the two new American battleships retained in the Atlantic. (3)

In response, the RAF mounted a bombing raid on the *Tirpitz* on the night of 28 January 1942. Nine Halifax and seven Stirling aircraft were dispatched, but thick cloud prevented their pressing home an attack.

---

1. Major M.R. Jefferies, RE. In December 1940 he was appointed as Superintendent of MD1, a department reporting directly to Winston Churchill and his chief scientific adviser, Lord Cherwell. Jefferies was responsible for developing novel weapons including proximity fuses and sticky bombs.

Tirpitz's first sortie from Norway was to attack convoy PQ12 in March 1942. However, before reaching the convoy she was ordered to break off the engagement as her position had become known to Admiral Sir John Tovey KCB, DSO, Commander-in-Chief, Home Fleet. He immediately ordered a torpedo attack by aircraft of the Fleet Air Arm flying from HMS *Victorious*. None of the torpedoes hit the ship, and she returned unscathed to port. After a period of maintenance she sailed on 3 July to engage convoy PQ17, but was ordered not to attack if there was any possibility of defeat. *Tirpitz* turned away, but the First Sea Lord, Admiral of the Fleet Sir Dudley Pound GCB, GCVO, believing she was still about to attack, ordered the convoy to scatter, an order that was met with almost disbelief by those in the convoy. The merchant ships became easy targets for U-boats and German aircraft, and over 150 men were lost along with huge amounts of military hardware. *Tirpitz* had wreaked havoc without even joining battle.

It was against this background in the summer of 1942 that Godfrey Place, having returned from the Mediterranean, was summoned by the Captain of Submarines of the 5th Flotilla, Rear Admiral R.B. Darke DSO, and asked, 'How would you like to sink the *Tirpitz*?' To which Godfrey Place replied, 'Yes.' When asked in 1988 why he had been chosen, Place replied, 'purely because I happened to be in Blockhouse at the time.' (4) It transpires that the interview actually took place at the Ritz Hotel, London; Godfrey Place had been invited for tea and it was apparent that when asked if he would like to sink the *Tirpitz*, an answer of 'No' was not an option.

Within weeks of the interview, Godfrey Place was appointed to HMS *Varbel* on the Isle of Bute in Scotland. *Varbel* was a newly established unit responsible for the development and deployment of submersible craft, including chariots (a form of motorised torpedo, with a two-man crew sitting astride the vessel wearing breathing suits, and armed with a detachable charge in the nose) and midget submarines, or X-craft. X-craft had been developed by Commander Cromwell Varley DSO, who had served in submarines in the First World War. An adventurer, he had commanded HMS *H5* in 1916 when, defying orders, he took the boat into the entrance of the Jade River in Germany (near to Wilhelmshaven), home to the German fleet. Here he sank a U-boat and then successfully sailed back to Harwich, where his exploits were rewarded with a dressing down for having left his patrol position. Varley left the Royal Navy in the 1920s following the introduction of the 'Geddes Axe'. He was a close friend of Admiral Sir Max Horton, Flag Officer Submarines. Horton had commanded the submarine HMS *E9* when, in September 1914, he had torpedoed the German cruiser *Hela*. On returning to base he initiated the tradition of flying a 'Jolly Roger' following a successful trip. Varley had also been in communication with Churchill about his ideas and plans. The first midget submarine, initially designated 'Job 82' but subsequently called X3, was built at Varley's marine yard at Brunsledon on the River Hamble. Constructed under conditions of strict secrecy, she was 50 feet long, about 5 feet 5 inches in height (at the highest point) and had a displacement of approximately 50 tons. She had three compartments: a forward control room, a Wet and Dry (W&D) compartment in the middle, which allowed a diver to enter and exit when it was submerged (and was the only route for entrance and exit), and the engine room at the stern. Commander Varley had originally designed X-craft for use in covert operations in mainland Europe, such as placing charges at the base of bridges over inland waterways.

In December 1941 a crew was assigned to X3, even before she was completed. The Commanding Officer was Lieutenant W.G. 'Willy' Meeke DSC, who had been the first lieutenant of HMS *Sturgeon*. He, along with Lieutenant Donald Cameron RNR (another former member of *Sturgeon*'s crew), were described by Godfrey Place as the 'two original stalwarts of X-craft.' The third member of the crew was Chief ERA[2] Richardson. Cameron was a Scotsman, born in 1916; he had entered the Merchant Navy before the war, but in August 1939 joined the Royal Naval Reserve. The following year he was appointed to the submarine service. He would spend a lot of time with Godfrey Place over the coming years, and they became good friends. He was a quiet, somewhat detached man, who at times almost appeared remote to those around him, but he had a keen sense of observation and when time afforded he would paint. Deep down, however, he was an officer with a sense of absolute determination.

X3 was launched on the River Hamble at 23.00 on 15 March 1942 and made her first dive on 24 March in Portsmouth harbour. Trials of X3 were undertaken over the following months, both at Portsmouth and in Portland harbour. At this time X-craft were very much a 'cinderella programme', and there was little support for the crew. As a result, Meeke and Cameron spent considerable periods of time ensuring that the boat remained serviceable. By mid-July 1942 it was apparent that the enemy were aware of some of the trials, having increased their activity in the Portland area. The decision was made to move to a new, more secure, base in Scotland, and trials were suspended. The trials' tender, HMS *Present Help*, sailed from Portsmouth on 26 August to the Isle of Bute, and at the same time X3 was transferred by train to Faslane, where she was launched and sailed to Bute. Meanwhile, construction of the second prototype, X4, had started at the naval dockyard at Portsmouth. (5)

2. ERA: Engine Room Artificer.

There were several new recruits to HMS *Varbel* in September 1942, and they varied both in experience and background. Godfrey Place was one the few full-time Royal Naval officers who joined in September 1942 and he recalled that the recruiters were looking for 'men who had about one year's practical experience, preferably regular officers who had been midshipmen and so were tolerably adept at coastal navigation'. The first call for recruits was made through Confidential Admiralty Fleet Orders 843/42, which requested: 'Volunteers for special and hazardous service, who are below the age of 24, unmarried, good swimmers and of strong and enduring physique.'(6)

Godfrey Place was remembered as a 'handsome man who was sloppy but incredibly cool under pressure' by Lieutenant George Honour, who shared a cabin with him for a time. He described how he once found Place with bits of machinery distributed all over his bed, having just dismantled an engine; this was reminiscent of his father's dismantling of a gramophone in the bath. He was popular at *Varbel* for his dry humour and kindness, although he developed a habit of borrowing items of clothing from other men, invariably without their permission. (7) Many of the recruits were members of the RNVR, but Lieutenant A.R. 'Baldy' Hezlet DSC, the Instructional Officer, commented that they were 'all extremely keen and determined'. (8) Recruits were also drawn from the South African and Australian navies, including Lieutenant Bruce MacFarlane, RAN, who had been the Officer of the Watch on board HMS *Queen Elizabeth* on the fateful night of 19 December 1941 when she was attacked by Italian frogmen in Alexandria harbour. After the attack, the ship's Commanding Officer, Captain Claud Barry DSO, said to MacFarlane, 'You had better go and do the same thing, hadn't you?'

Training for midget submariners took place at both Portsmouth and Bute, and Place recalled that the trials were hard work;

> We were in Scotland for a certain amount of work up and then came down to Portsmouth for a conference, doing trials for a day or so, trials having to be done at night because of security, then going along to the Keppel's Head[3] for breakfast, then, into the conference room for 9.30 and sitting down with a slide rule and looking at the results of the trials. I found I was as adept with a slide rule as anyone else.

The Isle of Bute lies to the west of the mouth of the River Clyde, and experiences a relatively mild climate, benefiting from the Gulf Stream.

---

3. Hotel named after Admiral Keppel, and frequented by members of the Royal Navy over many years.

Rothesay, the main town, lies on the more sheltered east coast, as does the smaller town of Port Bannatyne, about one mile north. Submarines of the Royal Navy had been based at Rothesay since the middle of 1940, when the 7th Submarine Flotilla arrived from Portland and were joined by the depot ship HMS *Cyclops* from Harwich. Rothesay became the major base for British submarine training in the Second World War. (9) In preparation for midget submarine training the Royal Navy requisitioned the Kyles of Bute Hydropathic Hotel in September 1942. This was one of three hydropathic hotels on the island, built on a hill above Port Bannatyne, and had its origins in a Victorian house called Swantonshill, built in 1855. A long wing was added to the west side of the house when it was converted to a hydropathic hotel, which opened in June 1879. A further wing was added around 1911 as part of the rebuilding programme following a fire on Christmas Eve 1909. Built in the Victorian 'gothic' style with ornate turrets and a central castellated tower, it commanded impressive views through tall windows to the east, over Kames Bay and up Loch Striven. The hotel had eighty-eight rooms for guests and, unlike the other 'hydros' on the island, did not serve alcohol to residents. In June 1942, in one of the last advertisements placed before it was requisitioned by the Royal Navy, it announced itself as 'a beautiful residence sitting in fifteen acres of sheltered grounds.' It prided itself on running water in all bedrooms, a swimming pond, hard tennis courts, badminton and golf.

The name HMS *Varbel* was an amalgam of Varley and Bell, the latter being Commander T.I.S. 'Tissy' Bell, who was responsible for training the crews. Commander D.C. Ingram DSC was the first commanding officer of *Varbel* and had served in submarines earlier in the war; in July 1940, when commanding HMS *Clyde*, he attacked and damaged the German battleship *Gneisenau*. Despite being a 'stone frigate', *Varbel* was an official naval establishment and possessed a ship's bell, which hung in the entrance hall. Made of solid brass, the bell had a notable history. It had been salvaged from a cargo ship, the SS *London Merchant*. Built in 1925 she was sold in 1935 and renamed the SS *Politician*. On 5 February 1941, on passage from Liverpool to America, the *Politician* became stranded on the island of Eriskay in the Outer Hebrides. The ship was carrying a considerable quantity of whisky destined for America, in payment for military hardware.[4] The forward section of the ship was towed to Kames Bay in

---

4. This was the basis for the novel (later filmed) *Whisky Galore*, written in 1947 by Sir Compton Mackenzie. It featured a ship called the *Cabinet Minister* which was stranded on the Island of 'Little Todday' while carrying a cargo of whisky. As in real life, the islanders salvaged the whisky.

August 1942 for salvage, and the ship's bell was removed and placed in HMS *Varbel*, where it remained until she was decommissioned in May 1945. The bell was later moved to the Isle of Bute Museum, Rothesay, where it hangs opposite the bell from HMS *Rothesay*, a frigate commanded by Godfrey Place in 1962–3. (10)

The base at HMS *Varbel* allowed easy access to the waters of Loch Striven, to the north-east of Port Bannatyne. It had already been demarcated as a restricted area for submarine exercises and its deep water and sheer sides mimicked the Norwegian fjords where the *Tirpitz* was moored. To aid training, a second base was established at the northern head of Loch Striven, in a requisitioned shooting lodge, Ardatraig House, renamed HMS *Varbel II*. This lacked some of the grander features of *Varbel* and provided a rather spartan base. Commander Bell was appointed the first Commanding Officer of *Varbel II*; he was described as a man 'of fantastic energy, but incapable of suffering fools gladly. He was constantly falling foul of higher authority and the very young.' Sub Lieutenant John Lorimer, RNVR, was one of the first recruits to join the midget submarine programme and remembered how they built up their stamina by cross-country runs, felling trees and swimming in the icy waters of the loch. He recalled meeting Godfrey Place at Bute, and remembered being told that he had obtained five firsts at Dartmouth without doing any work. As was typical of the man, Place did not discuss himself at all, and never mentioned his early life or his earlier service in the Royal Navy. However, he told John Lorimer that the award of the Polish Cross of Valour entitled him to 'a mistress, two cows and half a hectare of land in Poland.'

Another new recruit to *Varbel* was Sub Lieutenant Max Shean, RANVR, an Australian who had volunteered for midget submarine service, having previously served in the corvette HMS *Bluebell*. He recalled that Commander Bell was 'an energetic, single minded man who urged them to train until they were as "fit as tigers".' Shean described how 'many men rose early, ran on the hills and returned for breakfast – they used more energy than they consumed, and so hunger mounted by the day. Others felt that training for life in a poorly ventilated submarine was better achieved by taking all the rest available and spending off-duty time becoming accustomed to self-generated tobacco fug, sipping gin.' Writing after the war, Shean was of the view that 'experienced fug generators were the more successful at crippling battleships.' Whether this was meant to include Godfrey Place is uncertain, but he did enjoy the outdoor life in Scotland and often walked over the hills for the best part of a day when not in training.

At the same time as X3 and X4 were being used in training, modifications of the design were made by the Admiralty before placing an order for the production of six operational craft. They were to be built by Vickers

Armstrong at Barrow-in-Furness, for delivery in late 1942 and early 1943, and would be named X5 to X10. A critical feature of the craft was their strength, which allowed a diving depth of about 400 feet. In the operational design the forward compartment contained the batteries, and behind that was the W&D compartment. To the aft of this was the control room where the crew would be accommodated; this had a separate hatch as well as a periscope and induction trunk (for allowing air intake). At the stern of the boat was the diesel engine, a 32 horsepower Gardner, identical to that used in London buses at the time. The control room housed the magnetic and gyrocompasses, and in its roof was an armoured glass plate which allowed the crew to determine when they were passing under a target. There was also a small electric heater, referred to as the 'gluepot boiler', which allowed the crew to warm food. Conditions were exceptionally cramped on board, and it was soon recognised that there would be a need for a passage crew to man the boat on its journey to the target, with a changeover to the operational crew one or two days before an attack.

The original plan for X-craft operations involved a diver leaving the craft and placing limpet mines on the target. Place recalled that this was given up at an early stage; instead, the armament was two detachable streamlined side charges, each holding two tons of torpex explosive. The charges contained buoyancy tanks, which ensured that they were neutrally buoyant during passage. Once released the tanks would flood. The charges were to be detonated by a time fuse, which had a delay of up to six hours. X-craft had a range of about 1,200 miles on the surface and 150 miles when submerged, with a maximum speed of six knots when surfaced and five when dived.

In September 1942, A.V. Alexander, the First Lord of the Admiralty, provided Churchill with an update on the project. X3 was at Bute, there were twelve officers and twenty-four ratings in training and X4 was due to be completed in October 1942. Alexander remarked that the planned date for operations against the enemy was March 1943. (11) By November 1942 Godfrey Place was in command of X4, which was being used to 'train the trainers.' He recounted how there was 'more or less daily running, as well as trying to do an endurance trial to see what living conditions were like.' By this time some of the defects with the boats were becoming obvious; most were of an electrical nature, resulting from condensation forming on electric cables.

The earliest plans for midget submarines to attack the *Tirpitz* were devised in October 1942 by staff at Northways, the Office of Flag Officer Submarines. The operation required assistance from the Norwegian resistance, and Colonel J.S. Wilson, Head of the Norwegian Section of Special Operations Executive (SOE), became closely involved with the planning. Initial plans were to use six X-craft in the first week of March 1943, before the nights became too short. It was intended to attack the *Tirpitz* either at Trondheim or Narvik, and to use Norwegian fishing vessels to tow the X-craft to within 150 miles of their target, where they would slip and make their own passage to the ship. To ensure success, there was a need to practice and perfect towing of X-craft, and arrangements were put in place for trials to commence early in 1943.

X-craft were not the first submersible craft to be used in an attempt on the *Tirpitz;* in June 1942 'Operation Title' was authorised for November 1942. This involved charioteers being transported across the North Sea in the Norwegian trawler *Arthur*, commanded by Lieutenant Leif Larsen of the Royal Norwegian Navy. Two chariots were to be taken to Trondheim fjord, and then launched to attack the *Tirpitz*. The party, comprising two charioteer crews and two spare men, left the Shetland Islands on 26 October, two days after *Tirpitz* had arrived at Trondheim. The *Arthur* safely negotiated the German guards in the fjord, the crew making use of forged papers provided by SOE, but the operation came to an abrupt end when it was discovered that the two chariots had broken loose from their hidden position under the keel of the trawler. The mission had to be abandoned, and those involved made their way across Norway to Sweden and thence back to Britain. All reached safety except for Able Seaman Bob Evans, who was wounded whilst fleeing from German soldiers close to the Swedish border. After receiving medical care, Evans was interrogated and then shot as a spy.

Whilst in training, X-craft crews had to face many hazards, not least the inherent instability of the boat which often led to sea-sickness. Working in an X-craft was not for the faint-hearted. Conditions inside were unpleasant, as the damp air became stale from being recycled. There were also mechanical hazards, with crew members being injured by unguarded machinery. Hazel Lloyd-Jones, a Wren driver working at *Varbel*, remembered the casualties that had to be driven to the hospital on Bute. She recalled the case of ERA Ken Petty; the sleeve of his submarine jersey had become caught in the revolving engine shaft aboard the X-craft which took his arm off. 'After the CO had severed the few remaining strands of skin with a dinner knife he was rowed ashore, quite conscious, by the torpedo man Elijah Whittaker. His arm followed in a cardboard box.' (12)

In October 1942, when under the temporary command of Sub Lieutenant John Lorimer, X3 sank in 110 feet of water in Kames Bay, the result of a partially open valve on the induction trunk. All three crew members (John Lorimer, 'Taffy' Lates and Len Gay) escaped, and the attending vessels, *Tedworth* and *Barfield*, were able to rescue the submarine and raise her to the surface. The submarine was sent by train to Portsmouth for overhaul and repair in early November. The sinking of X3 led to a Board of Inquiry whose report was sent to the Flag Officer Submarines. On 17 November, clearly appreciating the taxing and demanding conditions associated with midget submarine operations, he wrote:

> I have directed the Commanding Officer HMS *Varbel* that Sub-Lieutenant Lorimer to be admonished for the errors on his part which led to the sinking of X3; but at the same time I agree that Sub-Lieutenant Lorimer's subsequent conduct was highly commendable and I have also directed that he is to be so informed. The quick salvage and slipping of the submarine reflect credit on the commanding officer HMS *Varbel*, who is also to be congratulated on a very clear report. (13)

X4 arrived at Bute in November 1942 and the following month was involved in a tragic accident. On 11 December 1942, whilst she was exercising in Inchmarnock Water (to the west of Bute) on a five-day endurance trial, the weather suddenly deteriorated. Godfrey Place had just been relieved on watch by Sub Lieutenant I. M. Thomas, RNVR. Thomas was standing in the hatchway ditching rubbish when he was caught by a strong wave and washed over the side. Water entered the W&D compartment, causing the boat to sink rapidly. Place was in the control room in the bow, with ERA W.M. 'Bill' Whitley in the engine compartment at the stern, and neither could communicate with the other. Not for the first time, Godfrey Place was trapped in a submarine. Fortunately he was able to send out distress signals to one of the attendant vessels, and within two hours X4 had been located and was being raised to the surface. Godfrey Place later recalled the incident and described how it was due to the inherent defect in stability of the boat. Following this, they went over to 'harbour running' (where boats were only exercised in more sheltered waters). Thomas's body was never found, and he was one of thirty-nine members of the 12th Flotilla who lost their life on active service.[5] He was just twenty-one and had interrupted his studies at the Royal Veterinary College, London, in order to join the navy. This tragedy led to modifications to the X-craft, with the addition of a horizontal bar and buckled strap fitted to the induction trunk in order to secure the watch keeper to the casing in heavy weather. It was named the 'Hezlet rail' after its designer, Lieutenant Hezlet.

---

5. All thirty-nine members of the 12th Submarine Flotilla who lost their lives on active duty are remembered on a memorial unveiled in 2005 at Port Bannatyne, Isle of Bute and a cairn at Kylesku, Sutherland, unveiled in 1993.

Selection of crews for the operation took place towards the end of 1942, and all senior lieutenants received commands. These were:

X5   Lieutenant W.G. Meeke, DSC, RN
X6   Lieutenant D. Cameron, RNR
X7   Lieutenant B.C.G. Place, RN
X8   Lieutenant B.M. MacFarlane, RAN
X9   Lieutenant T.L. Martin, RN
X10 Lieutenant K. Hudspeth, RANVR

At the same time the first lieutenants were appointed:

X5   Sub Lieutenant H. Henty-Creer, RNVR
X6   Sub Lieutenant J.T. Lorimer, RNVR
X7   Sub Lieutenant L.B. Whittam, RNVR
X8   Sub Lieutenant W.J. Marsden, RANVR
X9   Sub Lieutenant J. Brooks, RN
X10 Sub Lieutenant B.E. Enzer, RNVR

Max Shean, who had been selected as a reserve for either an operational or passage crew, recalled that the announcement of the commands was followed by a wardroom party. It was, however, still some time before the attack on the *Tirpitz* would occur, and there would be a number of changes to the crews before then.

Soon after these announcements there was a change in command, as Flag Officer Submarines, Admiral Sir Max Horton, hauled down his flag on 9 November and was succeeded by Rear Admiral Claud Barry. Barry had served in submarines in the First World War although his most recent appointment had been Commanding Officer of HMS *Queen Elizabeth*, and this had included the night in 1941 when the ship had been attacked by Italian frogmen.

There were also members of the Women's Royal Naval Service (WRNS) at HMS *Varbel*. Both officers and ratings were posted to the establishment, undertaking a variety of jobs, including working as drivers, stewards and in communications. Petty Officer Jessie Wilson recalled:

> Men and women were accommodated in the Hydro and (it) gave one the feeling of working together and seeing familiar friendly faces day after day. It does not take much to evoke memories of *Varbel* for me and I can say that, unfashionable though it may sound today, 'I had a lovely war'. However cosy it may sound today 'We were like one big happy family.'

Lily Robbs was a mess steward at *Varbel* and commented:

> There was always an air of excitement about the place. When you first
> saw these special craft, and heard the stories the lads told of
> happenings and laughs against themselves, it made you realise just how
> close knit a community *Varbel* had become. You found yourself
> conversing on the same level and you knew you'd been accepted. (14)

Amongst those appointed to HMS *Varbel* was twenty-one-year-old Third
Officer Althea Tickler, WRNS, who had joined the service in 1942. Althea
was born and brought up in Grimsby, and was the second of three daughters
born to Harry Tickler and his wife Bertha (neé Anningson). All three
daughters were accomplished sportswomen, having been Junior Tennis
champions for Lincolnshire. Althea also had a passion for horses, having
hunted before the war with the Brocklesby Hunt. The Ticklers were a well
established and respected family in Grimsby, and Althea's father was the
third son of Thomas George (T.G.) Tickler, himself descended from a family
of local mill owners. Thomas Tickler had established himself as a grocer and
confectioner in Grimsby in about 1880 and then developed the company,
T.G. Tickler Ltd. The business expanded into the production of jams and
preserves, running factories in both Grimsby and Southall. Their most
famous product was 'Tommy Tickler's Plum and Apple Jam' which was
supplied to soldiers serving in the trenches in northern France during the
First World War.

   After initial naval training at Greenwich, Althea served at Grimsby, close
to home. However, she was advised that she would only really progress in the
service if she was willing to serve away from home. Almost to call their bluff,
she agreed to do so and before long was travelling to Glasgow by train.
Althea, being very personable and out-going, easily struck up conversation
with another Wren officer in the train. From their conversation it was
apparent that the second officer had been appointed to a naval establishment
on Bute. However, since this was a single appointment she needed a female
companion; she chose Althea, and before long they were both serving in
HMS *Cyclops* at Rothesay.

   The arrival of the elegant Third Officer Tickler on Bute 'turned heads' all
over the island, not least that of Godfrey Place. Many years later he described
her arrival on the island as electrifying to all the young men. He was
desperate to ask Althea out, and approached her with a ruse of asking for
some change for the bus. Althea did not have any money, but rather than just
say 'no' she spent considerable time searching her handbag, trying to find
some for him. In fact, she was so concerned for the apparently penniless

officer that she offered to ask someone else if they might have some change. Unbeknown to Althea, Godfrey Place had plenty of money all the time. After this initial encounter, he asked Althea out for a walk, to which a 'love rival', fellow submariner Sub Lieutenant Bruce Enzer, invited himself along, much to Place's chagrin. The competition was on. Althea later described the hilarious behaviour of the two suitors attempting to outdo each other by showing off their athletic prowess, vaulting gates and standing on their heads. Place had to push himself to the limit to keep up, and this was not helped by his relatively small stature. However, it was now apparent to Althea just how serious Godfrey Place was about her, and their friendship grew. Soon after arriving on Bute Althea was, conveniently, appointed to HMS *Varbel*, where she served as Signals Officer of the flotilla.

Place travelled to London at the end of December 1942 for the New Year celebrations, although he appeared not to have requested leave from any senior officer before departing. He met his mother and sister, both of whom were serving in the ATS. Peggy was based at Droitwich, having joined the Army in May 1941, and Helen (Bunty) was leading a team involved with making newsreels to be sent to troops serving abroad. In October 1942 Helen had become engaged to Major Ernest Kenber, Royal Artillery, who had been a master at Marlborough College. Peggy did not approve of their relationship and had made her feelings very clear, much to the embarrassment of both her children. On New Year's Eve Godfrey wrote to Althea; their relationship was such that he obviously felt able to tell her about the tensions in his family. He described the uncomfortable time as they had dinner, Peggy was described as being in 'one of her blackest moods,' and he continued:

> Bunty was more or less in tears most of the time and Mum grew more vitriolic as time progressed. The pianist – in lieu of cabaret – played Rhapsody in Blue very well and that was about the only bright thing of the evening. Oh dear – some people have difficult mothers. She doesn't approve of Bunty's boyfriend and considers it beneath her dignity to go and see his people.

In the same letter he wrote of his feelings about the progress of the war, and of war itself:

> I think propaganda is getting worse – all the evening papers tonight exultant over the execution of a Belgian Nazi spy and the odd 130,000 Germans killed at Kotclnov. If I were made Archbishop of Canterbury tomorrow – an office I feel I'm unlikely to hold, I would revive the 'love your enemies' line as I don't think hate is liable to get anyone anywhere.

After returning from London, Place travelled to Vickers Armstrong where the operational submarines were being completed. X5 was launched on 31 December 1942 and the remaining five craft followed, with the last, X10, being launched in the middle of February 1943. Writing to Althea from the Victoria Hotel, Barrow, he asked if she would perform the naming ceremony for his boat, X7, and explained the situation:

> When we arrive we shall never have been wet and it is essential to perform the ceremony prior to the first insertion. If you were to get Ingram [Commander Ingram] on the sly with a whisky and soda, I'm sure you could wheedle him into consenting to a female going over to do this – you see it must be a female. All sailors are superstitious and regard the bad luck attendant on the absence of this ceremony, not as a possibility but certainty. Think of the good this will do – and suppose the chances were ruined just because this simple action was not performed.
>
> BUT
>
> If he doesn't agree – which he probably won't if you don't switch on charm – we'll get a dazzling blonde from Bell's joint [Commander Bell] to do it when we arrive ... but it wouldn't be very lucky.

Althea did perform the naming ceremony for X7. Godfrey Place had chosen the name '*Pdinichthys*', a prehistoric 'fearsome' fish which laid two eggs. The boat also had a motto: 'Not to our friends, only fearsome to our enemies.'

The start of the new year brought both the towing trials and a name for the operation; the attack on the *Tirpitz* was given the codename 'Operation Source'. In early January the Norwegian trawler MFV *Bergholm*, commanded by Leif Larsen (who had returned from the ill-fated 'Operation Title'), arrived at HMS *Varbel* from Shetland to commence towing trials. Operational X-craft were not available, so X4 was used. It did not take long for more problems to be identified, and Larsen and others concluded that it would only be possible to tow with a trawler in calm waters. They were also concerned as to the suitability of fishing vessels for the task, and questioned how X-craft crew would find their way to the target in a steep-sided fjord on a dark night. Responding to these concerns, the decision was made to plan the raid for when there was a half-moon, to aid the crews in finding their goal.

At the beginning of February 1943 a new plan was produced, involving just three X-craft which were to be towed from the Shetlands on 5 March;

each would have a passage crew and an operational crew. The X-craft would be towed by Norwegian trawlers along independent routes to slipping positions off the Norwegian coast. All X-craft were to attack in daylight, over a period of forty-eight hours. After completing the attack, X-craft were to return to the Shetlands under their own power or, if they were unable to do so, would rely on the LARK organisation, which was part of the Norwegian resistance, to aid their escape to Sweden. It was helpfully pointed out to Colonel Wilson at SOE that 'none of the X-craft crew can speak Norwegian or ski.' Within a week plans had changed yet again, and on 14 February Admiral Barry wrote to Colonel Wilson to inform him that the operation had been postponed until the autumn, the reason being: 'Materiel failure with the craft so interfered with training that it was impossible to get even three of the craft operationally fit for operations before the hours of darkness get too short.' (15)

Nearly 400 miles from *Varbel*, Winston Churchill continued to demand progress on plans to destroy the *Tirpitz*. On 16 February 1943, writing to the Chief of Combined Operations, First Sea Lord, Chief of the Air Staff and Commander-in-Chief, Bomber Command, he made his views quite clear:

> Have you given up all plans of doing anything to *Tirpitz* while she is at Trondheim? We heard a lot of talk about it five months ago, which all petered out. At least four or five plans were under consideration. It seems very discreditable that the Italians would show themselves so much better in attacking ships in harbour than we do.
>
> What has happened to the chariots and to the diving mines?
>
> I should be much obliged if you would take stock of the position, if possible together, and thereafter give me a report. It is a terrible thing that this prize should be waiting and no one able to think of a way of winning it. (16)

Tirpitz had been based at Trondheim over the winter of 1942-3, allowing essential maintenance to be carried out which was followed by gunnery trials. In early November 1942 the German navy had become aware of 'Operation Title', and responded by moving the ship between berths at frequent intervals and having divers regularly inspect the hull. Within a month of Churchill's letter, the *Tirpitz* sailed from Trondheim to northern Norway, arriving at Alten fjord on 24 March 1943 in the company of the battleship *Scharnhorst* (31,800 tons) the 'pocket' battleship *Lutzow* (12,100 tons) and eight destroyers. *Tirpitz* anchored in Kaa fjord, an arm of Alten fjord, some 50 miles inland. Over the next five months she undertook further planned maintenance as well as a number of repairs. In Kaa fjord she was even further from the midget submariners' base, making any attempt to attack her even more challenging.

Back on Bute, the midget submarine programme was continuing to expand, and amongst those joining HMS *Varbel* in March 1943 was a young Northern Irishman, Able Seaman James Magennis. He had joined the Royal Navy in 1935 as a boy seaman aged sixteen and initially served at HMS *Ganges*. He had already seen action; in December 1941 he was on board HMS *Kandahar*, part of Force K, when she struck a mine off the coast of Tripoli attempting to help the cruiser HMS *Neptune* which had struck a series of four mines and then sank with the loss of 764 officers and men, including Sub Lieutenant David Bevan. Magennis joined the submarine service in 1942 and registered at HMS *Dolphin* for special service on 15 March 1943. Four days later he arrived on Bute, where he recalled meeting Godfrey Place and Donald Cameron and making his first trip in a midget submarine, X7. He was to go on to play a critical role in midget submarine operations, both in Norway and later in the war in the Far East, for which he would receive due recognition. (17)

There was high security at HMS *Varbel*, and all those working there were told not to talk about their work. In early 1943 the population of Bute had risen due to an influx of civilian evacuees and the billeting of Polish and Canadian troops. Bill Lavender lived in Port Bannatyne and was fourteen when HMS *Varbel* was established. He recalled seeing the midget submarines exercising in Kames Bay and berthed alongside at the newly constructed jetty at Port Bannatyne. 'People accepted them' he said, and added 'many of us did not realise that they were any different from a standard submarine.' He pointed out that access to the island was totally reliant on some form of shipping, and the authorities had complete control over the ferries.

Integral to the successful operation of the midget submarines was a depot ship, and HMS *Bonaventure* was to fill this role. *Bonaventure*, a merchant vessel, had been built for the Clan Davidson line but after her launch in 1942 was requisitioned by the Royal Navy. The ship, with a displacement of 10,000 tons, had a large crane which allowed X–craft to be lifted onto her deck. Her first Commanding Officer was Captain W.E. 'Willy' Banks DSC, who had served as a submarine commander during the First World War. *Bonaventure* was to act as a depot ship both at Kames Bay and at the more northern base, Loch Cairnbawn.

For Godfrey Place a relationship that had started with a request for a bus fare had developed into love; early in March 1943 he asked Althea to marry him, and she agreed. As was to be a feature of much of their married life, they were soon parted, when he travelled from Bute to Loch Cairnbawn for midget submarine trials. Place had both work and pleasure on his mind; Althea's acceptance of his proposal made him exceptionally happy and he wrote to her to describe his feelings:

> It seems incredible that one word – 'yes' – should make you my fiancée, and us engaged and going to be married and live happily ever after all in one. It's the most marvellous thing that ever happened since green slime became a living organism. I can hardly wait to get back, it won't be very long now. I want to tell you over and over again that I love you and I want to hear you say 'I love you too, Godfrey' because that's the most beautiful thing anyone has ever said to me … I think love is a wonderful thing, love and understanding will break down all barriers – in fact if only everyone loved and understood everyone else how happy the whole world would be.

As with any engagement, there was the issue of the two families and how they were to be introduced to each other. Godfrey Place became engaged before he had met Althea's parents; certainly he did not ask Harry Tickler for his daughter's hand. In Althea's case, it was unusual for someone of her standing and background from Grimsby to marry a man from outside the town, and her family were keen to know all about her fiancé as soon as possible. It was, however, only after they had become engaged that Godfrey told Althea about his family, although by this time she had met his sister Helen. Althea had already gained some insight into Peggy from his letter of New Year's Eve, but in March he described his mother's life in more detail to her.

Godfrey Place's relationship with his mother was undoubtedly fraught, and by 1943 spending more than three days in her company was a trial for both parties. After Pat's death Peggy had struggled to keep her son at school and then Dartmouth. Initially, Peggy had worked for the Duchess of Portland at Welbeck Abbey near Worksop. She then moved, first to Bewdley in Worcestershire and then to Stourbridge, where she worked for the church. Here she had managed to settle in a home of her own. However, Peggy had always had difficulties in managing money; there had been numerous rows between her and Pat about her excessive spending. When the war started and there was a financial downturn, Peggy had a three-figure overdraft and packed up home in an attempt to run away from her problems. In May 1940, when Godfrey Place was on leave from HMS *Newcastle*, he and his sister endeavoured to sort out things with the bank. Of the two, it was Helen who appeared to have a greater grasp of the financial situation along with the ability to deal directly with the banks and creditors. Her brother did not have the same financial acumen, and it would be many years before he acquired it. Place wrote of Peggy's response to her financial difficulties: 'She was quite hopeless at this time – whenever we tried to get down to brass tacks she burst into tears and we were afraid she'd lose her reason.'

Peggy joined the ATS in May 1941, a move that appeared to provide her with some degree of stability. In March 1943 Godfrey Place conveyed his feelings about Peggy to Althea:

> I'm frankly very worried about her – because she recognises that her life is now past. Like all her family her only interest was her husband – when he died she strove to educate her children as it had been planned ... now, with both of us self supporting (at least Bunty's married which amounts to the same thing) she realises that she is not working to a definitive aim in life and the meaning seems to have dropped out of any existence on this earth. Being nervously energetic the ATS does, I suppose, provide a certain amount of outlet for her energy. But she does not make friends easily now and what she will settle down to after the war God knows. She says she intends to wander through Europe with Olive Mackin – a cousin of my father's – while Olive paints. Perhaps that is best, she is not strong and sunshine will be good for her ... but it terrifies me to think of someone wandering, unsettled, eternally looking for something she knows she can never find. And there is nothing Bunty and I can do.

Had he been too candid with his fiancée so soon after proposing marriage? Trying to allay possible concerns on the part of Althea, who had yet to meet Peggy, he added: 'I hope I haven't frightened you over my mother but if you don't like her you need have no more to do with her than politeness demands. Deep down I know I am very fond of her indeed – but I know she can be difficult.'

He also described his grandmother, Mabel Stuart-William, who was known as Dame in the family: 'There are people who seem determined to be miserable. Dame, when you said good luck to her over a glass of sherry, used to look gloomy immediately and say how much we needed luck but it wasn't much good anyway and I used to practically throw the decanter at her. Dame is Peggy's mother- I'm afraid you'll meet her sometime.'

Godfrey Place also used his letters to Althea to describe himself: 'I am an obstinate person, I like arguing, dogs and fried onions, and loathe religious fanatics, masculine women and carrots.'

Marriage appears to have come slightly earlier than either party had foreseen, and Godfrey Place wrote:

> It's funny you should mention that you didn't bank on marrying before you were twenty-four because I had always (rather cynically) maintained that I would marry a girl of seventeen when I was about thirty or thirty-five and life had little else to offer. But this is much more satisfactory.

On board *Bonaventure* he was already making arrangements for the wedding and had asked Sub Lieutenant Henty Henty-Creer, RNVR to be his best man:

> Henty says that he'll be best man, and Terry [Lieutenant T.L. Martin] wants to be an Usher – I suggested he dresses up in a small boy's sailor suit to be a page boy but he said 'Whoever heard of a page at a wedding being mildly inebriated?' In a somewhat alcoholic mood last night he told me he loved you and did I mind?

The 'best man to be', Henty Henty-Creer, came from a naval background; his father had been an officer in the Royal Navy who had married an Australian girl. Henty-Creer was noted for his winning personality, good looks and a 'twinkle in his eye'; Godfrey Place considered him a 'very good friend.' Henty-Creer was later described as a 'finely tuned eccentric' who always wore his cap at a jaunty angle. Even in 1943 he was writing his autobiography, an undertaking that Max Shean felt was consistent with Henty-Creer's own statement that, 'An impression is better than the solid fact.' He was born in 1920 and left school to work in the film industry before and during the first year of the war. With the commencement of hostilities he had been desperate to serve his country and, despite being offered exemption from service, joined the RNVR. Officer training was undertaken at HMS *King Alfred* in Hove, Sussex, where he passed out in the top echelons of his class. From there he was appointed straight to the submarine service, in which he was detailed to join the X-craft programme in the autumn of 1942. (18)

Back on board *Bonaventure*, Godfrey and Althea exchanged several letters over the following weeks. He was missing his fiancée dreadfully and described his response to receiving three letters from her in one day:

> Mail – you couldn't see me for dust when they piped 'hands of the mess muster for mail.' Three letters – one for each day at the beginning of the week. Thank you so much – I did not know it was possible to

look forward to mail so much or to be so excited at the sight of three envelopes.

You should have seen me when I got my mail ... I was busy in the fore hold at the time and I fairly ran and came back with it, tore open all three envelopes at once – got all the letters mixed up and the engineers and shipwrights, who I was dealing with at the time, had to wait nearly an hour while I had a first view through them all.

Letters were now to be welcomed, although this had not always been the case, as he wrote:

Always before it has been with a vague fear that I have approached the mail bin to find a letter from my grandmother – 'suppose you must have gone abroad again' or Mum 'do hope you aren't ill ... no better for two months.' Well, they can't complain now as I've written to the whole lot to tell them all about it.

Official notice of the engagement did not appear until 16 April 1943 in *The Times*:

Lt B.C.G. Place RN and Miss A.A. Tickler The engagement is announced between Lt Basil Charles Godfrey Place Royal Navy, son of the late Major Godfrey Place, DSO, MC and Mrs Margaret Place ATS, Pirbright Camp, Woking, and Althea Anningson Tickler, Third Officer WRNS, daughter of Mr & Mrs Harry Tickler of Danesbury House, Bargate, Grimsby.

The midget submariners' northern training base, Loch Cairnbawn, also called Port HHZ, is a sea loch in a remote part of north-west Scotland, just north of the Assynt peninsula and about fifteen miles south of Cape Wrath. It extends inland where it divides into two, Loch Glendhu and Loch Glencoul. The remoteness of the region helped in ensuring security for this and other military operations taking place in the area. Those living in the area remember how the roads were closed by the military authorities. Max Shean described how in the summer, crews went ashore at every opportunity, walking the hills and visiting nearby villages. To the east was Kylesku, a small hamlet with a pub next to the ferry, remembered by the crews as somewhere they could get bacon and eggs every day, a most uncommon event due to rationing. To the west was another hamlet, Nedd, and a little further on, the village of Drumbeg, where dances were held and romances occurred; one officer later married a girl from the village.

Place was in *Bonaventure* in March 1943 in order to take part in exercises to assess the sea-keeping, navigational and attacking qualities of X-craft. X5, X6 and X7 took part and their target was *Bonaventure* herself, moored in Loch Cairnbawn. The plan was for X-craft to be towed south to Loch Kishorn, a distance of about 80 miles, from where they would travel back alone to attack the *Bonaventure*. The journey time to Loch Kishorn and back was less than twenty-four hours, so it was decided that the whole exercise was to be carried out by the operational crews. On 28 March X5, commanded by Willy Meeke, was towed, submerged, from Loch Cairnbawn by HMS *Tedworth*. Once at Loch Kishorn, she slipped and returned to make an undetected attack on *Bonaventure*. Place was unable to undertake the full exercise due to a serious defect in the induction trunk in X7. By 31 March the repairs had been completed. Due to time constraints, the new plan allowed for X7 to travel about 10 miles to the west (close to the Point of Stoer) and then return and attack. At 11.45 X7 left *Bonaventure* and dived. A full westerly gale was blowing and the sea was very rough. By 15.15 the boat was off the Point of Stoer, but the crew heard noises indicating the port charge was working loose and banging against the boat's side. Undaunted, Godfrey Place steered X7 to commence the attack, but by this time the sea was very violent and all the crew were seasick. To make the conditions more realistic, *Bonaventure's* defences were enhanced by the trawlers *Port Ryan* and *Heland* undertaking anti-submarine patrols at the loch's entrance. Anti-submarine nets were also placed around *Bonaventure*. X7 dived to 40 feet for the attack but with periodic visits to periscope depth; however, Godfrey Place found keeping the boat at periscope depth very difficult due to the prevailing sea conditions. At 16.05 X7 inadvertently broke the surface but was not seen, and about one hour later she avoided the *Heland* to enter the loch at periscope depth. She remained undetected and commenced her attack from the port side, passing under the anti-submarine nets, so that by 18.23 she was under *Bonaventure*. The two charges were released within thirty seconds of each other, and less than ten minutes later X7 surfaced, clear of the nets, and returned alongside *Bonaventure*, having been away for some seven hours. *Bonaventure* was lying in about twenty fathoms of water, and divers were sent down to recover the charges to determine their positions and relate these to their point of release. X7's first charge was lying 150 feet from the stern, under the port side of the ship and the second was 110 feet further forward, but 10 feet clear of the starboard side. There had been no difficulty in releasing the port charge, despite the problems noted earlier. The report by Admiral Barry on X7's activities concluded that 'the attack is considered to be highly successful.' (19)

After the exercise it was concluded that more practice was required, and from this, recommendations on methods of attack could be produced for all X-craft commanders. The problem of charges drifting after their release was of concern, and further trials were scheduled at Rothesay. A similar exercise would be undertaken by the other X-craft (X8, 9 and 10) in May or June, again at Loch Cairnbawn. Admiral Barry, when forwarding his report to the Admiralty in April 1943, noted, 'the results and the high standards of efficiency attained by X-Craft Commanding Officers and crew are most gratifying.' This was, however, to be the last major involvement of Willy Meeke in the operation. Place described him as 'the grand old man of the party at twenty-eight years old'; but when it was decided not to undertake the attack in the spring Meeke moved back into ordinary submarines. He left a legacy of high standards that he and Donald Cameron together had set, and which were to be expected of all the crews in future.

Bonaventure sailed from Loch Cairnbawn, arriving at Kames Bay on 5 April. Later that month there were changes to the organisation of midget submarines, with the formation of the 12th Submarine Flotilla. Captain Banks relinquished his command of *Bonaventure* to Acting Captain P.Q. Roberts and then made his way ashore to command the new flotilla. His headquarters were to be at HMS *Varbel*. The 12th Flotilla comprised all operations and training involving midget submarines, chariots and Welmans (the latter being one-man midget submarines designed for use in combined operations). Although strongly supported by Admiral Mountbatten, they had limited use and no tangible successes in the war.

The components of the Flotilla were:

HMS *Varbel*: Shore establishment at Port Bannatyne, Rothesay, Flotilla headquarters: X-craft training.
Commanding Officer, Captain W.E. Banks DSC

HMS *Varbel II*: Shore establishment at Loch Striven, based at Ardatraig House. Tender to HMS *Varbel*, X-craft training.
Commanding Officer, Lieutenant Commander J.F.B. Brown DSC.

HMS *Bonaventure*: X-craft depot ship. Advanced X-craft, Chariot and Welman training at Loch Cairnbawn, and other sites as required.
Commanding Officer, Captain P.Q. Roberts.

HMS *Titania*: Depot ship for Chariot training and preliminary Welman training. To be based in Loch Corrie.
Commanding Officer, Commander W.R. Fell OBE, DSC. (20)

With the expansion of the flotilla came changes at some of the establishments, and enlargement of facilities. At Port Bannatyne there was dredging of part of the harbour and requisitioning of the pier for use by X-craft. Nearby at Ardmaleish, just to the north of Port Bannatyne, a slipway allowed X-craft to be taken out of the water for servicing and repair, and there was to be a new road to the yard as well as the construction of a weatherproof store.

In April there was further good news for Godfrey Place, when a signal arrived at Bute from Flag Officer Submarines:

Please convey my heartiest congratulations to Lieut. Comdr. WOODWARD on award of 2nd Bar to his DSO, To Lieut PLACE on award of DSC.

At this time, Teddy Woodward was in command of the Submarine Commanding Officers' training course based at Rothesay.

Following the departure of Willy Meeke, Captain Banks appointed the recently promoted Lieutenant Max Shean as Commanding Officer of X5, in April 1943. Henty Henty-Creer was to remain as first lieutenant and to concentrate on penetrating the nets that protected the *Tirpitz* at her anchorage. There were two types of nets:

1) Anti-submarine nets, found at the entrance to a mooring or harbour. These were normally made of three-inch wire in a mesh of about three foot square, which extended from the surface to the seabed.
2) Anti-torpedo nets, sited around a berthed ship, which were usually made of hard steel rings, about one foot in diameter, closely resembling chain mail. (21)

Successful penetration of anti-submarine nets would be vital to the attack. The W&D chamber allowed a member of the crew acting as a diver (either the first lieutenant or the ERA) to exit the X-craft and cut through nets. Godfrey Place recalled net cutting as both 'fascinating and entertaining' but he and others questioned the practicality of doing it in an enemy harbour. It took some time to discover a suitable technique and it was Max Shean who finally developed and demonstrated the method. The technique was, however, applicable only to anti-submarine nets, and Place was of the opinion that the possibility of cutting through an anti-torpedo net was 'absolutely nil'; it was planned that X-craft should pass under these. The diver used a hydraulic cutter attached by flexible piping to the midget submarine, and five or six cuts in an anti-submarine net allowed the submarine to pass through. Place commented that this was 'quite exciting, but if one thing goes wrong, everything goes wrong', and felt that the diver was actually a sacrificial lamb. Despite the success in developing a strategy for cutting nets, tragedy struck the flotilla again when on 31 May Sub Lieutenant David Locke, RNVR, a crew member from X7, failed to return from a net-cutting exercise in Loch Striven, and was presumed drowned.

In June 1943, command of X5 passed to the First Lieutenant, Henty Henty-Creer, who would not be promoted to Lieutenant for another two months. Max Shean moved to command X3 and continued training other officers and men. There was obviously some displeasure at these changes on the part of Shean who, after the war wrote of Henty-Creer's appointment:

> I received my 2nd strip i.e. Lieutenant, after two and a half years as a Sub Lieutenant during which time I had gained a watch-keeping certificate and had been successful in an attack which had probably sunk a U-boat, while Henty achieved rapid promotion without such experience. It did not concern me at the time, but I believe is a matter of some significance in view of subsequent happenings. (22)

The loss of David Locke highlighted the problems associated with non-specialist divers attempting to penetrate the anti-submarine nets, and there needed to be changes to ensure that the attack could take place. The solution was to recruit specialist divers to the X-craft crews, but this meant each boat would have a crew of four; conditions on board would be even more cramped.

Towards the end of June 1943, all officers who were training as charioteers at Loch Corrie were summoned by Commander Fell to a meeting on board HMS *Titania*. Amongst those attending was Sub Lieutenant Roland Hindmarsh, RNVR, who had joined the Royal Navy on leaving school and had delayed his studies at St Catherine's College, Cambridge until after the war. Despite being only twenty years old he had already served with the Malta convoys in 1942. Under conditions of utmost secrecy they were informed about the existence of midget submarines and of the need for six divers to volunteer for the mission to act as net cutters. An immediate decision was not required, and they were asked to write their names on a piece of paper once Commander Fell had left the room. Another diver at the meeting was Sub Lieutenant Robert Aitken, RNVR, also aged twenty. He initially thought 'no thank you' to the idea of transferring to midget submarines, but with some persuasion, and the offer of transport to Glasgow and a few days' leave, he agreed.

Six divers volunteered and were soon on their way south to HMS *Varbel*.
Their introduction to X-craft was rapid, and before long they were diving in
Loch Striven, making their first attempts to exit and enter a midget
submarine, at a depth of 15 feet. After this they headed north to Loch
Cairnbawn, where they joined HMS *Bonaventure* and met the crews of the
midget submarines. Hindmarsh remembered the atmosphere in *Bonaventure*
as 'severe and purposeful, buzzing with activity and tense with deadlines.'
This was the antithesis of *Titania*, where the divers had enjoyed 'boyish
buffoonery in the wardroom'. Not long after their arrival, Roland
Hindmarsh became all too aware of the different atmosphere and dynamics
in *Bonaventure* when encountering Godfrey Place.

> I remember throwing off remarks loudly to Geordie [Nelson, a fellow
> diver] on the second day, as he sat beside me, about those X-craft types,
> and making myself obnoxious. I think I felt disturbed by the change
> from being the centre of attention on Tites [*Titania*] to simply one of
> a much larger team, and a somewhat unwelcome late arrival at that.
> Certainly I remember no warmth towards us from the X-craft crews,
> when we arrived. So if they were going to be stand-offish, we could be
> hostile in return. This led to a sharp exchange I had in the wardroom
> at lunch with an RN lieutenant who took exception to the style of my
> remarks, and snubbed me in public. I learned afterwards that this was
> one of the X-craft commanders, Lieutenant Godfrey Place. I hadn't
> experienced this kind of nastiness since my training at King Alfred,
> and I found it particularly unwelcome in the context of an imminent
> hazardous operation. (23)

Godfrey Place did not suffer fools gladly throughout his career and was not
averse to using his acerbic tongue when he believed it was called for. Roland
Hindmarsh may have been the first to get such a dressing down; he would
not be the last.

Many years later, Hindmarsh remembered that first meeting with Godfrey
Place and described him as decisive, not at all cheery and with an authority
about him which created an atmosphere of respect; he was decisive in his
statements, a man who knew that what he was saying was right. This was in
marked contrast to Donald Cameron, who came across as a much more laid-
back individual.

The divers who joined the midget submarines received a less than friendly
reception from the established crew members. It was immediately obvious
that there was a definite hierarchy and that segregation amongst officers

extended to the depot ship. Here the commanding officers ate together as a group, as did the first lieutenants, and soon the divers did likewise; there was little interaction between the groups in the wardroom. Before long, each diver was assigned to a boat. Following his earlier encounter, Hindmarsh was keen not to be enclosed in the confined space of an X-craft with Godfrey Place and was certain that 'Place wouldn't want to have me as his diver.' He was assigned to Bruce MacFarlane's X8. The diver assigned to X7 was Robert Aitken, described as a man of 'strength and solid calm'. It did not take long for Aitken to encounter his Commanding Officer's determination to get a job done, and done properly. One night he was at the helm of X7 and Place gave the order to dive. Aitken was still fumbling with the valves when Place appeared and opened the valves rapidly to ensure the boat dived correctly. The first lieutenant of X7, Bill Whittam, was unusual amongst the X-craft crews in being appreciative of the divers, perhaps because he had some experience of diving himself. He was twenty-two years old and had previously served with the commandos. Noted as a genial character, he was, at six feet five inches tall, perhaps not best suited to the midget submarine. A public schoolboy, he had stories as 'tall as himself'. Whittam was also a man with an eye for the ladies, and Shean noted him on the train to Glasgow in September 1942 reclining across the laps of 'some six or seven Wrens'. Whilst at *Varbel* Whittam had become close friends with a Wren who was serving alongside Althea, Third Officer R.D. 'Ruth' Barham. The fourth member X7's crew was ERA Bill Whitley, aged twenty-eight and described by Place as 'a gay lad whose father was waiting for him to take over his engineering works in the Midlands.' (24)

One of the many challenges still facing the operation was how to tow the midget submarines to Norway. The early trials had involved X-craft being towed by trawlers or similar vessels, but there were significant problems, not least the violent motion in the submarine. In June 1943 towing trials involving a conventional submarine were initiated by the Admiralty Research Department. HMS *Thrasher*, Commanding Officer, Lieutenant A.R. Hezlet, and X7 started the trial at Kames Bay and Loch Striven. On 11 June X7 was towed to Loch Cairnbawn by *Thrasher*, remaining submerged en route for up to seven hours, but surfacing for brief periods to ventilate the boat. After five days of towing trials in Eddrachillis Bay, X7 was towed south, arriving at Kames Bay on 17 June. The trials allowed an estimate of the towing pull engendered at different towing speeds, and the impact on fuel consumption by the submarines. However, even before the trial had been completed, Admiral Barry had written to the Commander-in-Chief, Home Fleet to advise that his intent, as at 16 June, was to tow the six X-craft using two 'T' class and four 'S' class submarines of the Home Flotilla. There would also be a need for a further two 'S' class submarines to be available at Scapa Flow, held as spares at twenty-four hours' readiness to sail. Altogether the eight boats represented nearly the entire strength of operational submarines in British home waters, and all the boats would have to have completed operational patrols by 24 August for them to join 'Operation Source' in early September. The submarines would be required for six weeks, during which time there would only be four submarines left available in home waters.

On 9 July 1943, a signal was sent to the Norwegian resistance: 'FOS informed me that Submarine has proved ideal way of towing. He did not appear interested in further trials with fishing boats.' (25)

Although the trials involving X7 and *Thrasher* had been a success and allowed a more suitable means of towing to be developed, inspection of *Thrasher*'s log revealed problems with the telephone communication, carried through the tow rope to X7, with it breaking on several occasions. (26)

After completing the towing trial, Godfrey Place travelled to London. On 22 June 1943 he received the Distinguished Service Cross at an investiture at Buckingham Palace. The occasion was notable for a number of reasons, not least the absence of the King. King George VI was on a tour of the Mediterranean, the highlight of which was his visit to Malta GC on 20 June. In the King's absence, Queen Elizabeth took his place for what was the first time since the reign of Queen Victoria that a queen had held an investiture. *The Times* reported that 'the recipients of the medals and their families waiting in the grand hall for the ceremony to begin were surprised when the Queen, attended by officials, walked onto the dais.' More than 270 people attended, and the first recipient of an award was Wing Commander Guy Gibson VC, DSO*, DFC. A month earlier he had lead the Dambuster raid by 617 Squadron and was at the Palace to receive the Victoria Cross along with a bar to the Distinguished Service Order.

Less than a month after attending the investiture in London Godfrey Place married Althea Tickler. The card from Mr and Mrs Harry Tickler invited guests to the wedding at 2pm at St James Church, Grimsby on Tuesday, 20 July 1943. However, on 13 July (Althea's birthday) the church was severely damaged by enemy bombs and the wedding had to be rapidly rescheduled for Saturday 17 July 1943 at Holy Trinity and St Mary the Virgin Church, Old Clee, Grimsby. The marriage was performed by the Vicar of Grimsby, Canon Lisle Marsden. Henty Henty-Creer was the best man, and both Althea's sisters were bridesmaids. A reception was held at the Tickler home, Danesbury House at Bargate, and was followed by a brief honeymoon in the Lake District, at the Borrowdale Hotel near Derwent Water. However, it was short-lived, since before long Godfrey was back in training in the north of Scotland.

As part of the final preparations for the attack, the battleship HMS *Malaya* was used as a target. A sister ship of HMS *Queen Elizabeth*, the *Malaya* had also served at the Battle of Jutland in the First World War, and with a displacement of 42,000 tons was slightly smaller than the *Tirpitz*. In July 1943 she was stationed at Scapa Flow, but sailed to Loch Cairnbawn on 25 July. For the next two weeks she lay at anchor, serving as a target for the attacking X-craft. Place recalled that all six X-craft attacked and there was only one possible detection by men on board the ship, which had posted special submarine look-outs during this period. (27)

During August there were further intensive exercises involving all six X-craft at Loch Cairnbawn. Exercises often took place at night, with several entries in *Bonaventure's* log showing X7 returning in the early hours of the morning. It was during this period that Place carried out the only trial using live side charges. He recalled how he laid two in Loch Glendhu and watched to see 'a very impressive explosion to a tremendous height.' His viewing point was just outside the Kylesku Inn.

Winter came early to Loch Cairnbawn in 1943, and by early September there was already snow on the peaks of the surrounding hills. HMS *Titania* sailed from Loch Corrie to Loch Cairnbawn on 30 August to act as the depot ship for the six towing submarines which were to take part in 'Operation Source'. The towing submarine for X7 was to be HMS *Stubborn*, Commanding Officer, Lieutenant A.A. 'Anthony' Duff, which had recently returned from patrols in the Mediterranean. Anthony Duff had passed out of Royal Naval College, Dartmouth in April 1937 as Chief Cadet Captain. He left the Royal Navy in 1946 as a result of failing an eyesight test and entered the Diplomatic Service, before finally, as Sir Anthony Duff, being Director General of MI5 from 1985 to 1987. Godfrey Place was to describe him as 'the cleverest man I have ever known.'

Stubborn arrived at Loch Cairnbawn on 31 August and was joined by the other five submarines over the following twenty-four hours; all had been fitted with special towing devices. At the same time all leave was cancelled and security tightened even further. During the next ten days *Stubborn* and the other submarines undertook towing trials with their nominated X-craft. The time spent towing was, in retrospect, remarkably short, and no attempt was made to tow for several days, as would be required later that month. Some crew members later reflected that more time should have been spent perfecting towing; this might well have prevented some of the difficulties that befell 'Operation Source'. The crews also practised the changeover of operational and passage crews, undertaken in inflatable dinghies that were in fact life rafts used by the RAF. John Lorimer recalled how they actually spent very little time practising this part of the operation.

Final preparations for 'Operation Source' involved filling the side charges; on 10 September X5, X6 and X9 were hoisted on board *Bonaventure*, and on the next day the remainder were brought on board. (28) Fitting the live side charges involved spot welding, and when X6 was on board a spark started a fire amongst the side charges. John Lorimer rushed for the fire hoses and extinguished the blaze, despite being told by the workmen to flee the scene. It later transpired that the threat was minimal, since if the fire had reached the explosive it would merely have melted; initiation of an explosion required a detonator. (29)

With the impending departure of the crews there were a number of visitors. Commander G.P.S. Davies from Northways, who had been responsible for planning the mission, arrived on board *Bonaventure* on 4 September. He had visited the ship earlier in the year, when he was described by Place as 'a pleasant sort of bird but he is most insignificant really.' At this time all those involved were told that, in the view of the Admiralty, this was to be the most significant naval encounter of the whole war. There were three targets. *Tirpitz*, 'the pride of the German fleet' was to be attacked by X5, 6 and 7; *Lutzow* by X8 and *Scharnhorst* by X9 and 10. X-craft, having completed their attack, would sail back out to a rendezvous area, where they would be picked up by one of the towing submarines. Godfrey Place recalled that the briefing was 'very well done, and they had got every bit of information they could, including vertical sketches, to give a vertical view of the targets.' He felt that the intelligence was very thorough. On 10 September Admiral Barry arrived and flew his flag in HMS *Bonaventure*. He had come to see off the men of the 12th Flotilla on their mission. That night was to be their last in Britain for some time, and he hosted a dinner for the officers on board HMS *Titania*. Churchill sent a telegram wishing the crews 'God Speed'. Despite the heightened security, Bill Whittam had been able to telephone his girlfriend Ruth, who later told Althea that Bill was 'in terrific form.' Captain Fell recalled that there was a 'tremendous dinner party, and a remarkable evening followed in the wardroom with nearly all hands in little more than bow ties and underpants, but with morale sky high.' (30) Admiral Barry was also to comment on the confidence of the men when he recalled how 'any doubts I might have entertained as to the outcome could not possibly survive the infectious confidence of these young men who were just leaving us. They were like boys on the last day of term at school – their spirits were so high.'[6]

6. The ERAs involved with the mission went ashore from *Bonaventure* to a bar, although ERA Ralph Mortiboys, X5 operational crew, remained on board and wrote to his recently widowed mother; he had a premonition that he would not return from the raid.

For Godfrey Place there was no opportunity to say goodbye to his wife, although in one of their last conversations before departure she asked him to be aware of the anti-torpedo nets, telling him that 'they might be deeper than you think'; prophetic words in the light of events to follow.

Chapter 6

Operation Source: Attacking the German Battlefleet

U nbeknown to the men of 'Operation Source', as they were completing preparations for departure, their targets had moved from their anchorage. Would this result in the operation being abandoned?

After a prolonged period in the north, the German battleships were about to undertake an operational sortie. The British, in conjunction with both Soviet reconnaissance flights and members of the Norwegian resistance, had kept a vigilant watch on the ships. On 3 September reconnaissance flights identified the *Tirpitz*, *Scharnhorst* and *Lutzow* all moored in Alten fjord, and Admiral Barry decided that the conditions were appropriate for the operation. Four days later, a reconnaissance flight over Alten fjord by a Spitfire, flying from Vaenga, a base in northern Russia, identified only the *Lutzow*; on the previous day both *Tirpitz* and *Scharnhorst* had left their anchorage to take part in 'Operation *Sizilien*', an attack on the island of Spitzbergen. On 7 September *Tirpitz* arrived off the island, flying the White Ensign, and commenced a bombardment of the weather station and coaling facilities. German troops were put ashore and captured sixty Norwegian and three British prisoners. The ships left the area the next day, and *Tirpitz* arrived back at her anchorage in Alten fjord at 17.30 on 9 September. (1) The intelligence received by Admiral Barry on 7 September had to be put into the context of 'Operation Source'. If the X-craft were to reach their targets at the planned time, they had to leave Loch Cairnbawn on 11 and 12 September; it was only possible to delay their departure for a maximum of three days due to the waning moon. Fortunately, visual reconnaissance on the morning of 10 September confirmed that both *Tirpitz* and *Scharnhorst* were at anchorage in Alten fjord. The mission could begin.

The six submarines, each towing a midget submarine, commenced their journeys from Loch Cairnbawn on 11 September. They were to follow similar, but separate, routes north to the coast of Norway, where at predetermined positions they would slip their tows. The first to depart were HMS *Syrtis*, (Commanding Officer, Lieutenant M.H. Jupp DSC) towing X9 and HMS *Truculent* (Commanding Officer, Lieutenant R.L. Alexander

DSO) with X6 in tow, which departed at 17.35. HMS *Stubborn*, towing X7, departed at 21.30, and the last to leave was HMS *Sceptre* (Commanding Officer, Lieutenant I.S. McIntosh MBE, RAN) with X10, which left at 14.00 on 12 September. (2)

The passage crew for each X-craft consisted of a Commanding Officer and two ratings. In X7 the crew was Lieutenant P.H. Philip, SANF, Able Seaman James Magennis and Stoker John Luck. Peter Philip was a South African, a short, stocky, hook-nosed man with great stamina and natural enthusiasm and very popular with his colleagues. As a child he had suffered from polio, leaving him with a limp. Before the war he had been a radio presenter of children's' programmes in South Africa and had acquired the nickname 'Uncle Peter.'

Much of the ultimate success of 'Operation Source' was undoubtedly due to the hard work and professionalism of the passage crews. They lived for eight or nine days in appalling conditions, most unable to stand upright, only being able to stretch out straight in one place and being tossed, jerked and rolled by the sea, as well as being cold, damp or even soaking wet. Despite this, they succeeded in keeping their craft in working order for the operational crews. James Magennis described some of the problems that faced the crew of X7 during the passage:

> From the start we ran into trouble, we were zooming up and down, first breaking the surface, then plunging dangerously close to the 150ft limit that would damage the explosive charge and blow us up. Philip, our South African captain, flooded in more ballast. The weight gain gave us greater stability. We were kept up by the pull of the tow. (3)

For the first three days of the passage *Stubborn* remained on the surface whilst X7 was submerged, surfacing for twenty minutes at 05.00 and 13.00 and for two hours at 20.00. All went to plan during this part of the journey, and progress was aided by the prevailing fair weather. However, sea conditions started to deteriorate from the fourth day, so that when surfaced it became dangerous to open the X-craft hatch because of the risk of flooding or a man being swept overboard. When surfaced there was also the risk of colliding with the towing submarine which could easily have sent the X-craft to the bottom. Working in the cramped conditions of the X-craft also led to problems, and James Magennis almost severed his thumb while working with a knife behind a switchboard.[1]

1. Able Seaman James Magennis was mentioned in dispatches, and the citation read: 'AB Magennis was a member of the crew of HM Submarine X.7 during the passage from the base to the vicinity of the attack. The fortitude and devotion to duty of this rating

On 15 September at 12.13 the crew of *Stubborn* spotted a U-boat about three miles away, and dived. They surfaced about one hour later, and the patrol report noted, in retrospect, that this submarine was probably X8, which had parted company with her towing submarine, HMS *Seanymph* (Commanding Officer, Lieutenant J.P.H. Oakley DSC) at 04.00 that day. Further problems were encountered three hours later. Whilst proceeding on the surface at 7 knots it was noted that the tow to X7 had parted. James Magennis described the episode:

> Before long, the tow rope broke and we had a terrific scare. I was operating the planes; John Luck was sat at the steering and periscope controls, Lieutenant Philip was dozing on our one bunk above the batteries. Lieutenant Philip ordered us to blow all tanks. The depth gauge still rose, 120ft, 130ft. I was in a cold sweat as it approached 150ft, and slowly we started to surface. (4)

X7 surfaced, and Peter Philip opened the hatch to be greeted by the sea sweeping in and washing his legs from under him; he clung precariously to the periscope, just managing to stay on board. With *Stubborn* stationary, an auxiliary hemp tow was passed to X7 by placing one end in a rubber dinghy manned by Robert Aitken. Aboard X7 there was difficulty in securing the tow, and it had to be secured to the towing clench on the vessel's casing. This operation took nearly two hours, and no sooner had *Stubborn* proceeded on her course that X8 was spotted, alone on the surface, about two miles away. *Stubborn* closed towards X8 in the hope that she would encounter HMS *Seanymph*. That night, *Stubborn* continued north along her planned route, now with two X-craft; she was towing X7 and had X8 in company. Lieutenant Duff sent a wireless report to Flag Officer Submarines. At the time *Stubborn* was just inside the 'wireless transmission silence' area, but it was considered, since she was 105 miles from the coast, that 'breaking of (radio) silence in the hope of forwarding another four tons of explosive to the enemy was considered justified.' That night, problems beset X8, which developed faults with her compass and was only able to achieve 3 knots. During the night *Stubborn* lost contact with X8, despite having switched on her bow lights, and Lieutenant Duff made the decision that he could not delay his passage any further for the sake of X8, as it was likely to prejudice X7's chances of attack.

during an extremely arduous voyage lasting some 9 days, contributed to a considerable degree towards the success of the whole operation.' He, along with Lieutenant I.E. Fraser RNR, would later be awarded the Victoria Cross for the attack by midget submarine XE3 on the battleship *Takoa* in the Johore Straits, Singapore in May 1945.

Early on 16 September, at 03.15, *Stubborn* spotted a submarine four miles away. She was challenged and identified herself as *Seanymph*. Information about X8 was passed to her so that she could continue the search. A relatively peaceful day was interrupted at 21.10 by radar contact with an aircraft closing towards *Stubborn;* she dived and surfaced twenty minutes later. The next day, 17 September, *Stubborn* spent most of the time dived as she was now close to the Norwegian coast. At 15.00 *Stubborn* sighted *Seanymph* with X8 in tow, but a little under two hours later a loud explosion was reported, followed by a second explosion at about 18.45. The charges on X8 had flooded, and it was decided to release them in order to try to salvage X8. However, when released, both charges had exploded. X8 was scuttled in the early morning of 18 September.

It had originally been planned to transfer the operational crew to X7 in the evening of 17 September, but at 18.00 the transfer was delayed due to rough sea conditions and a favourable weather report for the following day. On 18 September *Stubborn* again spent most of daylight hours submerged, and surfaced at 18.00. That evening, at 20.15, under a starry sky, the transfer of the crews started and was completed about an hour later. During the transfer Godfrey Place spotted Peter Philip's boots, and asked if he could borrow them, despite being size 12 and far too large for him. Philip duly obliged, parting with what he described as 'enormous fleece-lined jobs, which cost five guineas at Gieves and the apple of my eye.' Although the boots would serve Place well, their owner would never see them again. (5)

No sooner had the transfer taken place than yet another disaster occurred. The tow had broken again, this time parting close to the towing link on *Stubborn*, and left nearly 600 feet of hemp hanging from X7's bows. This time there appeared to be no quick way of re-using or repairing the broken tow, so both ends were freed and a third tow, a two-and-a-half-inch wire normally employed for berthing, was employed. Philip undertook the transfer, again using a rubber dinghy. When X7 first tried to pick up the dinghy she rode over the wire and pulled it from Philip's grasp. The wire was recovered and again passed to the dinghy. After nearly two hours, it was finally secured to X7. As *Stubborn* got underway it became obvious that X7 was adrift again, due to the screw shackle on X7's casing coming adrift. Just after midnight X7 moved close to *Stubborn* and, as *Stubborn* drifted down on to her, a heaving line was thrown across and the tow line was then pulled onto X7. At 00.50 X7 reported that the tow was secured. Lieutenant Duff later wrote, 'The interval of 35 minutes had been a little breath-taking owing to the very close proximity of the two craft in a very heavy swell, but no bump was made.' (6)

Describing the problems of placing the wire tow, Place recalled:

> It was no joke securing this in the sea conditions that prevailed and Bill
> Whittam and I – secured by lines to the boat against being washed
> overboard – spent three exhausting hours on the casing before X7 was
> finally in tow again. We were neither of us dry nor in good humour
> when we went below, but the orderliness within was a delight to be
> seen. One would hardly have known that three men had spent a week
> in this confined space, and the mechanical efficiency of the machinery
> was in keeping – the passage crew could not have done a better job. (7)

The operational crew spent much of their first day on board X7 sleeping,
until the evening when the weather cleared and X7 surfaced. It was not long
before *Stubborn* and X7 faced a further challenge. At 01.05 on 20 September
a mine was sighted on the port bow. Bill Whittam was keeping watch in X7
and the rest of the crew were down below having supper. He reported that,
'*Stubborn* is flashing and there is something bumping up against the bow.'
Place looked through the periscope to see that there was indeed something
bumping against the bow, but could not make out what. He said to Bill
Whittam, 'I'll go and have a look,' to which the reply was, 'You'd better
hurry – it's a mine.' The mine's mooring wire had caught on the tow and
slid down until it was bumping on X7's bow. Place recognised that the mine
was 'a German one, it was half hitched around the tow and had come to rest
against X7's bow.' He noticed it was painted green and black and one horn
had already been broken. To keep it off the casing he gingerly placed his foot
on its shell and loosened its mooring wire from the tow rope, breathing more
deeply as it floated astern. This action was later described in Admiral
Barry's report as 'deft footwork which allowed him to clear the unpleasant
obstruction.' It was the first time that Place had kicked a mine away by its
horns; perhaps his knowledge gained in answering questions about mines in
the Torpedo examination in March 1939 had come in useful? In 1988
Godfrey Place recalled, almost nonchalantly, that it was a 'perfectly safe sort
of mine.' After this episode he went below and thought 'a tot wouldn't do
us any harm,' so they toasted the Geneva Convention and Minerva – the
mine with the crumpled horn. (8) After dealing with the mine, *Stubborn*
dived at 02.00 and did not surface again until 19.00. At 19.40 *Stubborn*
stopped and gathered in the tow, drawing X7 close to her in order for Place
to receive the latest information. At 19.55 on 20 September they said
goodbye and X7 slipped her tow and proceeded inshore; she was now on her
own.

By this time 'Operation Source' was depleted in numbers, with only four midget submarines preparing for the attack, X5, X6, X7 and X10; Admiral Barry later admitted that this was more than he had ever anticipated. Tragedy had struck X9 on 16 September. At 09.00 HMS *Syrtis* reduced speed to allow X9 to surface, but there was no X-craft, only a slack tow. This was recovered by *Syrtis*, but it snagged under her stern. Max Shean, X9's diver, was told to clear it, but his diving suit was in X9. Dressed only in overalls and attached by a line, he went into the cold sea but found it impossible to get down to the propeller. Fortunately, he was able to clear the obstruction by letting more rope out, whereupon the tow floated off. *Syrtis* then retraced her tracks looking for X9, but nothing was found. All three members of the passage crew were presumed lost. (9)

It had been a remarkable feat by the crew of *Stubborn* to arrive at the specified slipping position on time, despite all the problems that had arisen en route. All four X-craft slipped from their towing submarines at about the same time, and made their own independent way into Stjernsund, going in on the surface over the top of a declared German minefield. At this time the weather was improving, and Place remarked that it was 'quite calm'. At 23.15 X7 sighted another X-craft near by; this was X5, and Place exchanged calls of 'good luck and good hunting' with Henty Henty-Creer. This was to be last time he had any contact with his good friend and best man. (10)

X7 dived early, at about 02.30, on 21 September, and proceeded steadily up Stjernsund into Alten fjord itself. Place recalled that this was 'a quiet day, dived at 90 feet and out of sight, with very pleasant weather indeed.' Later in the day, at 16.30, he saw the *Scharnhorst* sailing out for a gunnery exercise; as she was not X7's target she was disregarded. By contrast, the ship's movement caused consternation in London. On the night of 21 September at Northways, Admiral Barry summoned Lieutenant Commander Alistair Mars DSO, DSC, a former submarine commander who was deputising for Commander G.P.S. Davies. Reconnaissance had just been received that the *Tirpitz* was in her birth, but neither *Scharnhorst* nor *Lutzow* could be found. It was reported that the Commander-in-Chief, Home Fleet, Admiral Sir Bruce Fraser KCB, KBE, flying his flag in HMS *Duke of York*, was raising steam in order to pursue the ships, and had asked the Admiralty to cancel 'Operation Source'. Admiral Barry asked Mars what would he do? Mars replied that if the *Tirpitz* was there at dusk she would be there at dawn, because the Germans would not move her at night. He pointed out that the target for the operation was the *Tirpitz*, and that the operation could not be remounted. It was suggested that the Admiral might like to remind the Admiralty that they could not afford another '*Bismarck*'. The operation was to proceed. (11)

X7 surfaced just after dark and spent the night of 21 September at her waiting positon, in the lee of the Bratholm islands, just outside the main fleet anchorage. This provided an opportunity to charge the batteries and undertake repairs. Place recalled another 'little problem', namely that the diesel exhaust pipe was leaking, causing the boat to fill with fumes. The spare pipe did not fit, but Bill Whitley saved the day by making a joint with tape, canvas and chewing gum. (12)

Wednesday, 22 September was the day of the attack, and X7 left her overnight mooring early in the morning, diving at about 01.30, to make her passage through the anti-submarine boom to reach the *Tirpitz* at the head of Kaa fjord. Place recalled that it was a trip made with 'seemingly all the time in the world; as the first explosion was due to be between eight and nine, we had five and a half hours to do the four or five miles.' He went on to describe how 'we hung about a little bit to make sure it was fully daylight before going through the opening in the anti-submarine boom across the neck of Kaa fjord.' In the plan of operations the diver in the X-craft would be responsible for leaving the craft and cutting the anti-submarine nets. This was to have been Robert Aitken's task and in 2004 he described the sequence of events:

> Just before dawn we set off to the first challenge, the antisubmarine (a/s) net. This was the one the diver had to cut if the CO [Commanding Officer] couldn't get through it in any other way (which all the COs were quite determined to find). As we approached, the CO saw the gate in the a/s net had been opened to let a trawler through. We dived underneath its wake and got through without having to cut the net. Having got through the gate the CO, looking through the periscope, saw another boat was about to cross our path. We had to dive below periscope depth and whilst unsighted hit a bunch of anti-torpedo (a/t) nets moored in the fjord. In the reconnaissance photograph these nets were protecting a German battleship which had gone to sea. (13)

The nets stretched around an anchorage for the *Lutzow*, but this was now empty as she had departed on exercises. Place described how 'in going deep to avoid a little minesweeper that was coming out of the anchorage, we ran into a boom, and got lodged in the anti-torpedo nets.' He went on to relate how they freed X7: 'it took quite a while to get out with quite a lot of pulling and pushing and blowing and so on, but I don't think we broke surface, but I was a little bit cautious that we had revealed our presence.' Robert Aitken recalled this challenge:

The bow had caught on something we couldn't see and we couldn't move. All we could do was to shuffle the boat forward and astern, making it alternatively more and less buoyant, hoping to shake off the net. With no success after about 30 minutes the CO told me to get dressed and go and see what the problem was. Getting into a diving suit in an X-craft without assistance took a long time and was quite exhausting. Before I was ready to dive the CO said, 'Take it off. I don't know how it happened, but we're now free,' and we were on our way again.

Although free of the nets, there was now a defect in a trimming pump and the gyrocompass was faulty. X7 proceeded towards the target and at about 05.45 Place caught his first sight of the *Tirpitz*, then submerged about 200 to 300 yards from the anti-torpedo nets. Just prior to reaching the nets, at 07.10, Place ordered the fuses on both charges to be set for one hour; there was now real urgency to the attack.

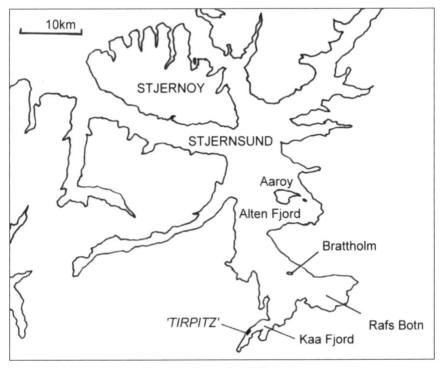

Passage route for midget submarines September 1943

Based on the results of photographic reconnaissance, X-craft commanders had been told that German anti-torpedo nets consisted of two lines, supported by buoys, and that it was unlikely that they would be deeper than 70 feet. As the water in Kaa fjord was 120 feet deep Godfrey Place believed he would easily be able to pass under the nets. However, it soon became apparent that the nets were constructed of a very fine mesh and that they went much deeper than reported. The situation was even more complex as there were, in fact, three lines of nets, one of which was secured to weights on the floor of the fjord. Althea's words to him about the nets a month earlier were ringing true. Passing through the nets took considerable perserverance and involved five minutes of 'blowing and wriggling.' After this, Place recalled, 'miraculously when we came up to the surface there were no intervening nets and the *Tirpitz* was 50-60 feet away'. Robert Aitken recalled their passage through the nets:

> The CO tried to find a way through the a/t nets protecting the *Tirpitz*. He tried one way after another and I don't think Godfrey Place was ever absolutely sure how but he suddenly found we were inside the nets surrounding the *Tirpitz*. Without knowing it, the CO may have slid over the top, found a gap or the open gate.

X7 was now very close to the target, but a further problem had arisen since the gyrocompass had stopped working. Undaunted by the obstacles and

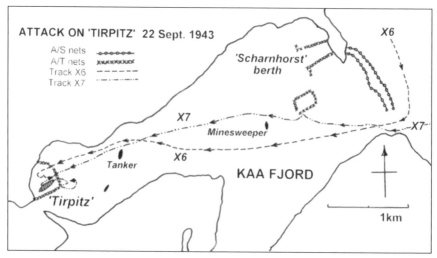

Passage at Kaa Fjord

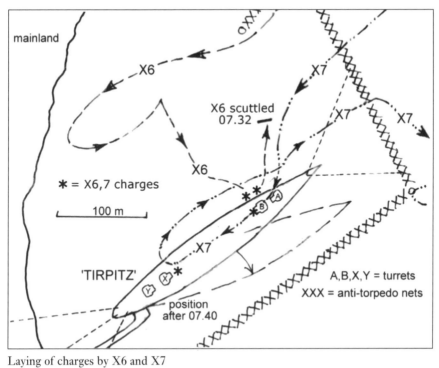

mainland

X6

X7

X6 scuttled
07.32

X7 X7

X6

* = X6,7 charges

100 m

X6

X7

'TIRPITZ'

A,B,X,Y = turrets
XXX = anti-torpedo nets

position
after 07.40

Laying of charges by X6 and X7

setbacks encountered so far, Place ordered X7 to dive to 40 feet and then proceeded at full speed towards the *Tirpitz*. X7 made contact with the ship on her port side, below B turret, at 07.22, and then slid gently under the keel where the starboard charge was released in the full shadow of the ship, under B turret. As a result of the collision X7 had swung to port, and Place now found himself proceeding along the keel of the *Tirpitz* towards the stern. After 150-200 feet the second charge was released under X turret. With both charges released, Aitken recalled how, 'the job done, the CO set a course for home!'

Slightly before X7 had laid her charges, X6 had attacked *Tirpitz* and laid hers. She had been dogged by problems, not least the flooding of one of her charges on 11 September, although skilled seamanship enabled the crew to maintain the trim of the boat for the next eleven days. On the passage to Alten fjord the periscope flooded and the crew had been forced to strip it down and re-assemble it at least three times. X6 passed through the opening in the anti-submarine nets approximately 90 minutes after X7. At 07.05 she passed through the boat opening in the anti-torpedo nets travelling on the surface, astern of a small coaster which was entering the enclosure. Donald

Cameron then dived and made for the *Tirpitz*. However, X6 then ran aground on the north shore of the enclosure and broke surface. She was spotted by a junior member of *Tirpitz's* crew, who informed a senior officer, but was advised that he had probably seen a porpoise. Undeterred, Donald Cameron manoeuvred the boat clear of the shore and in the right direction to make an attack. In doing so, X6 broke surface again about five minutes later; there was no mistaking her for a porpoise this time, and the alarm was raised on board the *Tirpitz*. By now X6 was totally unserviceable and Donald Cameron, realising escape was impossible, proceeded to destroy sensitive equipment and documents and scuttle the boat, releasing his charges next to B turret. He surfaced close to the *Tirpitz* where fortunately she was unable to bring to bear any of her main armament. X6 was met by a German patrol boat, commanded by Lieutenant Leine from the *Tirpitz*. Leine attempted to get a tow rope on to X6, but as he was doing so the crew were opening all the valves to scuttle the vessel. The crew then left X6, with Donald Cameron the last to leave and forgetting to pick up his pipe and tobacco. All four crew members boarded the patrol boat, barely getting their feet wet in the process. As they did so, X6 sank at 07.32, and the Germans were forced to release the tow rope to prevent their vessel being dragged under as well.

The attack by the midget submarines had caught the crew of the *Tirpitz* completely by surprise, and their response was both slow and confused, with some crew members believing that the alarm was another exercise. The first sighting of a submarine was recorded at 07.07, and ten minutes later the order was given to close all watertight doors. At 07.36 the ship was placed at action stations, and the order given to raise steam. However, it was apparent that it would take some time before she could proceed under her own power. At 07.40, recognising the seriousness of the situation, the Germans attempted to move the *Tirpitz* away from where X6's charges were believed to have been dropped, by heaving on the mooring cables, causing the *Tirpitz's* bows to move to starboard. This also moved her slightly away from X7's first charge.

The four crew from X6 were taken on board the *Tirpitz*. As they arrived, John Lorimer asked Donald Cameron, 'Skipper, shall we salute the German flag?' To which the reply was, 'Why, of course.' And much to the Germans' displeasure, they did. (14) Strange as it may appear, the crew from X6 were not the first members of the Royal Navy to have gone aboard the *Tirpitz* that month. That distinction belonged to Coder Esmond Dabner, who had been injured and captured at Spitzbergen on 8 September and was taken to Norway on board the *Tirpitz*. (15)

Godfrey Place, unaware of X6's progress or fate, faced a further dilemma:

> Being somewhat in doubt as to how we got in I thought we would go
> back to the point where we had penetrated the nets. But it was very
> difficult, the nets came to within ten yards of the *Tirpitz* and in that area
> it was very difficult to pinpoint yourself precisely. So in fact we spent
> most of the next three quarters of an hour trying to find the way out. I
> think we passed under the ship two or three times. Our charges were
> set for an hour and by then it occurred to me that we needed to take
> somewhat drastic measures to get out, so in fact we did a sort of flop
> operation of hitting the net, holding ourselves down, blowing the bow
> tank to full buoyancy as fast as we could, so we came up with a terrific
> angle and at the same time going full ahead on the motor, scraping the
> top of the net and got out.

In his report, Place described this as a 'a new technique for getting out of
nets,' and at 07.40 X7 slid over them. He wrote that he did not look at the
Tirpitz at this time as this method for overcoming net defences was 'new and
absorbing.' X7 was not, however, free of nets; Place wrote, 'it was extremely
annoying to run into another net at about 60 feet.' At this moment, X7 was
seen from the *Tirpitz* as she broke the surface, and the Germans responded
by dropping hand grenades and opening fire with machine guns.

At 08.12 the eight tons of amatol, which had been so carefully brought the
1,200 miles from Britain and placed under Europe's largest battleship,
exploded. On board the *Tirpitz*, the ship's log recorded, 'Two heavy
consecutive detonations to port, at one-tenth second interval. Ship vibrates
strongly in vertical direction and sways slightly between the anchors.' At the
time of the explosions John Lorimer was below decks being interrogated by
the Germans. He later recalled that 'the ship was lifted seven feet in the air,
but only one sailor died.' The Germans became very hostile and lined up
members of X6 crew on the deck as if to shoot them. Lorimer remembered
thinking, 'I wouldn't give a sixpence for my life right now,' but was also
'bloody furious' that the ship was still floating. His colleague Sub Lieutenant
Richard Kendall, the diving officer, who was on the quarterdeck, recalled his
reaction to the explosion:

> My knees buckled as the explosion hurled the ship out of the water.
> Steam gushed from broken pipes. Oil flowed from the shattered hull
> and covered the waters of the fjord. All around was confusion. (16)

The explosion caused all the electric lights to be extinguished and doors became jammed. Broken glass was everwhere, and many of the fire extinguishers discharged, depositing white foam throughout the ship. Although electricity was restored quite rapidly, there was other, more serious damage. All four main turrets had been lifted off their supports and were out of alignment, and several armour plates of the hull had been breached, with water entering some compartments and oil leaking out into the fjord. The optical systems of the range finders and the sighting systems for the armament had all been smashed by the explosion. Both the port propulsion system and the port rudder were damaged, and the aircraft catapults were unuseable. All the bottles of schnapps on board were broken. One sailor was killed and about forty wounded as a result of the explosion.(17) Captain Meyer, the Commanding Officer, flew into a rage and ordered the four prisoners from X6 to be shot at once as saboteurs, but he changed his mind when it was pointed out to him that they were just soldiers doing their duty.

The explosion also affected X7 and Place recalled: 'A quite considerable amount of noise, really rather too close to us for any comfort, but by no means lethal. The aft hatch lifted and quite a volume of water came in and there were one or two small spurting leaks, but nothing too dramatic.'

X7 was backed out of the net and surfaced, and again he recalled that 'we had a look around and it was galling that *Tirpitz* had not seemed to have settled in the water and in fact I had some doubts as to whether the explosion had been our charges going up or a depth charge from a surface ship.' However, the explosion had freed X7 from the nets and Godfrey Place described the next stage as, 'we went back to the bottom again and thought about it for a while and then decided we would have to get further away.' By this time all the diving gauges and compasses were out of action, but there was little structural damage to the boat. He continued:

Unfortunately in the next half hour, we were unable to maintain any sort of depth, there was so much water inside the boat that as soon as you got a bow up angle it all swished down to the back end and you came up to the surface, and as soon as a bow down angle it swished down to the other end and went rocketing down to the bottom again.

Place was now worried that with the loss of the periscope and the compass they might run the boat up on to the beach and so present the enemy with a complete X-craft. At this point he decided that the crew ought to bale out. He recalled how they considered going out by Davis Escape, but concluded that it was better for one person to wave a white flag on the surface. By now there was a lot of firing at the surface, so Godfrey Place decided that he should go outside and wave a sweater. He went up through the W&D hatch, waving a rather grubby white sweater and saying to Robert Aitken, who was immediately behing him on the ladder, 'Here go the last of the Places!' Aitken remembered that the shooting stopped just as he left the boat. Place turned to shut the hatch in haste, concerned that with so little buoyancy the boat would be flooded, but at the same time Robert Aitken was trying to push it open from below. Unfortunately, enough water entered to cause X7 to start to sink. At 08.35 Godfrey Place clambered on to a nearby practice target and was then picked up by a small German vessel and taken to the *Tirpitz*. On the short journey Place said 'Incredible.' 'What is incredible?' replied an officer in the boat. 'That the ship should still be afloat.' Place gratefully accepted cigarettes from the Germans but the tobacco was not entirely to his taste. Feeling ridiculous in little more than underclothes, sea boot stockings and oversized boots, he was taken to the quarterdeck of the *Tirpitz*, where he found himself surrounded by chaos and received threats that he would be shot. He replied that he was 'an English naval officer and expected to be treated with due courtesy.'

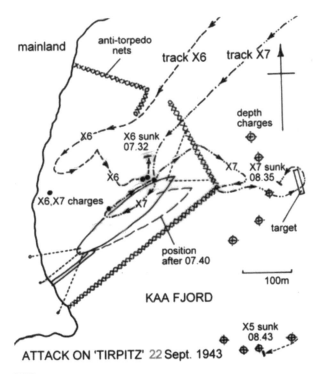

The fate of X7

Godfrey Place had taken the unusual decision for the commanding officer of a vessel to leave it first, naval tradition being that he should leave last. However, the fact of being under attack may have influenced his decision; by leaving X7 when he did there was a high possibility of his being injured or killed by enemy fire. As he was standing on the practice target, X7 sank with his three colleagues on board. Only Aitken escaped and events in X7 at this time can only be described by him:

> The three left on board discussed what we should do. The two alternatives were to try to get the submarine back on the surface again, or to escape using the Davis Submarine Escape Equipment, which was an oxygen breathing set. We were apprehensive about trying to get the boat to the surface because it had been damaged and by running compressors and motors we were going to make noise, which we felt would immediately attract depth charges. We decided that it would be wiser to escape using the breathing apparatus. We all put one on and started to flood the boat (the hatch could not be opened until the boat was fully flooded to equalise the pressure inside the boat with that outside). Unfortunately this took longer than we anticipated because some of the valves couldn't be fully opened. As the water crept up it reached the batteries which fused, giving off fumes, and we had to start breathing oxygen before the boat was fully flooded.
>
> During that time there was nothing to do except wait. As soon as we went onto oxygen (after the fumes came) we could not talk to each other, the oxygen mouthpiece prevented that. There were no lights, we couldn't see each other and we were left with our own thoughts. I remember throughout that I was very confident I would escape. 'It couldn't happen to me, I was going to survive,' I thought, and that's the way it turned out.
>
> Initially we decided Bill Whittam should get out through the after hatch, he was very tall which made it more difficult for him to get through the W&D. Bill Whitly [sic], the ERA, would get out through the W&D and I would use whichever hatch became available first. However, when Bill Whitly and I tried to exchange places we found the oxygen bottles and the periscope prevented us getting past each other. Bill signalled, 'It's OK, you carry on.' I went into the W&D to try the hatch, but the pressure hadn't equalised and when I returned to the control room I couldn't feel Bill until I stumbled over his body on the deck. I bent down and felt his breathing bag which had two small emergency bottles of oxygen in it. Both had been emptied which indicated Bill had run out of oxygen.

I went back to try the W&D hatch again. Fortunately the pressure equalised just after I'd broken my first emergency bottle. I opened the hatch, climbed out and jumped. As the pressure began to reduce, the oxygen expanded, leaving me with far too much. I made what I thought was a correct escape. I unrolled and held out the apron (provided with the escape kit for use as a brake) so I didn't go up too fast and blow out my lungs.

When I surfaced I first looked around to see whether Bill Whittam had got out of the rear hatch and was floating about. There was no sign of him. Then I looked up and saw the *Tirpitz*. I didn't get an awfully good view, bouncing about on the surface, but it was a great disappointment to see her afloat. She was very large, the pride of the German navy, and I had been very hopeful she had been sunk, but she looked intact from my limited viewpoint. (18)

Aitken reached the surface at 11.15 and was picked up by a German vessel and taken to the *Tirpitz*. Bill Whittam's body was recovered from X7 when part of it was raised from Kaa fjord in October 1943. His body was buried in Tromsø Cemetery, and later marked by the Commonwealth War Graves Commission. Bill Whitley's body was not recovered; he is commemorated on the Plymouth Naval Memorial

As to the fate of the other midget submarines that entered Alten fjord, it is known that at 08.43 on 22 September a third midget submarine was sighted approximately 500 yards outside the anti-torpedo nets. This was X5 and was was seen both by Germans on board *Tirpitz* and by some of the British prisoners. X5 was attacked by gunfire from the *Tirpitz* as well as depth charges, was seen to sink and was never recovered. None of the crew was ever found. There has been uncertainty ever since as to whether X5 completed an attack on the *Tirpitz*.

X10 did not reach her target. Soon after slipping there was a major problem with a clutch, which was repaired whilst the submarine hid in a deserted fjord. On the run into Alten fjord one of the side charges flooded, there were severe electrical problems leading to a fire and failure of the gyrocompass. The magnetic compass flooded and the periscope failed. Lieutenant Hudspeth realised there was no way he could make an attack and made his way back to the rendezvous area and *Stubborn*. Despite transferring crews (the passage crew from X7 were transferred to X10) in an attempt to tow X10 home, there were further setbacks, with the tow rope parting and X10 colliding with *Stubborn*. On 3 October, with a gale forecast, orders were received to transfer the passage crew and scuttle X10. All the crew of X10 arrived back safely in Britain, although the journey home in *Stubborn* was far from comfortable after the heads failed.

The *Tirpitz* had caused considerable anxiety for Winston Churchill throughout the war, and his earlier correspondence indicated just how determined he was to ensure she was destroyed or at least crippled. On the day after the attack, 23 September, he received a copy of an intercepted German message dated 22 September, which reported: 'A midget submarine was destroyed inside the *Tirpitz's* net barrage at 07.30. 4 Englishmen were taken prisoner.'

More encouraging news was received on 24 September, from a second intercepted signal:

> Heavy explosion 60 metres to port of *Tirpitz* at 10.12. (Submarine destroyed by time bombs) 500 cubic metres of water in ship. A second submarine was destroyed by time bomb; at 10.35 Commanding Officer was taken prisoner. A third submarine was fired on when 600 metres distant on the starboard beam, several hits being observed.[2] (19)

One week after the attack, Churchill met with his Chiefs of Staff and the Foreign Secretary to discuss convoys to northern Russia. He was now aware of the effects of 'Operation Source' and wrote:

> There was an agreeable new fact before us. The *Tirpitz* had been disabled by the audacious and heroic attack of our midget submarines …Thus we had an easement, probably of some months, in the Arctic waters. (20)

Although the *Tirpitz* was not sunk, the damage inflicted by the midget submariners was considerable. The Germans decided to repair the ship in Kaa fjord, and several vessels were dispatched north, along with hundreds of workers. As early as October 1943, the German navy had accepted that it might not be possible to restore her to full operational activity. In November 1943 it was reported to the German Naval War Staff that 'as a result of the successful midget submarine attack the battle cruiser *Tirpitz* had been put out of action for months.' (21) *Tirpitz* left Kaa fjord under her own power on 15 March 1944 for sea trials and was able to reach a speed of 27 knots. News of her departure was signalled to London by the Norwegian resistance. She was attacked on 3 April at anchor in Kaa fjord, where Barracuda aircraft from the Fleet Air Arm hit her with fifteen bombs; the

2. The timing was local time for Norway, which was two hours ahead of GMT; all times given in the Admiralty reports were GMT.

damage resulted in her being out of action for a further three months. During July and August 1944 there were further attacks on the ship by aircraft of the Fleet Air Arm, followed, on 15 September, by an attack by RAF Lancaster bombers. Dropping 12,000lb bombs, they inflicted severe damage to her bows as well as damaging her boilers. In response to this, combined with the Allied advances in Europe, *Tirpitz* was moved south to Tromsø to act as a coastal defence battery. On 12 November 1944 whilst at anchor she was attacked by Lancasters of 617 Squadron, which dropped 'tall boy' bombs. The mission was a success, and the ship capsized with the loss of over 1,000 men. Winston Churchill wrote to President Roosevelt on 15 November 1944, 'it is a great relief to us to get this brute where we have long wanted her.' (22)

Although the X-craft attacks had not sunk the *Tirpitz*, there is no doubt that the damage inflicted by Godfrey Place and his colleagues ensured that the threat she posed to the Allies was significantly reduced. After the midget submarine attack she never mounted offensive actions against the Allies, and to that extent 'Operation Source' was completely successful. Although there was loss of life on both sides, it is important to put this into the context of the large numbers of Germans who were later killed on board the *Tirpitz* when she was finally sunk.

The final words on 'Operation Source' are best left to Admiral Barry in February 1944:

> My admiration for Lieutenant CAMERON and Lieutenant PLACE and their crews is beyond words.

Addendum
The members of the 12th Submarine Flotilla who died in 'Operation Source' were:

X5 (Operational Crew)

Lieutenant H.Henty-Creer, RNVR
Sub Lieutenant A.D. Malcolm, RNVR
Sub Lieutenant T.J. Nelson, RNVR
ERA R. Mortiboys

X7 (Operational Crew)

Lieutenant L.B. Whittam, RNVR
ERA W. M. Whitley

X9 (Passage Crew)

Sub Lieutenant E. Kearon, RNVR
Ordinary Seaman A.H. Harte
Stoker G. H. Hollett

Chapter 7

'For You the War is Over':
Life as a Prisoner of War

As part of their training in HMS *Bonaventure*, the crews of X-craft received lectures about possible capture from Major J.M. 'Jimmy' Langley and Lieutenant H.R.B. Newton DSC. Both men had first-hand experience of escaping from the enemy.[1] Godfrey Place received lectures covering evasion of capture and how to act if taken prisoner, as well the techniques for escape from prisoner-of-war camps. When asked in 1988 about his treatment and conditions in captivity he recalled:

> Oh, I think they were perfectly normal. It was quite useful to have been put in mind of the possibility of capture – in that it was pointed out to you that if you were standing on the deck of an enemy battleship and everyone was rushing around, doing their ordinary job, and if people started brandishing guns at you, although the Japanese might do it, the Germans would probably not shoot you. If they were going to shoot you, you could be reasonably certain they would take you to some quiet spot and that was the time to get frightened. So in fact any sort of hasty efforts to interrogation with a lot of waving of guns were not disturbing, because one had thought of that before the event. (1)

Earlier that morning, the crew of X6 had been accused of being spies. Donald Cameron described how he was accused of being a saboteur in league with the Norwegians or Russians, and the Germans threatened to shoot him. John

---

1. Lieutenant Newton was the Commanding Officer of the submarine HMS *Cachalot* serving in the Mediterranean. In July 1941 she was returning to Alexandria from Malta when she was rammed off Benghazi by an Italian destroyer, rendering her unseaworthy and forcing her to be scuttled. All but one of the ninety-two men on board were rescued and became prisoners. Major Langley had served with the Scots Guards as part of the British Expeditionary Force. At Dunkirk he was severely wounded, losing an arm, and was captured by the Germans but escaped from a hospital. He travelled via Paris and Marseilles to Gibraltar, from where he returned to England in March 1941 to work for Special Operations Executive and MI9.

Lorimer recalled that a German interrogator was under the impression that they were commandos.

After one night in the cells on board the *Tirpitz,* all the X-craft prisoners were moved south to Germany, a journey that took over two weeks. They were initially transferred in a minesweeper to Tromsø, by which time Place was aware that there were other prisoners, although he had not seen them.[2] Robert Aitken, the only other to escape from X7, recalled that they spent two nights at Tromsø, where they were held in German barracks. The prisoners were moved again by minesweeper, this time to Narvik, and during the passage prisoners were kept apart from each other. Aitken recalled one occasion when an officer entered his cabin, accompanied by a rating, the latter carrying a bowl of soup. The rating turned round and, out of the view of the officer, flicked a pack of cigarettes towards him; this left a lasting impression on Aitken, who remembered the crew as really quite friendly, although they undertook their duties in a most correct and proper way. On arriving at Narvik the prisoners were kept in a school building with all its windows wired shut. Lorimer recalled being interviewed by an old German commander, who gave each prisoner a comb, toothpaste and toothbrush. The journey continued to Trondheim, again by sea, and Place described how on arrival, 'they, the Germans, seemed to be determined to think that we were going to shoot them – there were floodlights and two guards per person.'

After three days in an 'ancient and wet dungeon' in Trondheim, the prisoners were taken by train to Oslo, followed by a ferry journey to Aarhus in Denmark, and then on by train to Germany. This time, the guards allocated to the prisoners came from prisoner-of-war camps and were described by Aitken as 'a less friendly lot' compared with those who had been responsible for their earlier captivity. Place described the rather exceptional circumstances of the train journey:

> We had specialist treatment, we had a first class carriage each, but German soldiers we saw going on leave were in cattle trucks. They had a chap there who spoke English and who encouraged us to get together in the hope that he could pick up something from us, that we might talk. But we had been quite well briefed on that.

The prisoners arrived at the naval interrogation camp, Dulag Nord at Westertimke (approximately 18 miles north east of Bremen), on 9 October

---

2. This is at variance with the account given by Donald Cameron in the *Daily Telegraph,* 23 June 1945, when he recalled that, after his capture, 'it was not long before I found Place beside me on the quarterdeck.'

1943. They were immediately put in solitary confinement, and Place became P.O.W. No. 1140. The camp was austere, surrounded by two barbed-wire fences. Accommodation consisted of two timber huts, each with a long corridor, off which there were a number of small cells, each about 6ft by 10ft. These were sparsely furnished with just a small stove, a bucket and a narrow bunk covered with a thin palliasse. Prisoners described 'a dreary solitary place, where small amounts of natural light penetrated into the cell.'

Amongst the many prisoners held in Dulag Nord was Sub Lieutenant John Worsley, RNVR, who became good friends with Godfrey Place, a friendship that continued long after the end of the war. They had similar upbringings; Worsley was born in Liverpool but grew up in Kenya on a coffee farm run by his father, before returning home to attend school. At the outbreak of the war he was recruited by Sir Kenneth Clarke to serve as a war artist with the Royal Navy. He was captured in November 1943 off the coast of Yugoslavia, arrived at Dulag Nord on 22 November 1943 and spent Christmas of 1943 in solitary confinement. He recalled how prisoners received 'one small briquette of coal each day for their stove and one bowl of soup.' They were perpetually cold and hungry, had no human contact and had neither music nor books. (2)

Although there had been speculation that the Germans had taken prisoners from 'Operation Source' there was no definite news. Althea had been appointed to HMS *Beaver II*, the Immingham naval base, in the middle of August 1943 and at the same time was promoted to Second Officer. She had been married for barely ten weeks before her husband set off on 'Operation Source' and by October she had no idea what had happened to him. Was he dead or alive? Was he a prisoner or was he hiding in the north of Norway planning to make his way home?

Althea received a letter in early October from Captain Banks, who suggested that there was no reason to give up hope about her husband, but also reminded her of the need to maintain security when talking about him. Admiral Barry also highlighted the bravery and initiative shown by her husband and concluded: 'You may well feel proud of him.' On 12 October 1943, three days after Place arrived at Dulag Nord, details of 'Operation Source' were reported in *The Times*. Under the headlines of 'Tirpitz hit in Fjord Raid', 'Gallant Midget Submarines' and 'Hazards of First Order', the story provided considerable detail about the operation, and emphasised its hazardous nature. The first lines of the report read:

His Majesty's midget submarines have carried out an attack on main units of the German battlefleet in their protected anchorages in Alten Fjord, northern Norway inflicting underwater damage on the battleship *Tirpitz*. This involved hazards of the first order. The attack was made on 22 September. Two days later the German official communiqué announced that an attack by submarines of the smallest type had been repulsed and that prisoners had been taken.

The report carried the names of the Commanding Officers of the three missing midget submarines, namely Donald Cameron, Godfrey Place and Henty Henty–Creer. It finished with a summary of the official view: 'The Admiralty consider that the crews of these midget submarines displayed the highest qualities of courage, enterprise and skill.'

A few days before these stories were published Althea received a communication from the Admiralty, advising her that:

They have learnt with regret that H.M. midget submarine of which your husband, Lieutenant Basil Charles Godfrey Place, D.S.C., Royal Navy, was in command has failed to return from the gallant attack on the main units of the German battle fleet in Alten Fiord, Northern Norway, in which the battleship TIRPITZ was damaged, and must be presumed lost. Your husband has, therefore, been reported missing on active service, but in view of the German claim to have taken some prisoners during this attack, My Lords hope that your husband may be reported as safe though a prisoner of war.

Meanwhile My Lords desire me to express their deep sympathy in the grave anxiety which this news must cause you.

The letter was signed by H.V. Markham, Permanent Secretary to the Board of the Admiralty, who nearly ten years earlier had been responsible for writing to Cyril Wodeman to report on Godfrey Place's 'star' performance in the interview for entrance to Dartmouth.

On the day after details of 'Operation Source' had been reported a small announcement appeared in *The Times*:

Missing – In October 1943 on active service, Lieutenant Basil Charles Godfrey Place DSC, Royal Navy, husband of Althea (neé Tickler) and only son of the late Major Godfrey Place DSO, MC and Junior Commander Margaret Place ATS.

Godfrey Place described his time at Dulag Nord as being 'very much the same thing' (presumably referring to the nature of the earlier interrogation). The guards were interested in the politics of the war, telling Place that 'we (the British) could not catch up on the United States on the building of big aeroplanes,' and then continued to ask questions about the midget submarines. Place said it was apparent that the Germans had raised part of X7 from Kaa fjord,[3] and recalled one series of questions:

Interrogator: *How many cylinders does your boat's engine have?*

Place: *I am sorry you know perfectly well I am not prepared to say anything about it, whatsoever.*

Interrogator: *Ah, you do not know how many cylinders your boat has?*

Place: *Of course I know how many it has got; you know that I know how many it has got.*

Interrogator: *Ah, you are mad at me?*

Place: *Too right!*

On 25 November 1943, after forty-one days of solitary confinement, Place was transferred to the main camp, Marlag und Milag Nord at Westertimke. The camp was originally situated at Sandbostel, approximately 16 miles away, alongside a camp for Russian prisoners, but was moved to Westertimke in the spring of 1942 following an outbreak of typhus. (3) There were three parts to the camp: Marlag-O, which in December 1943 housed 336 naval officers, and Marlag-M, which held about 550 naval ratings. They were separated by an area containing the German barracks and the camp's administration offices. The third part of the complex was Milag Nord, about one mile away, which held up to 10,000 merchant navy prisoners. The shower house, used by all prisoners, was about one-third of a mile outside the main compound of Marlag-O. (4)

Marlag-O consisted of four sleeping huts, each with eight rooms. Rooms normally held up to twelve lieutenants or ten lieutenant commanders; there were also a few single rooms for senior officers. There was a theatre hut, a library hut, a mess hut and a canteen. Rudimentary sports facilities comprised a cinder field, used for football, touch rugby and a form of cricket. A dam nearby, constructed to provide a reservoir for fire fighting, was used as a pond for sailing model boats, and when frozen, for skating.

The camp guards, all members of the *Kriegsmarine* (German navy), were relatively old (with an average age over forty-five) and had been posted to the camp after being deemed unfit for front-line service. At the end of the war it

3. The Germans managed to raise the aft section of X7 at the beginning of October 1943 using drag nets.

was felt that treatment of prisoners by the *Kriegsmarine* had been distinctly better than in camps run by the German Army. Armed sentries were placed on duty outside the perimeter fence, and their numbers were doubled at night, when dogs were also on patrol. Any guard observing an attempted escape had orders to call on the prisoner three times to halt, and was permitted to shoot if the challenge failed. Considerable thought had gone into planning the camp security. The perimeter fence was made of four parts: the first, a single three-foot-high strand of wire, was sited five yards from the innermost of the two tall fences, each of which was a sixteen-foot lattice of barbed wire; the second was separated from the first by a five-yard gap containing many wire spikes.

Unsurprisingly, Marlag-O was run along naval lines, and morale was described as 'outstanding' by the Senior British Officer, Captain G.F.W. Wilson DSO, in his report submitted at the end of the war. Captain Wilson was Commanding Officer of the Armed Merchant Vessel HMS *Van Dyke* and had been taken prisoner in June 1940 off the coast of Norway. He wrote that 'food was good, but was necessarily supplemented by IRRC (International Red Cross and Red Crescent) parcels, the sanitation was fair. Clothing was not very good and incoming mail was slow to arrive.' (5)

Amongst the prisoners interned at Marlag-O was Lieutenant David James, RNVR, who had served in Motor Torpedo Boats (MTB) in the North Sea. He described his experiences after the war in *A Prisoner's Progress*. (6) The routine of camp life commenced with the first roll call at eight in the morning (nine in the winter) and a parade with Kapitän Bachausen, the Kommandant of Marlag, described as a short fat red-faced man and known as 'Tubby', a gentleman who was 'genuinely out to do the right thing. But he was weak.' Lieutenant C.L. 'Charles' Coles, RNVR, had commanded a MTB in the Mediterranean but was taken prisoner at Galita Island and arrived at Marlag three days after Godfrey Place; he lived in the room next to Place and they became lifelong friends. He recalled that Bachausen had been a prisoner of war himself during the First World War and was a 'very decent chap.'

The morning parade was followed by breakfast, usually porridge, toast and marmalade and coffee. Lunch would be, for example, corned beef and potatoes or soup with bread and cheese. A second roll call at two in the afternoon was followed at half past three by tea with bread and jam. The third roll call took place at six, and was followed by a two-course supper. The day drew to an end with lights out at ten thirty. The food provided by the Germans was both limited and poor, and was mostly bread, potatoes, sauerkraut and beetroot. As a result, prisoners relied on Red Cross parcels for luxuries and a system of general messing evolved that allowed parcel contents to be shared as fairly and widely as possible.

Place recalled these arrangements as, 'Very peaceful, with a central dining hall and it was all very respectable. There were shortages of comforts that were supplied by the Red Cross; this was due to the prisoners coming from Italy which had swelled the numbers by a hundred.'

Each month prisoners were allowed to send three letters, each of twenty-four lines, and four postcards, each with seven. Lieutenant Commander P. N. Buckley had been Commanding Officer of the submarine HMS *Shark* which was sunk in July 1940, and had been one of the first to arrive at Marlag-O in June 1942. He described how, despite letters being censored by the Germans, messages were passed home, with a number of systems employed for concealing information. He recalled how, when the prisoners from the midget submarines arrived, 'We sent home practically the whole story of their attack on the *Tirpitz* by letters, to our parents' home which the Admiralty intercepted and they got the story. The letters appeared normal to our parents. There were only about ten concealed words in a letter.' (7)

The letters sent home by Godfrey Place to Althea describe his activities and feelings during his time in captivity. A constant feature, unsurprisingly, is his longing to be home with his wife. Writing on 30 November, he described the system of parcels, especially how to send cigarettes, asking for Benson and Hedges if possible. He was also in need of clothes and asked particularly for pyjamas. In December the weather turned bitterly cold and thick ice formed on the pond, allowing him and Donald Cameron to go skating. As Christmas approached Place found that he had to undertake his own laundry, and wrote, 'washing clothes is one of the most tiresome things.'

At Marlag-O many prisoners became involved in theatrical productions. Lieutenant Bill 'Houston' Rogers, RNVR, who had been a theatre producer and photographer before the war, oversaw much of the camp entertainment, as well as the theatre, which was built in a condemned barrack quarter. The first production seen by Place was the Christmas pantomime in December 1943. 'Diana in Wardroom Land' was a skit on naval life, and Place enjoyed it; some of the men dressed up as girls were said to have looked 'pretty snappy'. The orchestra was directed by Houston Rogers, and Charles Coles played the alto saxophone. This was Place's first Christmas as a married man, and he was spending it in captivity. He managed to describe the celebrations as 'quite decent'; all the prisoners had tried to make the best of the situation, and storing food during the year made it possible to provide three special meals on the day. Breakfast was porridge and sausages, lunch was sardines, bacon and scrambled eggs, and finally there was Christmas dinner of roast meat, roast potatoes with gravy, followed by Christmas pudding and custard sauce. Commander G.R. Lambert DSC, had been captured at Dieppe in August 1942 where he had served as Principal Beach Master. Writing to his wife, he described 'a nice carol service on Christmas Eve' and continued: 'We made the best of Christmas under the circumstances. We had a very good dinner, our stomachs are not used to too much food. The Christmas pudding was marvellous.' (8)

By January 1944 Godfrey Place was trying to settle in as best he could to life as a prisoner of war. It was not easy; for a man used to activity and adventure being inactive and cooped up in this way was a challenge. He had, however, read widely in his youth, and captivity afforded him the opportunity to read again. In Marlag-O he found a wide range of books and read an eclectic mix, including *Grapes of Wrath*, *The Temptation of Saint Antoine* (in French), *Whom God has Sundered*, Tennyson and his favourite *Canterbury Tales*. January was also a time for New Year resolutions, which Place felt were useful for the strong-minded, but having unsuccessfully renounced cigarettes once in his youth he had given up the very faintest hope of renouncing anything for any reason other than 'inadequate funds'.

With time on their hands, prisoners undertook a range of activities, many having the objective of escaping by one means or another. There were educational classes, and early in 1944 Place joined one on Physics; he found this very dull, covering material that he had studied before and wrote, 'There were so few there and the lecturer is so earnest I'll have to turn up again next week, not to disappoint the poor fellow.'

The 'Marlag forum' was a series of lectures held fortnightly and included talks on recent naval events. In order not to arouse the interest of the Germans, they were billed under the most innocent names. For example, 'Plymouth Hoe', by Lieutenant Commander S.H. 'Sam' Beattie VC, was the story of the St Nazaire raid on 27 March 1942. With the codename 'Operation Chariot', the objective was to render the Normandie dock unuseable, since it was the only site on the western coast of France which could accommodate the *Tirpitz*. Success would reduce the likelihood of the ship being able to operate in the Atlantic. 'Operation Chariot' involved both the Royal Navy and Commandos, and five Victoria Crosses were awarded, two posthumously, in a raid described by Winston Churchill as a 'brilliant and heroic exploit.' Other titles with a less obvious naval flavour, were 'The Beveridge Report' and 'National Insurance.' In June 1944, Donald Cameron gave what was described by Captain Wilson as 'an interesting talk', although neither its title nor contents were recorded.

In October 1943 Althea had started to write letters to her husband, but as she did not know where he was, or even if he was alive, the letters were recorded in a diary. On 23 October the first entry started:

Dearest Godfrey

I just thought yesterday that it would be a very good idea if I wrote to you in this book and then you will one day be able to read what had been happening while you're not here.

Over the ensuing months she recorded her feelings as well as noting important and, at times, not so important events. In October she had seen her husband become 'front page news with a vengeance', and as a result, she was snowed under by letters. Henty-Creer's mother was reported to have given a 'far too revealing interview to a reporter about Henty's work.' Althea attended a WRNS Handicraft Exhibition held at the National Gallery, London and exhibited a model of HMS *Nelson* made by her, with some assistance from her husband. She met the Queen and wrote how she had to 'curtsey and call her ma'am.' In the same letter she wrote, 'I do wish I knew where you are.'

Althea's appointment to Immingham allowed her to be near to her parents' home in Grimsby, but there were difficulties. When people realised that her husband had taken part in 'Operation Source' she was asked questions that were rather too inquisitive. Added to this, the job was not to her liking; by October 1943 she was hoping to join the signals course, but was concerned that she needed to improve her knowledge of Morse code before applying. She remained in contact with Ruth Barham and wrote, 'Ruth thinks that Bill and you wouldn't be taken prisoner, although I can't see any other hope.' Althea had obviously followed 'Operation Source' in some detail and wrote, 'I was most annoyed that the old ship didn't completely sink. It jolly well ought to have done.' A few days later, she wrote again of her concerns, 'I do wish I knew what had happened to you – I do hope you are not in a horrid dark cell.'

Her hopes were raised by reports in the papers in late October of claims that prisoners had been taken from the crews of the midget submarines, but she wrote that this had been claimed 'so many times.'

As well as serving as a Wren, Althea had acquired another job: acting as secretary for her husband. She answered letters from a number of people, many of whom she had only met once, if at all. Writing to Aunt Maisie, she was unsure whether she was a 'Miss or Mrs'. She wrote that her husband had caused her 'more letter writing in the last six months than in the rest of my life.' There was some rest from secretarial duties in early November, and she described how she had gone for a walk and 'came back to the base by the railway line – successfully crawled through the bases defence by crawling through the barbed wire.' It would not be long before Godfrey Place would be trying a similar manoeuvre, but in an effort to break out.

As the winter progressed, Althea became more and more disheartened with her job, finding that her colleagues talked only of 'Wrens, Wrens and more Wrens all day', and wished at times she could be discharged from the service. She received a letter from Ruth Barham, who hoped that Bill Whittam and Godfrey were 'snug and safe in a Norwegian house.' As Christmas approached, Althea was missing her husband dreadfully, and wrote, 'If only you were here for Christmas … I am so tired of waiting to hear what has happened to you. Please, please, hurry up.'

One of the visitors to Immingham was the Commander-in-Chief, Home Fleet, Admiral Sir John Tovey GCB, KBE, DSO, who was introduced to Althea at the wardroom Christmas party. As the conversation progressed he told her that he had 'lent her husband a battleship to practice on.' At the same party a colleague complimented Althea by describing her as 'an inspiration to the others,' leading her to write in her diary: 'See what you married, a twenty-three-inch waisted inspiration – not too bad. A pity you are not here to be appreciating it all.'

The application for the signals course was submitted, and just after Christmas Althea travelled to London for an interview; whilst there she met up with Peggy, Helen and Helen's husband. The next day she learnt that she had been successful and was to start at the Signals School, HMS *Mercury* near Petersfield, Hampshire, in the middle of January. There was also news from the Royal Navy. Althea wrote in her diary: 'Oh the *Scharnhorst* was sunk the night before last. Jolly good isn't it. In the naval review of the year – 'your affair' was the outstanding feat.'

Early in 1944, the Admiralty became aware of those members of 'Operation Source' that had been taken prisoner. On 6 January Admiral Barry wrote to the First Lord of the Admiralty:

> I know you would like to know straightaway that we have just got the names of the six fellows in SOURCE who are prisoners of war. Their names are:

> Lieut D. Cameron RNR
> Sub-Lieut J.T. Lorimer RNVR

Sub-Lieut R.H. Kendall RNVR
E Goddard C/MX 89069 ERA4

Lieut B.C.G. Place DSC RN
Sub-Lieut R. Aitken RNVR

The letter also indicated that parts of the story of the attack had been received through the coded letters sent from Marlag-O, and that Admiral Barry was hoping for the rest of the story to be obtained through the same route. Detailed information on the attacks by X6 and X7 reached London by the end of January, allowing Barry to write a detailed account of 'Operation Source' on 2 February 1944 which included operational details from both midget submarine commanders. (9)

The news that Althea had been waiting for had finally arrived, and on 7 January she heard that her husband was safe. A letter was received from Admiral Barry and Althea was 'quite overcome on reading it.' She wrote: 'I just can't believe it properly. Oh darling I am so pleased, I just can't explain. I feel twenty years younger. Gosh the weight off my mind is so terrific, I feel in a dream.'

Althea was soon to receive many more letters. Captain Banks wrote: 'Godfrey's skill and bravery is legend – I simply long for the whole wonderful story to be made known to the world.'

Admiral Sir John Tovey, who had 'lent' a battleship to Godfrey Place in 1943, wrote, by hand, to Althea: 'You must be enormously proud of him and you can tell him from me that he has every reason to be proud of you for the courage you have shown during what must have been a desperately anxious time.'

News soon arrived for Althea that both Donald Cameron and John Lorimer were prisoners, but there was, however, no news of Bill Whittam. Ruth Barham wrote soon after from *Varbel* and informed Althea that she had been told that there was 'very little hope for Bill'. The loss of Bill Whittam and Bill Whitley would dwell with Godfrey Place throughout his time in captivity. In December 1943 he wrote: 'I am going to write to Ruth [Barham] one of these days but letters are appallingly difficult to write.' And in April 1944: 'Poor Ruth – I should so like to write but don't know what to say so I think I'll leave it till I see her when I am home ... your letter makes me think a lot of the two Bills – I do wish they were here.'

In Marlag-O, Place and a number of colleagues were planning an escape for late January 1944. The others involved were Lieutenant F.W. Carr DSC, RNVR, Lieutenant A.B.K. 'Bill' Tillie, RNVR, and Lieutenant A.H.

Brookes; all were described as 'unusually resolute men'. Their escape involved cutting through the perimeter wire at a site where four other prisoners had tried, unsuccessfully, in December 1943. They argued that the Germans would least suspect a site only recently used 'and anyway there was no other way.' The attempt took place on the night of 28 January 1944. As they started, Tillie thought it was not dark enough, an opinion which was borne out by events, but the rest were determined to have a shot at the escape, especially as an air raid warning had caused the perimeter lights to be turned off. There was limited success. On reaching the outer wire the wire cutter became blunt and started making a noise like a pistol shot at each stroke. Place relieved Carr on the wire cutters and as he was cutting the last strand a sentry heard the noise, called out a warning and the lights were turned on. David James described how 'we waited for shots, but none came.' Guards came into the camp with instructions for their (the would-be escapers) bedding to be transferred to the cells. One of the guards said that the prisoners were all right but that the situation had been *verdammt gefahrlig* (damned dangerous). Place managed to throw his forged papers into the ratings' compound (Marlag-M), and Frank Carr put his in the guardhouse fire. (10)

This escape attempt was rewarded with a period of solitary confinement. Place described how he had already spent two months in his own company and so was 'not very enthusiastic for another twenty-eight days.' However, one advantage was 'the ability to have a bath in front of the stove on your own.' At this time Godfrey Place was not allowed to write letters home, and he took the opportunity to rekindle his interest in writing verse. All prisoners were given a YMCA pocket book, and most used it as a diary, but Place wrote poetry in his. The first poem, written on 1 February 1944, was entitled 'Spring Sunset':

I gazed at the setting sun and looked away.
But stayed the red-gold image 'fore my eyes –
A fading halo to departing day
Made Saint before it dies.

Twilight wore all the robe of death,
But with no bitterness.
As at the stake the faithful martyr showed no pain
So died another day –
Of greater birth again.

On his release from solitary confinement he found that all the prisoners in the camp had been affected by his escape attempt. The daily regime was more severe, and nobody was allowed outside his hut after five o'clock, or sunset. As the evening meal had normally been at seven o'clock, it now had to be taken in the huts. He recalled:

> One could not help being a little bit conscious of the old hands saying 'Oh there's that chap, he's only been here five minutes and now we have to suffer for him having a futile attempt at escaping.' ... You had to admit that they had a point of view.

He addressed the issue of escaping again in 1988:

> In a prisoner of war book, the impression is left that everybody is spending all their time working out some way of escaping – but I would doubt if anyone engaged [in], over their time in camp, more than half an hour a day on escaping. As for the rest of the time, life had to be lived, so there was a fair amount of give and take. This was in the back of the mind of the escape committee who would make reasonably certain that the enterprise people was going in for had a reasonable prospect of success, against what sort of retaliation the Germans were likely to take.

Escaping was not an easy task; Place now had first-hand knowledge of the problems. The water table was high, and both Marlag-O and Marlag-M were surrounded by a deep water-filled ditch, which the Germans had created to deter prisoners from tunnelling. Added to this, the ground was soft so tunnels would easily collapse. The camp lay in a densely populated military area, and this presented a further barrier to successful escape for those who managed to get away. Despite this, prisoners dug three long tunnels, starting in the autumn of 1942, not long after the camp had been established. In September 1942, Lieutenants Beet and Catlow escaped via a tunnel and Catlow managed to travel as far as Denmark before he was recaptured.

John Worsley's artistic talents were used widely during his time in Marlag-O. He helped create a number of forged documents, but perhaps his most memorable contribution was a collapsible dummy called 'Albert'. Talking with the escape committee, he said, 'I know I will make a dummy', and later wrote that it was an off-the-cuff remark, 'a flight of fancy.'[4] Every Thursday

---

4. The idea of imitating the presence of a prisoner was not actually new to the camp. Coward described in *Sailors in Cages* how Russian prisoners at Sandbostel were

afternoon, officers from Marlag-O were marched in columns of three from their camp, through the administration compound, to the shower block. They were counted on the way there and back. The plan was for the dummy to take the place of an escaper on the return march, whilst the latter would hide in the shower block, making their escape later under cover of darkness. Lieutenant Bob Staines, RNVR, John Worsley's room mate, helped build the dummy; Worsley made the head, which had ping-pong balls as eyes (attached to a pendulum system, ensuring that they occasionally blinked) and Bob Staines made the body. Albert, in pieces, was carried to the shower block by a number of prisoners, including John Lorimer who recalled carrying Albert's left leg. Albert was assembled in the shower room whilst the escaper hid in the roof space. When complete, the dummy was supported on either side by hooks to the shoulders of 'minders' (Worsley and Staines) and marched back to camp. The first prisoner nominated to escape was Lieutenant 'Blondie' Mewes, RNVR, who could speak German. On 2 June 1944 Mewes hid in the roof space of the shower house, changed into civilian clothes and made his escape after dark. Albert was registered in head counts three times a day for the next four days, during which time Mewes travelled by train to the port of Lübeck. He made his way on to a Swedish cargo vessel, but his plea for sanctuary was refused. Attempts to board a second Swedish vessel were also unsuccessful, and he was then arrested. Mewes was returned to Marlag-O on 23 June, having endured five unpleasant days in the hands of the Gestapo. (11) Following the apparent success of Albert, he was used again later that month. Lieutenant William Phelan, RNVR managed to escape, but only as far as the local neighbourhood before being apprehended. The escape had been disrupted by a German guard entering the shower block to use the lavatory and discovering Albert being assembled. Worsley recorded that Albert's downfall was due to 'German bowels and not to their brains.' Albert's head was subsequently mounted on a plinth and proudly displayed on the Kommandant's desk; it became a topic of conversation for many German visitors to the camp.[5]

treated very poorly by the Germans; if one died his body would be propped up between two prisoners on parade, in order to be counted alive so that comrades could receive the dead man's meagre rations. In addition, a dummy had been made for one of the cabaret evenings held in the camp and had been seen by John Worsley.

5. In 1945 Guy Morgan and Edward Sammis wrote a play entitled *Albert RN* about the escape from Marlag. This was performed in London after the war, and Houston Rogers was involved in the show's production. In 1954 a film of the same name was made, and John Worsley acted as technical adviser and created a new dummy. Guy Morgan had been a prisoner at Marlag-O; on repatriation to England in September 1944 he smuggled out some of John Worsley's sketches and the early drafts of his own book *Only Ghosts Can Live* under the plaster supporting his badly injured left arm.

John Worsley also drew and painted many scenes of camp life. He painted the portraits, in oils, of the three Victoria Cross holders in the camp, using sheets (originally intended to be used as curtains) as canvas. The first to be painted was 'Sam' Beattie, and in June 1944 it was Godfrey Place's turn. He admitted that he was rather amused when asked to sit for the painting and found it rather tedious, but wrote to Althea: 'He is, however, undoubtedly, an expert, the portrait is progressing well. Darling I do feel silly being painted.'

Place was concerned that the painting would hang in the War Museum and that people would only be able to look at it from time to time. The sheets used for the portrait had already been used for scenery in a theatrical production. The paintings of Godfrey Place VC, Donald Cameron VC and 'Sam' Beattie VC were successfully bought back to Britain by John Worsley at the end of the war and today are housed in the National Maritime Museum at Greenwich. Several years later Place and Worsley inspected the back of the canvas and clearly saw the poinsettias that had been painted when it was used for scenery.

Although forty-two officers successfully escaped from Marlag-O, only three managed to reach Britain. The first to do so was Lieutenant David James. On 8 December 1943 he escaped from the shower house disguised as a Bulgarian Naval officer, Lieutenant Ivan Bagerov (pronounced 'bugger-off'). He was recaptured at Lübeck five days later, having been unable to obtain passage on a Swedish ship. He was returned to camp and spent Christmas Day in solitary confinement. On 10 February 1944 he again escaped via the shower house and travelled via Danzig to Lübeck, where he boarded the *Canopus*, a merchant ship carrying a cargo of oranges. He stowed away under the boilers and endured hot and filthy conditions for nearly three days. Despite a search of the vessel by German police officers, he arrived safely in Stockholm on 22 February 1944 where he needed five baths in order to get clean. Following his escape, the guards were informed that if anyone else escaped, the guard responsible in the area would be shot. (12)

Having served his time in solitary confinement, Place described how, two days after being released from the 'cooler', he was approached by a prisoner who said: 'You are a wire cutter aren't you? And we have noticed you can get through the top wire in the dark now with a very good chance if there is an air raid, because that wire is only patrolled until eight o'clock, by one sentry doing the whole length of the thing, including the ratings' camp and the bit in between – will you come with us?'

Place said 'No' since at that time he had no plain clothes and no cigarettes to buy anything with. On 20 February 1944 250 guards were withdrawn from the camp, and two days later four officers attempted to escape. Sub Lieutenant T.J. McLister, RNVR, and Lieutenant D.B. Taylor were recaptured a week later, whereas Lieutenants Dennis Kelleher, RNVR, and Stewart Campbell,

RNVR, who had asked Godfrey Place to join their escape, reached England. Their route followed that of David James, and they arrived in Stockholm on 8 March 1944. The success of their escape was all the more remarkable since they appeared to have undertaken few, if any, preparations. (13)

Despite missing out on a possible escape, there was, however, good news for Godfrey Place and the others involved in 'Operation Source' The *London Gazette* of 22 February 1944 carried the announcement of the award of the Victoria Cross to Godfrey Place and Donald Cameron. The announcement was unusual in that it was a joint citation for the two commanding officers:

The King has approved the award of the Victoria Cross for valour to

Lieutenant Basil Charles Godfrey Place DSC, RN (of East Meon, near Petersfield), and Lieutenant Donald Cameron RNR (of Lee-on-Solent)

Lieutenants Place and Cameron were the commanding officers of two of HM midget submarines X7 and X6, which on September 22, 1943, carried out a most daring and successful attack on the German battleship *Tirpitz*, moored in the protected anchorage of Kaafjord, Norway.

To reach the anchorage necessitated the penetration of an enemy minefield and a passage of 50 miles up the fjord, known to be vigilantly patrolled by the enemy and to be guarded by nets, gun defences and listening posts, this after a passage of at least 1,000 miles from base.

Having successfully eluded all these hazards and entered the fleet anchorage, Lieutenants Place and Cameron, with a complete disregard for danger, worked their small craft past the close anti-submarine and torpedo nets surrounding the *Tirpitz*, and from a position inside these nets, carried out a cool and determined attack.

While they were still inside the nets a fierce enemy counter-attack by guns and depth charges developed, which made their withdrawal impossible. Lieutenants Place and Cameron therefore scuttled their craft to prevent them falling into the hands of the enemy. Before doing so they took every measure to ensure the safety of their crews, the majority of whom, together with themselves were subsequently taken prisoner.

In the course of the operation these very small craft pressed home their attack to the full, in doing so accepting all the dangers inherent in such vessels and facing every possible hazard which ingenuity could devise for the protection in harbour of vitally important capital ships.

The courage, endurance, and utter contempt for danger in the immediate face of the enemy shown by Lieutenants Place and Cameron during this determined and successful attack were supreme.

Awards were also made to other members of the crews of X6 and X7:

His Majesty has also given orders for the following appointments and has approved the following award for gallantry, skill and daring during the attack:

DSO: Sub-Lt R Aitken, RNVR, Sub-Lt RH Kendall, RNVR, Sub-Lt JT Lorimer RNVR

CGM: ERA 4 CL E Goddard.

The original recommendation for the award of the Victoria Cross was written by Captain Banks on 14 October 1943, and read:

Cold blooded coolness, determination and gallantry of the first order were essential if this exceptionally hazardous attack was to be successful – it was also an outstandingly fine feat of leadership, required the highest degree of skill in handling the submarine and was performed by an officer who was for the first time in command of one of His Majesty's submarines. I consider no award too high. (14)

The King approved the award of the Victoria Cross on 13 February 1944. Althea was made aware of the award in a letter of 18 February; she was informed that it had to remain confidential until announced in the *London Gazette* on 22 February. The Admiralty asked if she was happy for her name and home address to be released to the press, to which she replied 'Yes' by telegram on 21 February.

When the award was announced Althea received many telegrams offering congratulations to her and her husband. Her sister Susan sent one alerting her to a radio broadcast to be made that night by Admiral Barry. The talk, entitled 'Midget Submarines', began:

One night last autumn in a lonely bay in the North, I wished good luck and said au revoir to a little band of officers and men who were setting off in their minute submarines known as the 'X' class, on what was undoubtedly one of the most hazardous enterprises undertaken during the war.

He described the journey and elements of the attack on the *Tirpitz* and went on to say:

> After many days of anxious waiting I learned that they had achieved some success, but only recently have we learned how great their success was – how great, too, the measure of their courage and endurance which has been recognised tonight with the announcement of the decorations which you have already heard.

Admiral Barry wrote to Althea of her husband, 'whose great bravery and total disregard of danger will go down in history as one of the most audacious and gallant acts in the whole annals of the Royal Navy.'

On 23 February 1944 there was widespread coverage of the attack on the *Tirpitz* and the recent gallantry awards in both national and regional newspapers. *The Times* carried a picture of midget submarines (these were the first pictures of X-craft released by the Admiralty) and of Godfrey Place and Donald Cameron. Other newspapers had headlines including, 'Midget Sub "Aces" sailed 1,060 death miles to VC', 'Treated Peril with Utter Contempt'. The *Manchester Dispatch* led with a quote from Althea: 'He's always thinking of the sea.' Some thirty years later Godfrey Place would describe the whole affair as 'a grossly over-publicized attack in a small submarine on the *Tirpitz* in 1943.'

Both Althea and Peggy gave interviews to the press; Althea was described as being 'somewhere on board a Royal Naval shore establishment' (which was HMS *Mercury*) and proudly rejoicing in the news that she was the wife of a Victoria Cross holder. When asked about the award, she said, 'Oh goody' and went on to say 'I am immensely proud of him and longing to see him again. I had a letter from him a week ago and he was very cheerful though worrying as to where he was going to get some tobacco.' She also said, 'I can't say I am really surprised that he has got the VC after all that he had done.' Peggy commented that her son 'had been married for seven weeks, and then missing for four months, but we never gave up hope and thought he was too full of life to have died. I'm terribly thrilled. How proud his father would have been. He has plenty of work to do yet and he will do it well.'

Godfrey Place learnt of his award via the camp radio, listening to the BBC, in February 1944. Robert Aitken heard of his DSO in the same way, but exactly when is unclear. Place later said that there was a 'little bit of a celebration, but I was too busy feeling hungry and thirsty to care very much about the award.' (15) Records show that on 14 March a number of officers, including Place, Cameron and Worsley, were sent back to Dulag Nord for further interrogation, and Captain Wilson was informed that they would

Godfrey Place's parents: Charles Morris Godfrey Place ('Pat') and Miss Anna Margaret Stuart-William ('Peggy') at the Grand Malahide Hotel, Dublin, May 1915

Godfrey Place with his sister, Helen, outside the Holderness Hotel, Folkestone, Autumn 1926

Godfrey Place with his mother (left of picture) and sister, Helen, crossing the bridge over the Zambezi, January 1927

Godfrey Place, aged about thirteen (1934)

Sub Lieutenant B.C.G. Place, 1941

Hood Term, Royal Naval College, Dartmouth, May 1935. Front row, fifth from right, Godfrey Place, sixth from right, David Bevan

Crew of HMS *Unbeaten*, at Hove Town Hall, August 1942. Godfrey Place, second from left, front row, with Lieutenant Commander E.A. 'Teddy' Woodward next to him

Marriage of Lieutenant B.C.G. Place, DSC, RN, to Miss Althea Tickler, 17 July, 1943, Old Clee, Lincolnshire. Immediately next to Godfrey Place is his best man, Sub Lieutenant Henty Henty-Creer

Godfrey Place on honeymoon, Lake District, July 1943

X-craft in Loch Striven

X-craft in Kames Bay, with the town of Rothesay behind

X7 crews. Standing, from left, Sub Lieutenant Robert Aitken, RNVR, Lieutenant Godfrey Place DSC, Sub Lieutenant Bill Whittam, RNVR, Lieutenant Peter Philip SANF. Front row, from left: Able Seaman James Mageniss, Stoker John Luck, ERA Bill Whitley

X-craft departing from Loch Cairnbawn, September 11, 1943

The *Tirpitz* at sea

Althea Place, March 1944, preparing clothes to be sent to her husband in Germany

Godfrey Place VC and Donald Cameron VC, following their release from prisoner-of-war camp

Godfrey Place on his arrival home from Germany, May 1945. To the left, his mother, Peggy, to his right, Althea, and his grandmother, Mabel Stuart-William

Godfrey Place with Robert Aitken (left) and Willy Meeke

Skiing in St Moritz, Godfrey and
Althea Place, 1948

Graduation ball, RAF Syerston, February
1952. Godfrey and Althea Place

801 Squadron, November 1952. Front row, third from right, Commander Godfrey
Place VC, DSC

Commander B.C.G. Place VC,
DSC, London, November 1957

Visit to Elstree studios to view the filming of Billy Budd, August 1961. Left to right;
Captain B.C.G. Place VC, Melvyn Douglas, Robert Ryan, Peter Ustinov, Captain E.M.
Brown

Laying of wreath at Malbork Commonwealth War Graves Cemetery, Poland, November 1963

Godfrey Place being 'towed ashore' at HMS *Ganges* in a Seahawk aircraft, October 1965

Godfrey Place on the bridge of HMS *Albion*,
February 1966

Entertaining local
Dayak leaders on
board HMS *Albion*,
April 1966

HMS *Albion*, Godfrey
Place at Divisions,
April 1967

'Crossing the line' ceremony, September 1967, Godfrey Place with 'King Neptune'

Godfrey Place inspecting the mixing of the Christmas cake in HMS *Albion*, November 1967. The ladies are both members of the RAF and had been serving at RAF Khormaksar until its closure

Rear Admiral Godfrey Place meeting a Sea Cadet on board HMS *Discovery*, 1969

'An admirable tow'. Godfrey Place on the occasion of his retirement from the Royal Navy, April 1970

Godfrey Place and Sir John Smyth presenting a gift to the Queen, on the occasion of her fiftieth birthday, April 1976, Windsor Castle

Godfrey Place with Joe Lynch GC, and the Prince of Wales, Savoy Hotel, London, 1981

'A Place of Honour'. Godfrey Place and members of the Victoria Cross and George Cross Association, with the Queen Mother, Clarence House, 1984

Godfrey Place VC

return within 48 hours. They returned to Marlag-O the next day, with no apparent reason for the interrogation. On 27 March, at appell, Captain Wilson announced the gallantry awards, and wrote in his diary:

> I announced the award of VC to Lt. Place RN and Lt. Cameron RNR and DSO to Lt. Lorimer RNVR. The subsequent applause greatly excited the nearest sentry outside the wire who thought it meant armistice had been declared!

There was less welcome news, however, on the same day. Wilson wrote: 'The renegade Joyce (Lord Haw Haw) came to Dulag and various officers were sent for to be interviewed, he did not get a good reception.' (16)

Although letters were slow to reach Marlag-O, many did arrive. Some of these contained coded messages, including on 3 March 1944 a letter written in 'backhand script with a relief nib' by Mr Angus Mackenzie of 39 Ross Place, Edinburgh, 10, to 'Lieut. Donald Cameron VC, RNR, P/W 1144, Marlag und Milag Nord (Marlag-O), Germany.' Although apparently a letter enquiring after Donald's well-being in the camp, one line read:

> This letter also brings Jane's and naturally my own congratulations on your nobly earned V.C. We're ever so thrilled.

The hidden message was:

> Admiral Barry expresses pride and admiration of submarine service and sends congratulations on your very nobly earned decorations. (17)

The presence of so many highly decorated naval officers at the camp was a source of comment by an Australian, Sub Lieutenant Kim Paterson, RANVR, a folbot raider, who was captured in Italy and arrived at Marlag in June 1944: 'There was such a collection of VCs and DSOs that if you weren't one you were very small fry.' (18)

Despite having to face the press and answer a large number of congratulatory letters, Althea still had a job to do, and her course at HMS *Mercury* was coming to an end. There were examinations to be passed and, writing in March 1944, her husband gave her some advice: 'don't do any work for it. It's always worked with me, at least the only time I did work I got a second which wasn't good enough – but I am sure you'll do all right.'

Althea passed the examinations and in the middle of April was appointed to HMS *Eaglet*, the Royal Navy shore base at Liverpool which flew the flag of Commander-in-Chief, Western Approaches, Admiral Sir Max Horton.

Her success was noted by Place when he wrote to his father-in-law, 'Althea appears to becoming a full naval officer while I am learning to wash and darn clothes quite well.'

During his imprisonment, Place took part in a number of theatrical productions, and Charles Coles remembered him as a person who was very willing to join in with such activities. In April 1944 he took to the stage for the first time, playing a Chinese bodyguard and servant in a production which involved singing a number of Gilbert and Sullivan songs; he wrote that it was 'great fun, but I do wish I could sing.' The audience enjoyed the show and many felt it was better than the Christmas pantomime. Place then played Gratiano in the *Merchant of Venice*. Despite his not being keen on either the play or the part and finding it very difficult not to laugh in the last scene, the performance in June was deemed a tremendous success. His friend Donald Cameron had also become involved in the productions, painting all the scenery. Place's next part was as Lady Helston in *The Flashing Stream*, performed in September, and in October, he took part in an extremely well received performance of *Hamlet*. Captain Wilson noted in his diary: 'A most impressive performance that took over three and a half hours ... Lt. Craven as Hamlet, Lt. Cdr. Hodson as Polonius and Lt. Place as Laertes were outstanding in an excellent cast.' (19)

After *Hamlet*, at the behest of Charles Coles, Place wrote lyrics to be considered for the Christmas pantomime; he was very pleased when one was accepted for the show. Christmas 1944 was celebrated with special meals, and Place demonstrated his culinary skills by making rock cakes and tartlets.

Although he admitted to being not very musical, Place attended many of the camp concerts, and commented on what an achievement it was to have a twenty-piece orchestra, especially when it was apparent that both the cellos had been made in the camp. Another form of musical entertainment was cabaret nights. In May 1944, the theme was fancy dress, and Place went as a Greek guard, 'the ones who wear frilly skirts.' Coles remembered that on a cabaret night the German guards extended the curfew to 11.00 pm: 'We shook on the agreement that no one would try to escape up until the end of the curfew; but what might happen at 11.01 pm was a different matter!'

Godfrey Place was of the view that 1944 would be his last year in captivity. He recalled: 'After the fall of Paris (August 1944), and the tunnel that we were digging at the time had been discovered – I have to admit the escaping season rather came to an end – we thought that the war would end in October or November, unfortunately it dragged on over the winter.'

Although apparently keen to join in with a number of organised activities in the camp, Place appears to have had mixed with only a few other prisoners in his free time. His letters indicate that he spent time with Donald Cameron and John Lorimer, and he agreed to become godfather to Donald Cameron's son, Iain. By contrast, Robert Aitken, the diver from X7, had almost no contact with Place during their imprisonment and is never mentioned in letters home.

In October 1944 Godfrey Place was in a 'black mood', finding the company of his room mates very trying:

> I feel at a very low ebb just now which I feel will almost certainly end up in a life size row with the rest of this room – if I read poetry because I like it, everyone thinks I'm trying to be an intellectual. I have spent two evenings recently talking to Charles [Coles] and the next day I can just see curiosity written on everyone's face, he is the only person I dare show a poem to – oh it makes me so angry at times – everyone likes one to be typecast and when one abandons the strain of the hearty fellow's mask, people are surprised and think 'Godfrey has changed recently.'

The black mood had lifted somewhat within a fortnight, but nagging tensions appear to have remained, probably not helped by the reduction in food and heating provided to the prisoners by the Germans as a result of the Allied advances in Europe. In February 1945 he was able to move rooms, a change that he welcomed, and was pleased that 'it is very nice to have new topics of conversation and discover new interests.'

With the advance of Russian forces in the east, the Germans decided to move the occupants of Stalag Luft III[6] in Sagan towards the west. On 27 January 1945 approximately 2000 RAF officers and non-commissioned officers set out on the 'Long March' in extreme sub-zero weather.[7] They walked the 60 miles to Spremberg, where they were entrained for Westertimke, arriving on 5 February 1945. In order to accommodate them in Marlag-M, approximately 700 naval ratings were transferred to Milag, while 250 went to Marlag-O. Before long, tragedy was to strike one of those who had recently arrived. On 19 February Flight Lieutenant C.K.L. Bryson was

---

6. Stalag Luft III at Sagan, Poland was the prisoner of war camp from which the 'Great Escape' took place on 24 March 1944. Some seventy-six men escaped, and three successfully made it to Britain; of the seventy-three who were recaptured fifty were executed on the orders of Hitler.

7. The RAF party included Squadron Leader Leonard Trent, RNZAF, who had been captured in May 1943 after parachuting from his burning aircraft over Holland. He took part in the 'Great Escape', having been drawn number seventy-nine, and was captured at the mouth of the tunnel. In March 1946 he was awarded the Victoria Cross for his actions in 'Operation Ramrod 17' in 1943.

approached by a German guard named Krause to engage in bartering. This took place after dark, at about 20.00, and Bryson, with the encouragement of the guard, stepped over the warning wire and crawled towards the perimeter fence. Witnesses recall hearing a burst of gunfire followed by the searchlights being turned on, and saw that Bryson had been shot, with Krause standing nearby holding an automatic weapon. Although Bryson received medical treatment he died on 9 April from septicaemia secondary to wounds to his liver and lungs. (20)

Early in April 1945 the Germans decided to move the military prisoners from Marlag to Lübeck, about 80 miles away. On 9 April Captain Wilson was informed by the Kommandant that all prisoners were to be evacuated on foot and they should be prepared to start that evening. Wilson protested strongly; he foresaw dangers for men on the road from Allied airforces, who now had control of the skies. John Worsley had to decide what to pack and he placed the three paintings of the Victoria Cross recipients in a makeshift protective container made from a number of empty dried-milk tins. Many prisoners decided to avoid this march, including Godfrey Place, who described his reaction to the suggestion:

> A number of us did not fancy this as the sky was dominated by (Allied) airforces – anything that moved was shot at; lately some Poles in the Merchant Navy camp had left the shutters open and someone switched the lights on, and one of our planes put three rockets into the hut – just like that[8] … a number of us said we didn't fancy walking about North West Germany, they (the Germans) said that walking wounded and sick would not go and so a number of us climbed under the huts, or I sat in a Red Cross box addressed to Sweden. When the camp moved out we went up to Milag Nord about one mile up the road. We took precautions to conceal ourselves – I went up under a straw mattress in a horse- drawn cart, but the Germans had lost interest in prisoners of war by then.

Place moved to Milag on 11 April 1945 along with Donald Cameron and John Lorimer; the latter recalled Milag as a 'mad house' housing some 6,000 prisoners from a number of countries and very different from the calmer atmosphere they had been used to at Marlag-O.[9]

---

8. Leonard Trent described how they saw a Mosquito being chased by two Me109s over the camp. The Mosquito shot up the bread lorry, causing the prisoners' bread ration to be reduced from one sixth to one eighth of a loaf per day.
9. In 1944 the British government had received reports that there was significant ill discipline at Milag, and made contingency plans for ensuring order in the camp at the time of liberation, plans that were to involve the officers at Marlag-O restoring discipline.

The march to Lübeck commenced on 10 April, with nearly 2,300 men under the command of Captain E.H.B. Baker DSO, the senior British officer. The majority were RAF officers, but there were nearly 500 naval personnel. Consequently, just 90 RAF officers and 70 naval officers remained at Westertimke. The decision by Godfrey Place to avoid the march was, in hindsight, wise. John Worsley recalled that the trek to Lübeck took about two weeks and there was a constant threat from Allied air attacks. Prisoners carried a white ensign, but often it was seen too late, if at all, by Allied airforces. On one occasion a Hawker Typhoon attacked the marching column, and six men at the rear were killed, including an elderly Royal Navy Captain who had served in the First World War and had been taken prisoner in 1940. On reaching Lübeck, the prisoners were herded into a military barracks along with Polish prisoners, before finally being freed by elements of the 11th Guards Division. (21)

At Milag it was clear to Captain Wilson that German control of the camp was fading. By 19 April it was, however, surrounded by both SS and other first-line troops who, Wilson suggested, would have welcomed an excuse to 'clean up the camp.' To prevent this, a Royal Marine guard was instituted, maintaining a continuous unarmed patrol inside the wire to prevent anyone leaving the camp. That evening two bombs were dropped on Marlag-M; six men were killed and four were wounded. On 26 April 1945 the Germans proposed a truce for twenty-four hours to allow all prisoners of war to be evacuated the five miles to Bahnstadt, where they would be turned over to the British. Wilson refused to have anything to do with this plan, believing it to be a further example of time-wasting by the Germans. Allied troops continued to advance and on 27 April they attacked the village of Kirchtinke, less than two miles from the camp. There was fierce fighting around Westertimke, and all the Germans fled the town by midnight. At 00.45 on Saturday, 28 April 1945, Wilson met Lieutenant MacGregor of the Scots Guards along with three soldiers at the main gate of Milag and was told that he was free. Wilson wrote that they 'got a warm welcome' (22), and Place described how, following his final period of captivity of two or three weeks in Milag, a sergeant of the Irish Guards cut through the back wire and said, 'Gentlemen, you are free.' At 11.00 prisoners in Milag paraded on the camp's square, hoisted the red and white ensign which had been made in the camp and gave three cheers for the King. On that day, Godfrey Place wrote a postcard to Althea:

I am in British hands.
I am well and safe.
Expect to be home soon, do not write.

Amongst those who entered the camp at liberation was a former prisoner; Lieutenant R.C.M.V. 'Micky' Wynn DSC arrived at the camp in a tank, flying the white ensign from its aerial. He had been a prisoner at Marlag-O but had been transferred to Colditz and was later repatriated to England on grounds of ill-health.[10] Other arrivals at the camp included Jimmy Langley (now Lieutenant Colonel) who knew that the prisoners from the attack on the *Tirpitz* were housed at Marlag. He found Donald Cameron and offered him his heartiest congratulations. Cameron replied to Langley, 'I congratulate you on your splendid simulated German interrogation. The real thing was so similar that I felt I was re-acting a part I had already played.' Donald Cameron also pointed out that 'your slap was harder than the one I received from the German interrogating officer!' (23)

Godfrey Place was now free, and drew together his belongings, including the poems he had written in captivity. A ballad of peace written in June 1944 was very pertinent to the situation that he and his colleagues now found themselves in:

Do not Sound your Trumpets

Oh do not sound your trumpets till the war is really won
This battle's but a prelude to a fight not yet begun:
We are fighting now for England – and that cause is true and just –
But victory brings its burden in a yet more sacred trust
We will have won by strength of arms, and thereby won the chance
To use our brains to form a peace which will all men enhance.

Within a few days of his release Godfrey Place was again in the news. The *Daily Telegraph* and *The Times* of 2 May 1945 both carried a picture of Place standing alongside Donald Cameron after they had crossed the Elbe at Lauenburg following their liberation. Godfrey Place was soon to be re-united with his family, but in the following month there would be a number of important invitations in London as well as the resumption of a career in the Royal Navy. In the words of his mother: 'He has plenty of work to do yet and he will do it well.'

10. Micky Wynn had been captured at St Nazaire in March 1942, and had been injured during the raid, losing an eye. His repeated escape attempts from Marlag-O led to his transfer to Colditz, where he feigned mental ill-health and was repatriated. He recalled how he went back to Marlag-O in 1945 in order to 'settle some scores with a few Germans.'

Chapter 8

'Plenty of Work to Do Yet':
Return to the Navy

Godfrey Place, like many prisoners of war, was flown home in a converted RAF bomber in May 1945. There is no doubt that his experiences had changed him; years later his sister would reflect that he was not 'so much fun as before the war.' Not only had he lost two crew members in 'Operation Source', but several of his term mates from Dartmouth had died in the conflict, including his best friend David Bevan. He had spent over eighteen months in captivity and now had to adapt to married life, something he had only experienced for less than a month. Moreover, he had not fared well on the camp diet and on his return was significantly underweight; on medical grounds he was provided with extra food ration coupons.

Godfrey Place was one of just eleven members of the Royal Navy awarded the Victoria Cross during the war and who had returned home. As such he would stand out, something that would often be uncomfortable for him since he was still a very modest and unassuming officer. He was not one for talking about the raid that led to the award of the Victoria Cross, especially to his colleagues in the navy. In this way he was very different from at least one other officer who had been awarded the Victoria Cross; the latter had a reputation for quizzing junior officers as to why, where and when he was awarded the medal, behaviour that was a complete anathema to Godfrey Place.

Once back in England, he made his way to Ampthill, Bedfordshire where his mother and grandmother had been based during much of the war, and where Althea was waiting to greet him. On 7 May, one day before the unconditional surrender of Germany, he sent a telegram advising of his plans: 'Arrive about 6.30. Please no fuss. All love – Godfrey.'

In June Place attended a garden party for prisoners of war at Buckingham Palace, hosted by the King and Queen. The exploits of the midget submariners featured prominently in the press at this time, and he and Donald Cameron were photographed talking to the Queen; the next day their picture was on the front page of many national newspapers. Soon after, he and Cameron attended a dinner for Victoria Cross recipients hosted by the *News of the World* at the Dorchester Hotel. The majority of those attending had been awarded their medal during the First World War (or before), but the guests included Captain Charles Upham VC*, who in 1942 became only the third man to be awarded a bar to the Victoria Cross, and the only combatant to do so (the other two were doctors).

On 22 June, two years exactly since he was invested with the Distinguished Service Cross, Godfrey Place was once again at Buckingham Palace, this time to receive the Victoria Cross from the King. On the day there were five recipients of the Victoria Cross, Lieutenant B.C.G. Place DSC, Lieutenant D. Cameron, Lieutenant Commander S.H. Beattie, Major F.A. Tilston and Lance Corporal H. Nicholls; all except Tilston had been prisoners of war. Despite receiving the nation's highest award for gallantry, Place would later tell his family that he had had doubts about collecting the medal; he remained upset by the number of his friends who had died in the war and was concerned that the medal in some way reduced the significance of these losses. However, he also realised that not receiving the medal would be exceptionally rude on his part. The King said, 'good show, good show' to both Place and Cameron. After the ceremony the Queen asked Place about midget submarines. Since they remained a top secret project, he was unsure how to reply. Remembering that the King had recently visited the midget submarine depot ship he was able to reply, 'His Majesty knows,' an answer that appears to have been both satisfactory and diplomatic. Again the midget submariners were the centre of publicity. The *Daily Telegraph* described the exploit of attacking the *Tirpitz* as 'David and Goliath', and Godfrey Place recalled how they had mended the exhaust in X7, and 'managed to patch it up with chewing gum and bandages.' In his self-effacing way he recalled, 'I didn't know how we got inside the nets and I didn't know how to get out of them.'

Following completion of leave, Place reported for duty with the Royal Navy and indicated, not unreasonably, that he wished to go back into the submarine service. He was told he could but would lose eighteen months' seniority, having not served in submarines for that period. This response was not well received, and Godfrey Place decided to pursue an alternative career 'above the waves'. He would never serve in submarines again, and there would be very few occasions on which he would even set foot in one.

After attending a number of short courses in Portsmouth, he was appointed to HMS *Goldcrest* in October 1945. This was the Royal Navy Aircraft Detection Centre, situated at Kete in South Pembrokeshire, close to St Anne's Head. HMS *Goldcrest* was responsible for training Fighter

Direction Officers (FDOs), and its location was ideally suited, as it provided uninterrupted radar cover over the adjacent waters of the Irish Sea. The development of fighter direction as a speciality started in the Norwegian campaign of 1940, and was due in no small part to the work of Lieutenant Commander C. Coke, serving as Air Signals Officer in HMS *Ark Royal*. It had been recognised early on that the best form of defence for ships against air attack was the use of fighter protection, controlled by specialist officers viewing radar information in their ships. They could then use the information to help fighter aircraft intercept the approaching enemy before they could attack. It was during this time that Place appears to have developed his interest in naval aviation, perhaps since he saw it as the way forward for detection and destruction of submarines.

Despite not being welcomed by the submarine service itself, Place was invited by Vickers at Barrow-in-Furness to the launch of the submarine HMS *Anchorite*. On 24 January 1946 he attended the ceremony in the company of two other midget submariners, Lieutenant I.E. Fraser VC, DSC, and Able Seaman J.J. Magennis VC. Both had received the Victoria Cross for their attack on the Japanese cruiser *Takao* moored in the Jahore Straits, Singapore in July 1945. *Anchorite's* launch received widespread publicity and provided an opportunity for Place to return to the yard where, three years before, he had inspected X7 as she neared completion. It was also an opportunity to meet James Magennis; the two had not met since September 1943 when the operational and passage crews had transferred to and from X7 in rough weather in the North Sea.

As well as attending the FDO course, Godfrey Place was able to enjoy the pleasures of married life. At the same time, Althea gained an insight into some of the rigours of life as a naval officer's wife, including moving from one quarter to another at frequent intervals and being confronted with archaic housing. It was whilst serving at HMS *Goldcrest* that Godfrey Place became a father, with the birth of a daughter, Andrea, in May 1946. The FDO course was successfully completed the following month, and the Commanding Officer noted that Place was 'an excellent officer on the course, who misses nothing, is keen and takes an intelligent interest. An instructively good influence on others. His modesty over his achievements is most pronounced.'

Place was appointed to HMS *Dryad* at Portsmouth to undertake the Navigation and Direction (ND) conversion course, which commenced in July 1946 and lasted six months. At the same time he and Althea purchased their first home, a farm, Lower Bradley, on the outskirts of the village of Withleigh near Tiverton. Place had suggested they buy a farm soon after their engagement in March 1943, when he wrote: 'Let's have a farm, too, You know I'm terribly fond of this world – I'd like to watch things grow and there's nothing I like more than the smell of England after some time at sea.'

The farm was situated in an idyllic location, on a hillside to the west of Withleigh, with views over the rolling countryside. This was a working farm, but the new arrivals found that conditions were rather primitive, especially as they now had a two-month-old daughter. There was no electricity, but Althea, with the help of her father, rapidly ensured they were connected to the mains. Althea relished life as a 'farmer and housewife' and managed not only the home but also the livestock on the farm. Amongst those employed on the farm was a former German prisoner of war who had remained in England. Despite his earlier enthusiasm for country life, Place was far from comfortable living at Lower Bradley; he felt he was not in control of the farm and did not have Althea's natural aptitude for country living. Possibly the final straw was being referred to as 'Mrs Place's husband' by neighbours. They had not lived long at Lower Bradley before he was appointed Navigating Officer in HMS *Cardigan Bay* in February 1947.

HMS *Cardigan Bay* was an anti-submarine frigate, launched in 1945, and in 1947 was serving with the Mediterranean Fleet. She had a displacement of 1,600 tons, a speed of 20 knots and a complement of nearly 200 men. In early 1947 she had just completed repairs at Malta. In command was Captain G.K. Collett DSC, who was also Captain of the 5th Frigate Squadron. Place relieved Lieutenant Anthony Bowen, who noted that 'it was not very often that one served with such a distinguished officer.' (1) In March and April 1947 *Cardigan Bay* visited a number of Red Sea ports, returning through the Suez Canal to Malta in the middle of April. It had originally been planned that she would sail to Aqaba to take King Abdulla of Transjordan on a fishing trip, but this was cancelled due to the potential political repercussions of such a visit. Despite this, the King sent a gift to Captain Collett, a silver cup from Christies which was inscribed 'In memory of my trip on HMS *Cardigan Bay.*'

As part of the Mediterranean Fleet, HMS *Cardigan Bay* was closely involved in operations to intercept illegal Jewish immigrants attempting to enter Palestine. The British mandate over Palestine was established after the First World War, and there had been numerous problems controlling immigration in the inter-war years. After 1945 there was immense pressure from Jews wishing to leave Europe and enter Palestine by whatever means. To circumvent the limits on immigration set by the British, Jews chartered boats, and it fell to the Royal Navy to intercept them. Sir Nigel Essenhigh, (First Sea Lord, 2001-2002) described this period:

In the aftermath of the Second World War, no task that fell to the Royal Navy was more demanding than the interception of seaborne illegal immigration into Palestine in 1945-48. Skilled ship handling was essential and boarding parties faced considerable hazards. (2)

In 1947 Jewish immigrants purchased the former Great Lakes steamer *President Warfield*. Ships of the Royal Navy tracked her passage across the Atlantic to the Mediterranean where, in July 1947, she entered the French port of Sete. There she embarked over 4000 men, women and children, mostly Czechs, Germans and Poles, all holding Colombian visas issued in France. Early on 11 July she slipped from her mooring and sailed towards Palestine, shadowed by ships of the Royal Navy. In an act that would go down in Jewish folklore, the *President Warfield* was renamed *Exodus*. The interception and boarding of the *President Warfield* was to be the most difficult so far attempted by the Royal Navy. The flotilla tasked with the interception included HMS *Cardigan Bay*, *Ajax*, *Chequers*, *Chieftain*, *Chliders* and *Charity*. At 08.15 on 17 July *Cardigan* Bay joined the flotilla and positioned herself two miles ahead of the *President Warfield*. As they approached Port Said, *President Warfield* turned north, towards the coast of Gaza. At this point the decision was made to board. On 18 July, at 01.52, all ships in the flotilla were placed at action stations, and boarding started about an hour later. *Cardigan Bay* was under orders to steam five cables astern of the *President Warfield* and have two boarding parties ready, if needed. She was to act as a 'long stop', being prepared for any lifesaving duties that might be necessary as a result of either naval personnel or immigrants falling overboard. In the ensuing three hours forty officers and men of the Royal Navy boarded the *President Warfield* and were met by fierce opposition. Women and children had been placed on the upper decks to act as human shields, and the counter-boarding devices included fireworks, smoke bombs, steam jets and barbed wire, as well as the contents of the heads. At least one naval rating fell from the *President Warfield* in the commotion of boarding and was picked up by the crew of *Cardigan Bay*. (3)

The intensity of the operation became apparent when it was realised that all four naval vessels directly involved had been damaged. Once the Royal Navy had gained control of the *President Warfield* she sailed to Haifa. Three passengers had been killed during the boarding and twenty-six required hospital treatment. The rest were transferred to one of three converted cargo ships, *Ocean Vigour*, *Empire Rival* and *Runnymede Park*, and they departed early on 19 July under escort to France. HMS *Cardigan Bay* sailed with the convoy but left on 27 July to take the Senior Military Officer to Marseilles for discussions with the French authorities about the immigrants. The following day, *Cardigan Bay* rejoined the escort, and, along with the transport ships, arrived at nearby Port de Bouc on 29 July. The French authorities had agreed to accept 'volunteer' immigrants from the ships; only fifty-six volunteered to land, the rest remained on board and sailed back to Germany. On 31 July *Cardigan Bay* sailed to Gibraltar, arriving on 4 August. She was held in readiness to intercept the illegal immigrant ship *Paduca*, but was relieved the following day by HMS *St Brides Bay*, allowing her to enter the dockyard at Gibraltar to undergo refit.

Ordinary Signalman 'Windy' Gale served on HMS *Cardigan Bay*, joining the ship at Gibraltar. Godfrey Place was his Divisional Officer and Gale remembered how very quietly he spoke. When a sailor had to report to him in his cabin they came away 'barely having heard half of what he was saying. If the sailor had been interviewed on a matter of discipline it was not unusual for Godfrey Place to blush when he told you off.' He also recalled that Place was so well known that on one occasion he was invited on to an American warship instead of the Captain. As Navigator, Place did not keep a normal watch but was available twenty-four hours a day when at sea. He was popular with the ratings in his division, a popularity that continued for many years. When he had retired, a rating from HMS *Cardigan Bay* was in trouble with the police and appealed to Place for help. Typically, he wrote a very supportive letter to the Chairman of the Bench who was to hear the case.

Godfrey Place had been away from home for nearly six months, and Althea sailed from Liverpool to join him at Gibraltar in August 1947. Andrea, now aged one, was left at home being cared for by Althea's elder sister Ann, who came to look after both her niece and the farm. A holiday was spent in Gibraltar before *Cardigan Bay* left the dockyard and rejoined the fleet at Malta. Althea also spent time in Malta, and 'Windy' Gale remembered how Place would wave to Althea as the ship entered Grand Harbour.

HMS *Cardigan Bay* next sailed to the Red Sea, visiting Massawa in Eritrea and Port Sudan, but a planned visit to Jeddah had to be cancelled because of an outbreak of cholera. The ship then returned to the Mediterranean and sailed to Benghazi to take part in the celebrations for the return to Cyrenaica of the Emir. Captain Collett reported that the 'presence and fine bearing of the naval contingent contributed materially to the success of the occasion.' Amongst the social highlights were a 'tea and sticky bun party' and an official dinner, at which it was noted that 'the language difficulty was embarrassing.'

Following the interception of the *President Warfield*, law and order in Palestine had deteriorated further, and Jewish terrorists kidnapped and killed two British non-commissioned officers. On the political front, the British mandate for Palestine was nearing its end. In September the United Nations

Special Commission on the future of the country proposed its partition between Israel and Jordan, as well as advocating that 150,000 Jews should receive visas for entry immediately. The proposal was rejected by all parties involved, but at the same time the Royal Navy remained as busy as ever. Details had been received of further illegal Jewish immigrant ships making their way to Palestine. The ships, the *Pan Crescent* and *Pan York*, (known as the *Pans*) were converted banana ships and would be difficult to board due to their high freeboard. There was also concern that the ships might be deliberately beached, so a cruiser was deployed to the flotilla in order to prevent this. The itinerary for the *Pans* became apparent at Christmas 1947, and *Cardigan Bay* was closely involved in their interception. The *Pans* sailed from Constanza in Romania at the end of December, carrying a total of 15,000 passengers. They passed through the Dardenelles on 29 December into a full-blown gale, and were shadowed by *Cardigan Bay* and *Whitesand Bay*. By 31 December the intercepting flotilla, comprising two cruisers and five destroyers (led by HMS *Mauritius*), boarded the *Pans*, which had stopped voluntarily. The ships altered course for Famagusta in Cyprus, arriving on 1 January 1948. The next day, *Pan York* received fuel from *Cardigan Bay*, but Collett reported that provision of fuel was difficult since the ships had different size hoses. Although there had been no problems with boarding, he also recalled that whilst alongside *Pan York*, the upper deck of *Cardigan Bay* was showered with 'Jewish Jetsam, discharge from Hebrew Heads which, added to the traditional Semitic Smell on an Illegal Jewish Immigrant ship, made conditions on board slightly nauseating.' The crew and passengers of the *Pans* were interned on Cyprus. (4)

After the encounters with illegal immigrant ships, *Cardigan Bay* took part in the spring cruise of the Mediterranean Fleet in March 1948 and visited a number of ports as guests of the French navy. These were described as having an atmosphere of 'entente discordiale', as the French still had sore and recent memories of the attack by the Royal Navy on the French fleet at Mers-el-Kebir in July 1940. The next month, Collett left the ship and his report on Godfrey Place indicated the high regard he had for his Navigating Officer, recording that 'he was willing to turn his hand to anything. The more unusual it is the better it pleases him.' Place continued to serve in *Cardigan Bay* in the Mediterranean, under two further Commanding Officers (Captain M. Hodges OBE, April to June 1948; Captain R.C. Medley DSO, OBE, June to October 1948), both of whom recognised his many talents. Place left the ship at Malta in October 1948 and Captain Medley wrote that he was 'an outstanding officer who should go a long way in the Service.' Despite having left the ship Place maintained contact with her. When she was paid off in 1961 the ship's bell was offered to former crew members. Several competed for it, including Godfrey Place. He lost out to Lieutenant T. Cruddas, an Engineering Officer, whose daughter Heather was the only child to have been christened on board, in July 1949. (5)

Having returned from over eighteen months away from home, Place was next appointed to the Radar Training ship, HMS *Boxer*, based at Portsmouth. However, before joining the ship he was faced with the death of his mother, Peggy, who died on 2 January 1949, aged fifty-four. She had moved from Ampthill to Kingswear in Devon in 1948 where she lived in a waterside property, Longford, which had superb views across to Dartmouth and, above the town, the Royal Naval College. Why she chose Kingswear is uncertain, but it may have allowed her to be reasonably close to her son and daughter-in-law, who were living near Tiverton. A memorial service for Peggy was held on Friday, 7 January at St Saviour's church in Dartmouth, and two days later Godfrey Place joined HMS *Boxer*. The ship's log recorded, '23.00: "Lt. V.S.G. Plaice [sic] VC, DSC" joined the ship.' (6) The ship was a hybrid, having originally been built as a tank-landing ship that served on the beaches of Normandy on D-Day in June 1944. During January and February she took part in exercises which involved her sailing out to Spithead most mornings and returning to harbour later that day. Exercises only took place in the week, and at weekends Place drove home to his family in Devon. In March the ship sailed to Rosyth for a two-week exercise and then returned to Portsmouth. Place left the ship in April and was posted to HMS *Dryad* to undertake the advanced section of the ND course.

Whilst at HMS *Dryad* Godfrey Place learnt to fly with the Royal Naval Flying Club based at HMS *Siskin*, RNAS Gosport. The club, despite its name, was a private concern. It had been established in 1948 to provide an opportunity for sub lieutenants of the executive branch, undertaking courses at Portsmouth, to gain experience of flying. It was hoped this might encourage some officers to join the Fleet Air Arm, which was expanding at the time. The aim was for up to forty officers per year each to undertake about seven and a half hours flying. (7) It is unlikely that the club's founders had envisaged that a lieutenant of seven years seniority, holding the Victoria Cross, would wish to make use of its facilities. On 7 July 1949 Godfrey Place flew a Fairey Tipsy dual-control aircraft alongside the Chief Flying Instructor, Flight Lieutenant K.W. Birt DFC. Less than three weeks later he piloted the plane alongside his instructor. Place continued to learn to fly until early August when he sailed in RMS *Queen Elizabeth* to America, where he spent nearly four months on the Command Operation Center Course at the Naval Air Station in Glenview, Illinois. At the end of the course he travelled home in RMS *Queen Mary*, arriving on 22 December.

During the four months that Godfrey Place had been away family life had changed. It had been decided to sell the farm, and home was now 11 Hamilton Road, Southsea. By the time Place left for America, Althea was expecting their second child, due in September. She had been very unwell after the birth of Andrea and was concerned that similar problems might occur after the second birth. She tried to persuade her husband that he should delay the trip to America, but to no avail; duty took precedence over family. Althea gave birth to a son, Charles, in September 1949, whom Godfrey Place did not see until he was three months old. This was reminiscent of his own childhood; his father did not see him until he was almost six months old.

In January 1950 the newly promoted Lieutenant Commander B.C.G. Place VC, DSC, commenced his next appointment, on the staff of Flag Officer, Air (Home), Vice Admiral Sir Reginald Portal KCB, DSC, at HMS *Daedalus*, RNAS Lee-on-Solent, an appointment that would help him to pursue a career in naval aviation. He made a good impression; his confidential report, written by the Chief Staff Officer, Captain A.N.C. Bingley OBE, declared that he was 'able to undertake a multitude of activities in a quiet, firm and effective manner.' Having been in post for six months, Place applied for the pilot's course with the Fleet Air Arm, but in August 1950 was informed that his request had been refused. Undeterred, he continued to fly with the Royal Naval Flying Club. Whilst at HMS *Siskin*, he attended a ceremony for the presentation of 'Wings' during which the visiting dignitary asked him about his red medal ribbon, saying that he had 'not seen one before'. Place told him that it was the Victoria Cross. The dignitary was highly embarrassed at his ignorance and somewhat annoyed with his hosts that he had not been informed that a Victoria Cross holder was to be at the ceremony.

Place's appointment to *Daedalus* finished on 8 March 1951 and from then he was effectively 'unemployed'. However, on 17 April 1951 the Admiralty relented in their opposition to his requests to fly, and his service record reads:

> T.L's [Their Lordships of the Admiralty] have given further consideration to request and now have agreed. To be appointed to No.23 Flying Training Course, RAF SYERSTON.

He had been accepted for the next training course for potential Fleet Air Arm pilots and was to commence at RAF Syerston in May 1951. By then he had gained thirty hours of flying experience, of which ten were as pilot. He would soon be learning to fly combat aircraft on and off aircraft carriers, and further service for the Royal Navy in a theatre of war was not far away.

Chapter 9

Wings, a Brass Hat and War in the East

After the Second World War, potential Fleet Air Arm pilots undertook their initial training at RAF Syerston, an airbase some five miles south-west of Newark, Nottinghamshire. The base had been built in the 1930s as part of Britain's rearmament programme, and early in the war had served as home for a number of squadrons of Lancaster bombers. Amongst those who flew from Syerston in 1943 were Wing Commander Guy Gibson VC, DSO*, DFC* and Flight Lieutenant Bill Reid VC. From the end of 1943 Syerston served as a base for training bomber crews, and in 1948, No 22 Flying Training School arrived, specialising in training pilots for the Fleet Air Arm.

Godfrey Place joined 23RN Flying Course at Syerston, Commanding Officer, Group Captain G.F.W. Heycock DFC, on 7 May 1951. He was one of twenty future naval pilots assigned to the course who ranged in age, rank, and military experience and included several members of the RNVR. Alongside 23RN course was No 5 (SEG) RAF course with twelve members. Following initial instruction, Place commenced flying at Syerston on 15 May on a cloudy day with moderate to poor visibility and light north-west winds. His first flights were in a Percival Prentice, the standard dual-control aircraft used for training by the RAF. At 11.35 Place took off as co-pilot, alongside his instructor Lieutenant Burden, on a flight that lasted some twenty-five minutes. He made rapid progress and on 28 May made his first solo flight, which lasted fifteen minutes. The next landmark in training was reached on the night of 21/22 June when Place undertook night flying. After three short flights with his instructor he undertook his first solo night flight on 22 June. Basic training continued until the end of July, by which time Place had recorded thirty-three hours of flying solo.

In August 1951, after summer leave, members of 23RN Course progressed to advanced training, during which they flew the Harvard IIB aircraft, an advanced trainer with dual controls. By the end of August Place was flying solo in the Harvard. As the course progressed, the hazardous nature of flying was highlighted to all members by two fatal crashes at Syerston in the autumn.

As part of advanced training there was a two-week camp at a Royal Naval Air Station, and for 23RN Course this was held in January 1952 at HMS *Nuthatch*, RNAS Anthorn, close to the Solway Firth, just west of Carlisle. Ten Harvard aircraft were flown up to the camp, and Place was responsible for flying one of them, with Lieutenant I.J. Brown, the officer in charge of the air party, as his passenger. Having returned from *Nuthatch*, the advanced course was completed at the end of January, by which time Place had completed ninety-one hours of flying solo, of which eight had been at night. On his assessment he was rated as 'above average' as a pilot and 'exceptional' as a pilot-navigator. On Friday, 1 February he was awarded his Flying Badge ('Wings') at a ceremony at Syerston, The reviewing officer was the First Lord of the Admiralty, Rt. Hon J.P.L. Thomas MP, and other guests included the Fifth Sea Lord, Vice Admiral E.W. Anstice CB, and Flag Officer Flying Training, Rear Admiral W.T. Couchman CBE, DSC. (1) Also in the audience was Captain G.R. Lambert, who had been a prisoner at Marlag with Godfrey Place, and was there to see his own son receive his Wings. Place had made a distinct impression over the preceding nine months. He was awarded a distinguished pass but failed to gain a mark of special distinction by less than one per cent in just one subject. The Senior Naval Officer reported that he was 'an exceptionally fine officer, who has set an outstanding example in personal effort and industry and this has had had no small bearing on the above average results obtained by those on the course.' He went on to note that 'Place is a person who inspires confidence. All his actions are clear-cut and logical.'

Having trained under the auspices of the RAF, Godfrey Place returned to the Fleet Air Arm and was appointed to 766 Squadron, Commanding Officer, Lieutenant Commander J.M. Henry, at HMS *Fulmar*, RNAS Lossiemouth. He arrived on Monday, 18 February along with eleven other officers to undertake Operational Flying Schools Course Part 1. They flew up from HMS *Siskin*, having just completed tests for flying at high altitude. Over the next three months Place learnt to fly combat aircraft, initially the Seafire, a naval variant of the Spitfire, but progressing at the end of March to the Sea Fury IIB. The latter was a fighter-bomber aircraft, the last propeller-driven combat aircraft to serve with the Royal Navy. It had a top speed of 460 miles per hour, a range of 700 miles and armament of four 20mm cannons along with either twelve rockets or a bomb load of 2,000lbs. This was the plane that Place would fly in combat, and it was a mainstay of the Fleet Air Arm combat squadrons. At the end of May Place was appointed to 736 Squadron, Commanding Officer, Lieutenant Commander P.H. London DSC, at HMS *Seahawk*, RNAS Culdrose for Operational Flying

Schools Course, Part II. Here the training with Sea Furies was intensive, and the pilots developed and perfected the skills required to undertake ground attack, learning how to strafe, rocket and bomb targets.

As the course at *Seahawk* came towards its end, Place was promoted to the rank of Commander on 30 June 1952. He was the first member of Hood term to reach this rank and was, at the age of thirty years and eleven months, the youngest Commander in the Royal Navy. He received many letters of congratulations, including one from David Woodward, a member of staff at the BBC who had been a war correspondent with the *Manchester Guardian* and *The Times* and had covered the liberation of Marlag in April 1945. Other letters of congratulations included one referring to his actions both above and below the waves and suggested, 'if you want something different, why not try learning Japanese?' Another well-wisher enquired, 'I hear you are a fully qualified bird man?'

As part of final training, Fleet Air Arm pilots spent a week on board the training carrier HMS *Illustrious*. The ship had the distinction of being the first aircraft carrier in the world with an armour-plated flight deck. She had served in the war and was badly damaged by the *Luftwaffe* in January 1941 as she was protecting a convoy supplying Malta. After a prolonged period of repair she served with both the Home and Pacific Fleets during the later years of the war. On Saturday, 19 July 1952 HMS *Illustrious*, under the command of Captain C.T. Jellicoe DSO, DSC, lay at anchor at Torbay and was open to the public. (2) In the afternoon Place, with thirteen other officers and nine ratings from 23RN Fighter Course, joined the ship for a week of intensive training. On Monday, 21 July, she sailed at 08.00 and undertook flying in Torbay until about 20.00, returning to anchor at Torbay for the night, a routine repeated throughout the week. Place first undertook a deck landing on 21 July in the early afternoon. On the next day he undertook two deck landings in the morning, and six in the afternoon, with a further ten over the following two days. His first catapult launch took place on Thursday, 24 July at 16.40, with a second about thirty minutes later. In all he undertook twenty-one deck landings in the four days on board, and his flying log showed no record of any problems. Harry 'Dusty' Miller served in HMS *Illustrious* and was in charge of the flight deck crash crew. He remembered an incident that week:

> We had numerous training parties on board; one task was the training of Sea Fury aircraft taking off and landing on. One aircraft missed all the arrestor wires and crashed into the flight deck barrier, ending up with one leg collapsed. I was first to the cockpit and asked the pilot if

he was all right? He looked at me, and in a calm, controlled voice said 'My, that was a jolly experience.' At that time to me he was just another pilot with the rank of Commander.

Harry Miller later recalled he had noted how polite and calm the pilot had been, only to learn later that he was in fact 'Commander Godfrey Place, VC'.

On 25 July *Illustrious* steamed to Plymouth, arriving in the evening, and very early the following morning, twelve officers and a number of ratings left the ship for *Seahawk*. The report from *Illustrious* recorded that Godfrey Place had; 'Steady approaches, A Shade Too Fast. After a poor start, did well.' At the end of August he had completed all his training, and in his final report it was noted that he was, 'A Potentially First Class Pilot. Keenness Exceptional.' Active service in a war zone was now only a few months away.

Although Place had thrived in training as a pilot, it undoubtedly had an impact on his family. In May 1951 his wife and two children (Andrea aged four years and Charles, eighteen months) moved to Newark with him and lived in a private flat. His reporting officer wrote in February 1952 that 'he has a very happy domestic life and his whole family are a fine example for all to see.' They next moved to Lossiemouth for four months, living in a naval quarter. On hearing the news of her husband's promotion in June 1952, Althea wrote congratulating him but also expressing her concerns: 'Your promotion has cheered me up a bit. I've been thinking the navy rather tiresome just lately - making you work so hard while we were with you. I do wonder what job you will get next - it must make it very awkward.' At the time, Althea was in Grimsby, attending Susan's (her younger sister's) wedding, an occasion that Godfrey Place was not able to attend due to his commitments at *Seahawk*.

Two months later, when it came for Godfrey to join a frontline squadron, Althea was very concerned about his being away from the family and facing the hazards of a combat zone. Her recollections of their lengthy separation after 'Operation Source', and the uncertainty that she had had to endure before knowing he was safe following the attack on the *Tirpitz*, were still fresh in her mind. From all reports she was far from happy with the situation and made her husband aware of her feelings.

The Korean War was the first conflict 'sponsored' by the United Nations. The Japanese had occupied Korea at the beginning of the twentieth century, and following the end of the Second World War, the country was partitioned at the 38th parallel, with the USSR supporting the regime in the north and the USA, that in the south. On 26 June 1950 North Korean soldiers, supported by Russia and China, invaded South Korea, and the United

Nations provided military support to the south. Although ninety per cent of the UN force came from the USA, there were significant contributions from Commonwealth nations, including Great Britain. The Royal Navy provided a total of five fleet aircraft carriers and fourteen Fleet Air Arm squadrons over the three years of the war. As the war progressed, there were a number of attempts at peace talks, but they all failed. By late 1952 there was an increase in the number of air strikes against North Korea, both from land-based and carrier-borne aircraft.

In August 1952 the Royal Navy aircraft carrier serving in Korea was HMS *Ocean*. Her relief, planned for November, was HMS *Glory*, at that time serving in the Mediterranean. *Glory* (13,400 tons) was a light fleet carrier of the 'Colossus' class, built at Harland and Wolff in Belfast. She was launched in November 1943, and commissioned in February 1945. She saw limited service in the war, exclusively in the Far East, and in August 1945 hosted the surrender of all Japanese forces in New Guinea. By September 1952 *Glory* had, however, obtained significant battle experience, having undertaken two tours in Korean waters (April to September 1951, February to May 1952) and was soon to sail east under the command of Captain T.A.K. Maunsell. Place would serve in *Glory* for five months, and forty years later summarised the conditions on board, as well as her history:

> HMS *Glory*'s active life covered little more than ten years, but it was a period of considerable significance; one might call these years 'Twilight of Empire' when Britain still had world wide responsibilities but no longer the wealth to support the largest and most powerful navy. The light fleet carrier was a cost effective compromise between mobility and the exercise of power, and economical operating and running costs – and as such, HMS *Glory* steamed many thousands of miles to meet actual and potential threats. One might call the ten years 'The Age of Transition' coming immediately before the leap forward to the most modern systems we recognise today. Radio and communication systems had made great progress since the ship was first designed but the thermionic valve had not yet been replaced by the micro-chip and printed circuit. The piston engined aeroplane had reached the peak of its performance but had yet to be superseded by the swept wing jet.
>
> And the sailor slept in his hammock, hemmed in and often overheated by more and more mechanical and electrical equipment … it is a great tribute to the fortitude of the British sailor that he worked so cheerfully in conditions varying from tropical heat to Artic cold, to the very peak of professional skills.(3)

Two Fleet Air Arm squadrons were embarked in HMS *Glory*: 821 Squadron with thirteen Fireflies and 801 Squadron with twenty-one Sea Furies. The latter was reformed in Malta in June 1952; the Commanding Officer was Lieutenant Commander P.B. Stuart and Lieutenant J.H.S. Pearce the Senior Pilot. Members of the squadron ranged in experience and age, and some were RNVR. Four new pilots joined the squadron in September 1952; all had just completed 23RN Fighter Course. They were: Commander B.C.G. Place VC, DSC, Lieutenant C.A. McPherson, Sub Lieutenant G.B.S. Foster and Sub Lieutenant J.F. Bellville. The squadron stood out in that the senior (and most highly decorated) officer was also the most junior pilot. Despite this, Place was well liked and respected by the members of the lower deck who were responsible for the servicing and maintenance of the aircraft.

HMS *Glory* sailed from Malta on Friday, 12 September to Barcelona, and undertook the first official visit by a Royal Navy vessel to Spain since the Spanish civil war. On the next day Place joined the Squadron at HMS *Falcon*, RNAS Hal Far, Malta, and remained there until *Glory* returned. On the same day, the potential hazards of carrier air operations became apparent to another newcomer, Lieutenant McPherson. Coming in to land on *Glory* he was too low and slow, stalled, landed awkwardly and bounced over the side into the sea. He was rescued by the shadowing destroyer HMS *Chieftain* and returned on board by bosun's chair. HMS *Glory* arrived in Barcelona on 15 September, and members of 801 Squadron described their time as 'an interesting and somewhat uproariously alcoholic official visit.' The ship was open to visitors on three afternoons, and the visit was considered an official success. Place, who had not travelled to Spain, spent his time in Malta in the air, with up to three sorties a day practising combat flying.

Lieutenant A.J. 'Spiv' Leahy, an experienced pilot who had served with the Fleet Air Arm in the Second World War, also joined 801 Squadron at Malta. In typically adventurous style he had driven down through Europe to Naples, and then travelled to Malta by ferry to join the squadron. When asked how the squadron responded to the appointment of Godfrey Place he recalled that the members were a bit surprised to hear they had been 'blessed' with someone who 'held a VC and DSC and had recently been appointed as Commander.' There was also some concern at Place's flying experience, since at the time he had a total of 378 hours flying (including 100 as co-pilot) and just 21 deck landings. On joining the squadron, Leahy recalled that Place was treated and behaved very much as a sub lieutenant. He did not mention the Victoria Cross and apart from the medal ribbon on his chest you would have not been aware that he had won it. Leahy also remembered that Place only once mentioned his service in submarines, when recalling his escape from X7 and stepping onto the gunnery target, saying 'here go the last of the Places!'

As for how the squadron members addressed their new pilot, Leahy called him 'Godfrey, or you!

HMS *Glory* arrived back in Malta on 22 September, and two days later Place performed simulated deck landings with the other new pilots and Leahy, followed by a night navigation exercise; the squadron log reported, 'there were no accidents'. The next day, the four new pilots all undertook bombing practice, dropping 500lb bombs on Little Filfla (an islet to the south of Malta, used for gunnery practice since the war). Lieutenant Commander Stuart noted, 'Unfortunately only two of the bombs exploded and the sight was not as impressive as it might have been.' On 29 September Place flew on to HMS *Glory* for the first time and performed four deck landings that day whilst she was steaming off the coast of Malta. Over the next ten days there was intensive flying practice, both at sea and at HMS *Falcon. Glory* would spend the night moored at Malta and then proceed to sea in the morning, commencing flying within about half an hour of departure. She would then return to harbour at night. This programme continued until the end of the first week of October. Prior to her departure to the Far East, *Glory* moored alongside at Grand Harbour, allowing time for a final 'run ashore' and hosting an official cocktail party on 7 October. The Commander-in-Chief, Mediterranean Fleet, Admiral Lord Mountbatten visited the ship on Thursday, 9 October, and later that day she sailed for Port Said in the company of the destroyer HMS *Daring*. On 13 October *Glory* passed through the Suez Canal, during which there was occasional rifle fire from the banks towards the ship. Flying operations recommenced in the Red Sea as the ship made her way to Aden. Arriving on 17 October, she moored in the harbour for a day before departing. She then sailed across the Indian Ocean towards Singapore and by 24 October was close to Ceylon (Sri Lanka), where Place flew a tactical reconnaissance mission over Trincomalee.

Three days after passing Ceylon *Glory* approached the coast of Malaya, and aircraft from both 801 and 821 Squadrons flew missions in support of the Army, who were fighting communist insurgents in the forests of Malaya. Two sorties, each of twelve Sea Furies and six Fireflies, flew with full loads to attack positions in the Kuala Langat forest reserve in Selangor. Place gained operational experience by flying in both. Although providing valuable practice for the pilots, the results of the operation were not clear. However, some pilots interviewed by journalists said, 'We found the target. There were huts in the jungle and we smashed them.' 801 Squadron received a signal from the Commanding Office of the 1st Battalion, Suffolk Regiment:

Thank you very much for air support. All Pongos much impressed. Good luck and happy landings.

William Thomas, a fitter with 801 Squadron, wrote to his mother in England, 'Yesterday our squadron took off and bombed the bandits in the hills, killed a lot of them, destroyed their huts and seven of them went and surrendered to the Army.' (4) By flying sorties over Malaya the aircrew involved, including Godfrey Place, became eligible for the Naval General Service Medal.

HMS *Glory* arrived at Singapore on 28 October and sailed for Hong Kong three days later. Shortly before her arrival on 4 November, she rendezvoused with HMS *Ocean*. Under her Commanding Officer, Captain C.L.G. Evans DSO, DSC, *Ocean* had served in Korean waters since June 1952 and was heading home. Her deployment had been marked by Lieutenant Commander P. 'Hoagy' Carmichael of 802 Squadron becoming the first (and only) pilot of a British piston-engined fighter to shoot down a jet fighter, when he was attacked by a MiG-15. After the ships had exercised together, eight aircraft were transferred from *Ocean* to *Glory* along with a number of aircrew, including Lieutenant D.G. 'Pug' Mather and Sub Lieutenant J.M. Simmonds, who had both served with Godfrey Place in 23RN Fighter Course.

Members of the newly arrived squadrons were briefed by those returning home on the threats they had faced during their tour. Aircrew received a lecture on escape and evasion and were issued with maps of Korea, along with pistols, ammunition and escape gear, the latter included a 'blood chit' written in Korean and English to encourage Koreans to give assistance. Leahy recalled that aircrew were fairly circumspect about the issue, since in the event of landing in North Korea escape would be almost impossible, since Europeans could not pass for locals. Despite having been a prisoner of war, Place did not mention the experience to anyone. Although preparing for flying in a combat zone, there was some time for relaxation. Whilst returning from a run ashore in Hong Kong, Place suggested to his colleagues that they should invite themselves to a party. On seeing a cruise liner in the harbour, he managed to get them all on board, telling members of the ship's crew that they knew the Chief Engineer (known as 'Mac'). Once on board, they toured the ship but left somewhat disappointed as there were no parties to gatecrash.

HMS *Glory* departed from Hong Kong on 6 November and sailed to Sasebo, a port on the southern island of Japan, one of two bases used by Commonwealth navies during the war, the other being Kure. After a brief period in port, *Glory* departed on 10 November to the China Sea off the west coast of Korea to relieve the American aircraft carrier USS *Baedong Strait* and assume the operational command of the task force. Patrols typically lasted twelve days, which included the time taken to sail to and from the base. Carriers were on station for nine days, during which the programme

involved four days of combat operations, a day for refuelling at sea, and a
further four days of flying. Due to the poor weather and high winds, flying
was delayed until the afternoon of 11 November. It started at 14.30, and just
over one hour later Godfrey Place flew his first mission of the war, in a sortie
led by Lieutenant Pearce, with instructions to attack a road bridge in the
Punchon area. They were faced with poor visibility at the target and so
headed south along the coast to attack another bridge, which they damaged.
During the patrol Place usually flew two sorties a day, one an attack on enemy
targets such as roads and railways in the north, the other a combat patrol,
providing air defence to the ships of the task force. (5) In the second half of
the patrol, Place flew sorties led by Lieutenant Commander Stuart.
Maintenance records indicate that Place's aircraft sustained a bullet hole in
the port wing on 17 November, although there was no record of this in his
own log. (6) The Sea Fury was a very tough aircraft, and it is possible that
the damage was only noticed by the engineers servicing it on its return. The
first loss of aircrew occurred on 18 November, when Lieutenant R. Nevill-
Jones of 801 Squadron crashed. His aircraft was hit by flak as he was pulling
out of a dive after attacking a railway bridge. Other members of the sortie
flew over the crash site for about ten minutes, but it soon became obvious
that there was no hope, since his aircraft had exploded on hitting the ground.
On the same day, Lieutenant D.F Robbins, flying a Firefly of 821 Squadron,
crashed into the sea. He was not injured, but rescue was hampered by his
dinghy failing to inflate correctly; when an American helicopter reached him,
they found that their lifting strop was too small to pass over the British
lifejacket. He was eventually pulled from the sea hanging on to the strop by
his hands. (7)

Some sorties were undertaken early in the morning in an attempt to locate
motor convoys travelling with headlights, and on 19 November Place flew in
a pre-dawn raid led by his Commanding Officer. Later that day, on board
Glory, the hazards of naval aviation operations were again apparent when one
of the flight deck crew was blown overboard by the slipstream of an aircraft
which was running up on deck. A helicopter was airborne within three
minutes, and a search was carried out, but he was not found. Thomas, writing
home recorded the incident: 'He sank in his heavy clothing and nothing
could be found when a helicopter got there. It was a shock to us, losing a
friend that way. And he has a wife and three children at home.' (8)

At his insistence, Place was treated as a junior member of 801 Squadron,
but the situation was slightly different in the ship's wardroom. Here he
tended to act like a sub lieutenant but was treated as a commander by other
members. His desire to have some fun, after hard work, was witnessed at a

'follies night', held after completing four days of flying. On one occasion there was a film show in the wardroom, and Place was having a drink in the bar with Lieutenants Leahy and Pearce. He suggested that they offer drinks to the audience, so they collected a range of bottles and glasses and went into the wardroom. Place asked the Commander, who was sitting in the front, what he would like. 'Crème de Menthe', was the reply, and Leahy was asked to bring it over. When he presented it to Godfrey Place, the latter proceeded to pour it over the Commander's head. Officers were somewhat aghast, but there was no comeback on any of those involved.

At the end of the first patrol, HMS *Glory* sailed to Sasebo on 20 November, having been relieved on station by USS *Baedong Strait*. During the week in port, Place, along with his Commanding Officer, gained an insight into the land war by paying a liaison visit to the 1st British Commonwealth Division. *Glory* commenced her second patrol on 28 November and immediately was affected by bad weather, which prevented flying on two days. The ship's log records that snow had to be removed from the flight deck on several occasions. (9) Place flew a similar pattern of sorties as in the earlier patrol, normally two a day. Overall, the patrol was somewhat uneventful, although nine Sea Furies and one Firefly were damaged by enemy flak. Only one plane was lost; Lieutenant Marshall ditched his Firefly in the sea some sixteen miles east of the ship, after his engine failed; he was rescued by a helicopter ten minutes later. On board ship, Captain Maunsell became severely ill at the start of the patrol and was transferred by stretcher to HMS *Consort* for onward transfer to Sasebo. Command of the ship passed to the Executive Officer, Commander D.E. Bromley-Martin, in the rank of Acting Captain. (10) Thomas wrote home: 'We're all sorry to lose the Captain – quite a nice chap – he was very considerate towards the men.'

At the end of the patrol *Glory* sailed to Kure, the base for Australian and New Zealand troops. The nearby Iwakuni aerodrome was run by Australians; it served as a shore facility for servicing planes which were then transferred to an aircraft carrier. In anticipation of being on patrol at Christmas, the ship's officers held their Christmas party whilst at Kure, and on 14 December a new Commanding Officer arrived, Captain E.D.G. Lewin DSO, DSC. He was an experienced Fleet Air Arm pilot who had flown from HMS *Ajax* at the Battle of the River Plate.

The third patrol of HMS *Glory* was marked by a number of unfortunate incidents. On 16 December two men were lost from a dragonfly helicopter that toppled over the side of the flight deck. Two days later it became apparent that aircrew were facing a threat from their own ammunition. Leahy, flying a Sea Fury, was forced to land on a beach after noticing an explosion in his port wing which produced a gaping hole he could see through. Initially, he thought he had been hit by flak, but after landing and inspecting the damage (the hole was large enough to stand up in) he realised it was due to an explosion of ammunition in the gun itself. He was flown back to the ship. Two days later a similar fault was believed to have caused a Firefly to crash, killing Lieutenant P.G. Fogden, who had only joined the ship one week before. There were significant concerns about this problem, and many attempts were made to elucidate the cause. The answer was found in January 1953, when aircrew examined another case of a gun stoppage and reported:

It was caused by an unstruck round, the cartridge case was found to have written on it in indelible pencil:

Iris Betson,
33 Stuart Street
Grantham
Lincs
23 years old, Sept 7, 1943

Give this one to Hitler for me. (11)

The use of old ammunition was the cause of the problem.

As well as flying sorties with the Commanding Officer and Senior Pilot, Place also flew with other flight commanders, including Lieutenant R. J. McCandless, another experienced pilot. He remembered Godfrey Place as an absolute gentleman, very pleasant to talk to, and a top class person who was very honest. As a pilot he thought of him as 'average'.

On 22 December Lieutenant V.B. Mitchell of 801 Squadron, flying his third sortie of the day in a Sea Fury, was hit by flak and forced to ditch in the sea. He spent nearly an hour in near-freezing water but was rescued safely by an American helicopter, so demonstrating confidence in the immersion suit issued to all pilots. Christmas Day was just another working day for the crew of *Glory*, and Place flew two sorties, the first a combat air patrol and the second a strike mission. Both were uneventful, and he returned to *Glory* at 14.05. One hour earlier, further tragedy had struck 821 Squadron when Lieutenant R. E. Barrett's Firefly was hit by flak when attacking a bridge. The aircraft went into a spin, crashed into the ground and caught fire on impact. It was a tragic Christmas for the ship's company. *Glory* departed to Iwakuni on 27 December, and after collecting a number of aircraft sailed to Sasebo, arriving on 30 December; Christmas and New Year were celebrated as one.

HMS *Glory* left Sasebo on 4 January 1953 to start her fourth patrol. There had now been a change in the plans for offensive air attacks: there would be no attacks on roads or rail bridges as the rivers and ground were now frozen and it would not be difficult for road transport to drive around any damage. Past experience had indicated that railway bridges were quickly repaired after being bombed, repair material usually being kept close by. Instead, the major targets were to be railway lines, and it was intended to bomb them in inaccessible parts of the country. Initially the policy was effective, but towards the end of the patrol it was noted that damage to tracks was repaired in about forty-eight hours. On the first day of flying, 5 January, Place had to abort his mission, being unable to attack due to bad weather. Unfortunately, on the same day, 801 Squadron lost three pilots. At 11.30 Lieutenant Mather's Sea Fury was hit by enemy flak and caught fire. The pilot baled out at about 400 feet, and the others in the sortie saw his parachute open correctly but were unable to see where he landed. A full-scale search was instituted, and an American rescue helicopter flew to the area, escorted by Sea Furies flown by Sub Lieutenants W.J.B. Keates and B.E. Rayner. At 12.47 radio contact was lost with Sub Lieutenant Rayner, and a fresh fire on a hillside was seen which was believed to be his crashed aircraft. Mather later wrote of his experience of baling out:

> I was free falling through the air so I pulled the ring on the parachute and that deployed rather suddenly. The next thing I knew I was dangling at the end of the chute moving rather rapidly towards the ground … the closer I got to the land I found I was being shot at. I returned fire and then thought it would be prudent if I didn't have the gun on me when I came down so I tossed it away. (12)

He was immediately taken prisoner by North Koreans and remained in captivity until September 1953, subjected to very harsh conditions and in solitary confinement for long periods. Further tragedy struck 801 Squadron later in the afternoon when Sub Lieutenant Simmonds became detached from his section leader during a reconnaissance mission. He was next seen in a tight turn which developed into a spin from which he did not recover. At 16.30 his aircraft disintegrated and burst into flames; there was no sign of the pilot.

Amongst the other duties performed by Sea Fury pilots was target spotting for the American Navy, and on 6 January Godfrey Place, flying with Lieutenant Pearce, carried out this task for the battleship USS *Missouri* as she bombarded selected gun positions. Although other pilots had experienced problems when performing this duty, it appears to have been rather dull for Place, and no hits were observed. At the end of the patrol *Glory* sailed to Iwakuni and then to Kure, where leave was granted. Twenty-one of the crew went off ski-ing, but Place took the opportunity to gain more flying experience, this time in Fireflies.

HMS *Glory* departed Kure on 19 January, on her fifth patrol; this was to be the last for Place as the ship had received a signal from the Admiralty: 'It is intended to relieve Commander (P) B.C.G. Place.' Air attacks during the patrol focussed on troop concentrations and stores. Flying was aided by fine weather on all but the last day on station, when high winds and heavy seas prevented take-off. The Squadron was, however, short of pilots; there were only eighteen, effectively seventeen since one was ill, whereas the full complement was twenty-one. Place responded to the shortage of pilots by often flying three sorties each day. On 26 January his second sortie had to be aborted as the aircraft had a fault, detected once airborne. The next day, he flew three sorties and landed at 17.30, completing his combat flying for the tour. Although there were no further losses of aircrew during the patrol, three planes had been damaged by enemy action. *Glory* arrived at Sasebo on Thursday, 29 January. Two days later, the ship's log recorded, 'Commander Place VC left ship at 18.20'. (13) He was on his way home, although took the opportunity to fly from Iwakuni aerodrome on a number of days before leaving for England.

In the five months with 801 Squadron, Place had flown 186 hours and carried out 97 deck landings. The report by his Commanding Officer stated:

> Considering his inexperience in air matters, this officer has evinced a remarkably keen and shrewd knowledge. Most adaptable and able.

He had also made a significant impression with Captain Lewin who recorded that, '[he] possesses marked leadership qualities, a keen sense of humour, and an ability to mix with all ranks.' Godfrey Place had served during five patrols, in which eight men had died and one was taken prisoner, and several pilots had crashed but been rescued. Apart from one bullet hole in a wing, he had been very fortunate, although later he would tell friends that overall the operational aspects had been rather dull.

HMS *Glory* served in Korea until May 1953, undertaking a further six patrols before being relieved by HMS *Ocean*. In this period a further four pilots were lost from 801 Squadron. *Glory* then sailed for home and arrived back at Portsmouth in July 1953; she had been away for nearly three years.

Godfrey Place was welcomed home in February 1953 by Althea and the children, not least because Althea was expecting a child in April. Aware that his next appointment was to be at RNAS Yeovilton, the family moved to the nearby village of West Camel, where they initially rented 'Riversmeet'. Melanie was born in April and soon after Godfrey commenced his next appointment as Staff Officer to Flag Officer Flying Training (FOFT), Rear Admiral G. Willoughby. He was one of two staff officers, the other being Commander S. 'Stan' Laurie, who had served in 824 Squadron in 1941 and, flying with Commander S.H. Struthers, had sunk the Italian destroyer *Daniele Manin* in the Red Sea. The two shared an office 'and many laughs' at Yeovilton from 1953 to 1955, and Laurie became a good friend of the family and godfather to Melanie.

Serving on the staff of FOFT, Place was responsible for advising on development and training of pilots once they had obtained their Wings, as well as for the numerous air divisions of the RNVR. Part of the job was to visit naval air stations around the country, and Place did not delay in flying to a number of these. In May and June 1953 he flew to several, including those in Scotland and Northern Ireland, and in doing so took the opportunity to fly a number of single-engine aircraft.

In August 1953 Place undertook a two-week conversion course at HMS *Peregrine*, RNAS Ford, to fly twin-engine planes, and trained on Oxford aircraft. Whilst on the course the party were posted to HMS *Pembroke*, Chatham, and travelled to RNAS Ford each day. Jack Harrall flew with Place on the course and remembered one night when they had finished late. Back at Chatham, they went to the wardroom, only to be told by the steward that, 'dinner was off'. Place fixed him with a look and said calmly and smoothly, 'It is on again now, Chief', and it was. Whether the steward knew who had spoken to him is unclear, but he obviously recognised that he was being addressed by a determined, and hungry, officer.

Serving with FOFT also afforded Place an opportunity to refresh his flying skills at sea from an aircraft carrier. In March 1954 HMS *Illustrious*, the training carrier, was in Weymouth Bay and he made four deck landings and launches from her on 17 March. (14) This was to be the last time he landed a fixed-wing aircraft on a carrier, but was far from the end of his flying career.

After having lived in rented property, the Place family purchased a house in the same village, West Camel House. This was a well proportioned family house with generous grounds. The move from nearby Riversmeet was overseen by Althea, with some household items being moved the half mile by her, pushing the pram. A feature of West Camel House was a walled garden adjacent to the local church, All Saints. The garden was rather overgrown and it was a struggle to keep it under control, alongside all the other family activities, so Place fixed a notice to the door, which was next to the entrance to the churchyard: 'Trespassers will be forgiven.' He claimed this was for the amusement of the elderly vicar. Regular visitors to West Camel House included Godfrey's sister Helen and her family. Her husband had returned to teaching at Marlborough after the war, and they had two sons, Christopher and Tony, who were of similar ages to Andrea and Charles. With long summer holidays, the Kenbers would come to stay for several weeks, bringing their caravan with them and camping in the grounds. The arrangement led to some friction between Godfrey and Althea, not least because it appeared that Helen and her family were getting more than a 'free lunch'. On one occasion, Tony and Charles were playing football in the garden, and Tony kicked the ball against a window; Godfrey was inside the room. The pane of glass swayed slightly before breaking and falling in. Place fairly exploded, and his anger led him to send a bill to his brother-in-law for the repairs.

By June 1955 Place was aware of his next appointment: he was to command an anti-submarine frigate, based in home waters. Time for flying would be limited, so to make the most of his time on the staff of FOFT he undertook a jet conversion course in June 1955 at St David's in South Wales. The course lasted two weeks and was based on flying the Meteor aircraft. In early July he returned to RNAS Yeovilton and was soon flying Vampires. His time with the Fleet Air arm was fast drawing to a close, although it was a case of *au revoir* rather than goodbye as he travelled to Northern Ireland to assume command of HMS *Tumult*.

Chapter 10

Surface Command

HMS *Tumult* was a 'Trowbridge' class destroyer, launched in November 1942. She was commissioned in early 1943 and initially served in the Mediterranean before sailing to the Far East in 1944. After the war she was converted into a Type 16 anti-submarine frigate and in 1954 joined the 3rd Training Squadron, based at Londonderry, the home of the Joint Anti-Submarine School. *Tumult* had a displacement of 1,710 tons, and a maximum speed of 36 knots. When she was converted in 1946 the open bridge was enclosed which made her 'top heavy'; as a result she tended to roll. Place relieved Commander J.R.R. Horne DSC, who had served in motor torpedo boats in the war, although his ability to command a frigate had not impressed the Admiralty. Eric Carter was the bosun's mate in HMS *Tumult* and recalled that the crew were pleased to hear that their next Commanding Officer was a holder of the Victoria Cross and felt that he must be efficient to have received the award.

Place assumed command at 09.00 on 15 July 1955 at Londonderry; the ship's log recorded: 'Commander B.C.G. Place. D.S.C., V.C., RN took over command.' (1) In the light of his attention to detail in ships' logs, it is surprising that he did not correct this entry. However, since its error related to the order of precedence of his own decorations he may have felt that it was inappropriate to do so. Later that morning he paid a courtesy call on the Squadron Captain, and then *Tumult* left Londonderry to sail to Rothesay, Isle of Bute. It was over ten years since he had last been to the island, which served as a base for *Tumult* whilst undertaking torpedo trials in the waters off the west of Scotland. The ship returned to Londonderry at the end of July and spent all of August in harbour.

In early September *Tumult* undertook two weeks of exercises in the waters off Londonderry, before sailing to Portland. After visiting Portsmouth in early October, *Tumult* sailed to Liverpool and spent three days alongside at Wallasey before departing to Londonderry. She next sailed to Milford Haven and from there to Devonport, arriving early on 21 October. Two days later *Tumult* sailed into the English Channel to rendezvous with the Portuguese warship *Bartholomeu Dias* which, escorted by the destroyers *Tejo, Vouga* and

Lima, was conveying the President of Portugal on a state visit to Britain. *Tumult*, in the company of the frigates *Vigo* and *Tyrian*, provided an escort for the group to Shoeburyness. They arrived on 24 October and all ships anchored over night. The next morning, *Bartholomeu Dias* proceeded up the Thames escorted by four fast patrol boats from the Royal Navy. She arrived at Tower Bridge, where President and Madame Craveiro Lopes were officially welcomed by the Queen. Place's involvement in the state visit was later recognised by his award of Commander of the Military Order of Aviz, and in February 1956 he was informed that the Queen had given him 'restricted permission to wear the insignia of the award.'

November was spent undertaking more exercises in the waters off the west of Scotland. *Tumult* returned to Londonderry at the end of November, and after ten days of exercises she sailed to Portsmouth, arriving on 12 December. One week later she was moved into dry dock and Place left the ship. His first command had been rather uneventful, but he was remembered by the ship's company as a very fair and pleasant Commanding Officer who never talked down to anyone. His Commanding Officer summarised his appointment:

> He is a man of very high ideals, and is a fine example to all those who do not possess his sense of vocation. Intelligent, versatile and utterly loyal, he had made his ship the happiest, most able, and smartest in the Squadron, deservedly winning the Efficiency Cup and most of the sports trophies.

In November 1956 Place had been informed of his next appointment, as Executive Officer in the aircraft carrier HMS *Theseus*, a 'Colossus' class light-fleet carrier and a sister ship to HMS *Glory*. Launched in July 1944, she initially served as a training carrier for the Fleet Air Arm. In 1950 she was dispatched to Korea, where she served from October 1950 to April 1951, and then returned to serve with the Home and Mediterranean Fleets. In early 1954 she was converted into a training ship when much of the hangar space was converted into classrooms and accommodation. She was assigned to the Home Training Squadron and with her sister ship HMS *Ocean* was responsible for all early stages of training for seamen in the Royal Navy, except for boys.

Throughout 1955 the Commanding Officer of *Theseus* was Captain A.C.C. 'Crap' Miers VC, DSO*, a former submariner who had commanded HMS *Torbay* in 1942. He was awarded the Victoria Cross for his actions in early March 1942 when attacking a heavily defended harbour in Corfu and sinking two enemy transport ships. An extrovert of immense proportions, his approach to people bordered at times on bullying. He was also renowned for his short temper. Miers was very keen to ensure that people he met knew that he had been awarded the Victoria Cross, and would often quiz them as to how he had won it. (2) This was the complete antithesis of Godfrey Place, whose modesty was such that he rarely if ever talked about his award, often to the disappointment of younger members of the Royal Navy who wished to know more about 'Operation Source'. Just after Christmas 1955, Captain E.F. Pizey DSO, relieved Miers of command of *Theseus*, knowing this to be his last appointment before retirement. He had served in submarines in the war and like his predecessor had the reputation of having a short temper; in a previous command he had shown his irritation by throwing his hat on the ground and stamping on it, in front of members of the crew. When he left the ship, the crew presented him with a door knocker in the shape of his hat, as a reminder of this incident.

In January 1956 *Theseus* was moored at Portland, and on 13 January Place joined the ship and the next day relieved the Executive Officer, Commander Geoffrey Carew-Hunt. Carew-Hunt was a very different person to Godfrey Place, being ebullient and outgoing, but short-tempered. Godfrey Place was now thirty-four, but still looked very young. Among those serving on *Theseus* at this time was Lieutenant J.J.R. Oswald,[1] who remembered that other commanders were somewhat taken aback to have what they described as a 'boy commander' as their Executive Officer. No sooner had Place taken up his appointment than he sent a memo to all commanders informing them of a run ashore that evening; there had been no discussion, but it was apparent that all would attend. The party left the ship in the early evening and returned well after midnight; Oswald was Officer of the Watch at the time and saw the boat return. First up the ladder, and apparently unaffected by the evening's entertainment, was Godfrey Place, who saluted Oswald and enquired how things were. Behind him, the rest of the party struggled to get aboard and all were very much the worse for wear; most failed to appear until much later that day. Godfrey Place had clearly shown them that although he may have been relatively small and apparently young, he was experienced in the ways of naval life.

The rest of January was spent undertaking exercises with the Home Fleet, initially in the Portland area; but on 23 January, in company with HMS *Ocean*, *Theseus* sailed to El Ferrol, in north-west Spain. C.P.O. Allan Ward remembered leaving Portland Harbour in a gale, and since the harbour entrance was quite narrow for a 'beamy' ship such as *Theseus* much of the

---

1. Later Admiral of the Fleet Sir Julian Oswald GCB, First Sea Lord, 1989–93.

manoeuvring was done by engines. He recalled that, 'I was very surprised afterwards to find myself told by the Commander (E) that I had a call on the internal phone. It was a thank you for my efforts from him [Place] on the bridge.'

His next encounter with Place was not quite so easy; Ward was the senior person responsible for the junior petty officers' mess and during 'commander's rounds' Place noticed a solitary sock drying on a mess pipe, and informed him that 'he would be having words with the culprit.' At El Ferrol most of the crew had the opportunity to visit local bars and night spots. Many of the trainee seamen had not been ashore since Christmas and made the most of the opportunity; it was remembered as 'an excellent run ashore'. *Theseus* was open to visitors during her time in Spain, then left on 31 January to sail, with *Ocean,* to Portsmouth. From mid-February to early May she underwent a refit at Portsmouth. Place took the opportunity to refresh his flying skills, having not flown since a week before assuming command of HMS *Tumult*, and in April spent time at HMS *Heron* flying Sea Balliols. As the refit came to an end, there was a change of command of the squadron, with Rear Admiral G.B. Sayer CB, DSC assuming the post of Flag Officer, Home Training Squadron and raising his flag in HMS *Theseus*. Over the coming months his responsibilities would extend far beyond training, as a result of political upheaval in the Middle East. After the refit *Theseus* left Portsmouth on 11 June with *Ocean*, sailed to Invergordon and on 19 June embarked helicopters of 845 Squadron. Four days later, both ships left Invergordon, accompanied by a screen of helicopters, and sailed east across the North Sea. During the afternoon, Godfrey Place disembarked by helicopter to RNAS Lossiemouth to travel to London and attend the centenary celebrations commemorating the institution of the Victoria Cross.

There were two days of official celebrations, starting on Monday, 25 June with a service of commemoration in Westminster Abbey attended by over 300 Victoria Cross holders from all over the world. After the service, those attending visited the House of Commons for tea. The following day, there was a parade in Hyde Park in the presence of the Queen. Among those standing behind the Queen was Admiral Sir Martin Dunbar-Nasmith VC, Vice Admiral of the UK, who nearly twenty years earlier had visited the Royal Naval College, Dartmouth and inspected cadets on parade, including Cadet B.C.G. Place. After the parade, the Queen Mother hosted a garden party at Marlborough House, where those attending could also visit the Centenary exhibition. Amongst the many exhibits on display was the portrait of Godfrey Place by John Worsley, painted in Marlag in 1944. The two of them examined the painting closely and located the poinsettia plants that had been painted on the back of the canvas, which had originally been used as part of the scenery in a play at Marlag. (3)

Whilst Place was in London HMS *Theseus* sailed to Kristiansand, Norway, arriving on 25 June, and undertook a number of official functions, including opening the ship for visitors. Derek Redman served as an Upper Yardman (Air) and remembered Captain Pizey's unusual skills in man management:

> One forenoon as we steamed up the sound to Kristiansand, from the bridge, over the tannoy, he [Pizey] bawled out a Lieutenant Commander on the Flight Deck, in front of several hundred trainees and some members of the crew manning the side.

This example of poor leadership was one that Derek Redman would remember for many years. Kristiansand was not a place for 'bright lights', as there were strict regulations on consumption of alcohol; it could only be obtained if purchased with food. This appeared to limit the crew's enjoyment of their time ashore. Place flew from London to Norway to rejoin his ship and arrived on board on 28 June, making his own entry in the ship's log: '22.45 Commander returned from V.C. Parade'. (4) *Theseus* left Norway on 3 July and sailed west, undertaking helicopter exercises en route, and rendezvoused with *Ocean* before arriving at Rosyth on 6 July. The two ships spent ten days there, during which the squadron held a sailing regatta and *Theseus* was open for visitors. It was to be the last time that the two ships were together as part of the Home Training Squadron, Admiral Sayer having received instructions that *Theseus* was to be paid off in January 1957. On 16 July *Theseus* sailed with *Ocean* to Tynemouth for an official visit before sailing to Portland, arriving on 24 July. During the passage *Theseus* played host to Mr Watson, the First Lord's representative at Admiralty Interview Boards. As part of an exercise *Ocean* sent a boarding party to *Theseus* with orders to search for a suspect civilian passenger; it is recorded that Mr Watson 'rapidly produced his Admiralty pass to members of the heavily armed boarding party.' On arrival at Portland, Lieutenant Commander A. Swainson joined the ship and soon after learnt that his sister Peggy had died. He later recalled that Godfrey Place kindly called up a helicopter and flew him to the funeral. He remembered Place's great kindness and later wrote that he was 'a wonderful man'. (5)

Whilst at Portland, *Theseus'* role as a training ship came to a rapid end. Recent political activities in Egypt had caused considerable concern to the British government. On 13 June the last British troops left the garrison of the Suez Canal area and ten days later Colonel Nasser was elected President of

Egypt. In July Britain, along with the United States of America, had withdrawn financial help for the proposed Aswan Dam. In response President Nasser nationalised the Suez Canal on 26 July, a move that sent shock waves through the British government and sent Godfrey Place to yet another war zone, this time fighting not below or above the waves, but on them.

Derek Redman remembered the night of 28/29 July, since a severe gale blew up and 'All Hands' was piped in the early hours of the morning in order to take down an awning across part of the flight deck that was being battered by the wind. One senior rating was using a marlin spike to loosen the ties when he put the spike through his hand, lost his grip and fell overboard. Place impressed all those by the way he handled the situation with 'calm, quiet, assured, professional and unflappable competence.' Later that day, he addressed the ship's company in the hangar, explaining the situation in 'clear and concise understandable language,' and advised that men under training would leave the ship later that week. At 10.45 that morning he made an entry in the ship's log, 'Immediate notice to steam', (6) and the next day *Theseus* left Portland for Portsmouth and disembarked the men under training. *Theseus* would be required to fulfil a number of roles during the forthcoming military operations, but not as a training ship.

The planning of operations to retake the Suez Canal involved two forward bases, Cyprus and Malta. Straightaway, *Theseus* embarked stores, ammunition, vehicles and men of the 16th Independent Parachute Regiment for transport to the Mediterranean. She departed Portsmouth on 5 August and sailed non-stop to Famagusta, Cyprus, arriving on 11 August. The voyage had not been without incident. One member of the embarked force found it difficult to find anywhere to sleep, so made himself comfortable inside a ventilation shaft. When the soldier lit a candle, smoke spread throughout the ship, and he spent the rest of the voyage in the chain locker. Lieutenant Graham Owens was serving with Royal Engineers, attached to the Parachute Brigade, and remembered one incident in particular. He was taken aback by Captain Pizey giving one of his officers a severe reprimand on the flight deck, in public. He was even more surprised when he saw that the officer on the receiving end was Godfrey Place; Owens later recalled that he was probably more shocked than Place that anyone could give 'such a bollocking to a VC holder.' Before arriving at Cyprus, one soldier was washed overboard during bad weather but was recovered swiftly, although the seaboat involved was swamped and had to be abandoned. Captain Pizey was not overly impressed by the collection of 'Pongos' that he had ferried to Cyprus. The next three days were spent disembarking troops and stores, mostly at night due to the heat, and then embarking 45 Commando, Royal Marines and sailing on 14 August to Malta, where they disembarked.

Theseus arrived back in Portsmouth on 22 August, and at the end of August senior officers were made aware of plans for the recovery of the Suez Canal, codenamed 'Operation Musketeer'. One of the roles for *Theseus* was to act as a 'casualty receiving ship', and in the initial plans the ship was to be prepared to receive up to 400 casualties in the first three to four days of the operation; this was later revised down to 75 over three days. At the end of September, further modifications to the ship were undertaken to allow the operation of an increased number of helicopters. As part of the training for helicopter-borne assaults, *Theseus* and *Ocean* spent two weeks undertaking helicopter trials at Spithead. These involved Whirlwinds of 845 Squadron and Sycamores of the JHU (Joint Helicopter Unit) and aimed to find the most effective method for operating a large number of helicopters to land 450 men at an objective some fifteen miles from the ships. During the two weeks over 1,000 landings were completed on the two carriers, and the only setback was poor visibility on the last day of trials that prevented a full rehearsal taking place, flying to RNAS Ford. There were, however, problems below decks with unrest among members of the crew who were concerned about their likely deployment to a conflict zone. This became apparent in HMS *Ocean* on 18 October, when eighteen retained seamen were discovered taking part in what appeared to be an 'unlawful assembly'. (7) The issue appears to have been dealt with locally, but after the helicopter trials were completed *Ocean* returned to Devonport where on 22 October there were further problems when twelve retained seamen attempted to leave the ship. They were prevented, arrested and, following a trial, imprisoned ashore. Meanwhile, *Theseus* had left Portsmouth and arrived at Malta on 26 October, to be joined by *Ocean* five days later. Together they were to be part of the Anglo–French force that attempted to recover the Suez Canal zone.

As part of the Anglo–French plan, Israeli forces attacked Egyptian forces in the Sinai desert on 29 October. Egypt failed to respond to the Anglo–French ultimatum to cease hostilities, and air attacks on Egypt commenced on 31 October, involving British aircraft from both the Fleet Air Arm and the RAF. On 1 November *Theseus* embarked 60 tons of ammunition, 36 vehicles, 350 men from the Army and half of 45 Commando Royal Marines (the other half were embarked in *Ocean*). The ship was now on a war footing, and a final co-ordinating conference was held that day on board *Ocean*, the flagship of the Home Training Squadron which had taken on the role of 'Task Group 345.9'. More helicopters were also embarked from RAF Hal Far.

Theseus was one of five Royal Navy aircraft carriers that took part in 'Operation Musketeer', the others being *Ocean* (also acting as a helicopter carrier), *Eagle, Albio*n and *Bulwark*, all of which provided fixed-wing aircraft. Two days later, at 11.00, *Theseus* sailed with *Ocean* for Port Said. The passage was relatively uneventful, although on board there was considerable tension amongst the crew and the embarked troops and speculation as to whether the invasion would lead to a world war. A possible submarine contact was detected on 5 November which caused *Theseus* to take avoiding action; it later transpired that this was an American vessel. At the same time, airborne troops were being dropped in the Port Said area in order to secure the El Gamil airfield; the invasion had started. In the early afternoon there was a visit from the Commandant General, Royal Marines, who arrived by helicopter. Later Admiral Sayer sent a signal to the ship's company:

We should all be very proud that the Home Fleet Training Squadron had been selected to play such an important part in the enterprise which will start at dawn tomorrow. We do not know what enemy opposition or difficulties we may run into but there must be no relaxation of alertness or effort till the job be thoroughly finished. I look to all hands to ensure that it is done supremely well, and I have every confidence that it will be. Good luck to you all. (8)

Theseus approached the north coast of Egypt later that evening, and those on board could see the fires and explosions on land; it appeared to be a real-life 'Guy Fawkes night'. Morale in both ships was reported to very high, but Admiral Sayer was later critical of a speech made by Hugh Gaitskell that night, reporting that, 'The speech broadcast by the Leader of Her Majesty's Opposition received on the eve of battle, was most ill-received by the majority of those on board.' Gaitskell's speech had called for the resignation of the Prime Minister, Sir Anthony Eden, and an immediate halt to the invasion of Egypt. The ships arrived in the operational area at 04.00 on 6 November, and *Theseus* anchored seven miles outside the port. Conditions were good, with fine weather and calm seas. The chaplain said prayers, and within an hour the first helicopter had taken off, followed closely by another nine as they commenced the first helicopter landing of troops in a conflict zone. By 10.00 all the embarked Royal Marines had been flown off, along with some twenty tons of ammunition and stores. At the same time, *Theseus* started to receive casualties. The first had arrived by helicopter at 09.45, a marine who was wounded as he left the helicopter, was evacuated and arrived back on board just nineteen minutes after his departure. Among the casualties received by *Theseus* were marines who had been wounded by 'friendly fire'. In the next three hours *Theseus* received forty casualties, most by helicopter but a few by sea (although this proved to be a painfully slow process). It was noted how the arrival of seriously wounded casualties on *Theseus* (and *Ocean*) had adversely affected the morale of those troops waiting to be deployed, and it was recommended that in future operations vessels undertaking helicopter-borne operations should not have to act as casualty receiving ships.

Early in the afternoon, *Theseus* weighed anchor and proceeded into Port Said, through a passage cleared by a minesweeper; she was the first large ship of the Royal Navy to enter the port. She continued to receive casualties throughout the day, although at one point refused a request for a helicopter to land as her flight deck was occupied by stores and vehicles. On board *Theseus* there were three surgical teams, drawn from the Royal Navy and the Army, who worked over the next forty-eight hours, treating not only British casualties but also French and Egyptian, some of the latter appearing to be only about fourteen years old. Whilst at Port Said, Army personnel were disembarked, and at 18.00 a second signal was received from Admiral Sayer:

> Please pass to ships' companies and embarked squadrons my heartiest congratulations on a splendid day's work. (9)

At 21.00 news was received of an impending ceasefire, which was to be effective at midnight. Political support for the occupation had drained rapidly following President Eisenhower's interventions, coinciding as they did with the American Presidential election. With the offensive operation completed, *Theseus* took on the role of a casualty ship, and in the morning of 7 November departed for Malta with seventy casualties on board. En route, the body of Marine Fowler, who had died of wounds the night before, was buried at sea at a ceremony attended by both Captain Pizey and Godfrey Place. (10) *Theseus* arrived at Malta on 10 November and secured alongside. Ambulances drove on to the flight deck, were lowered into the hangars on the aircraft lifts to allow casualties to be collected, and were then driven off the ship, away from the prying eyes of the media. 845 Squadron was also disembarked, and later that day men of the Duke of Wellington's regiment were embarked and *Theseus* sailed to Cyprus. Initially, she was ordered to sail to Limassol, but then rerouted to Famagusta, where she disembarked the troops and their vehicles. *Theseus* then sailed back to Malta, arriving on 17 November, and spent the next two weeks at Grand Harbour, until on 5 December she sailed to Port Said and embarked over 1200 men who were transported to Malta, from where they took an onward passage home by troopship.

Theseus returned to Port Said and on 15 December departed for the last time, having embarked over 1000 men and 100 vehicles; she then sailed non-stop to Britain, arriving at Portsmouth early on 21 December. Her entry to Portsmouth had been delayed due to fog in the English Channel on the previous night which had caused her to collide with a Norwegian tanker, but the resulting damage to *Theseus* was slight and only involved her paint work. HMS *Theseus*' commission was nearly at end, as was her service in the Royal Navy. On Christmas Eve Captain Pizey left the ship, and Godfrey Place was appointed Commanding Officer; he held the command until the end of January 1957, when he left the ship and she was placed in reserve.

Godfrey Place's initial appointment to a training ship had led to his becoming second in command of a ship that was at the forefront of a new method for deployment of troops. He made a significant impression with his peers, and despite a public reprimand from Captain Pizey, the latter wrote glowingly of him:

> I have been fortunate in having such an accomplished and efficient officer as my second in command, as a result of his careful planning and forethought I knew that the ship would be able to compete with any eventuality. He has set a wonderful example in the ship. A most impressive officer in every way, who will go far ... a most determined person who will allow no difficulty to get in his way, and is always prepared to try something new.

After leave in early 1957, Place travelled to Malta to take up his next appointment. He was to be Commanding Officer of HMS *Corunna*, a 'Battle' class destroyer. She was built on the Tyne in the Second World War and was launched some three weeks after VE Day. *Corunna* had a displacement of 3,315 tons and was armed with five four-and-a-half-inch guns and eight anti-aircraft guns. Her maximum speed was 32 knots. In 1956 she had been in refit at Malta during 'Operation Musketeer', much to the frustration of her Commanding Officer, Commander T.T. Lewin DSC. By February 1957 the refit was complete and *Corunna* was attached to the 4th Destroyer Squadron in the Mediterranean. Place joined the ship when she was moored in Sliema Creek on 26 February, and later that morning addressed the ship's company. (11) Lewin had served in *Corunna* since October 1955 and had made an immense impression, being almost idolised by his crew; their regard of him was summarised by one officer who wrote, 'Every single person on board

Corunna wanted to do well, so as not to let Terry [Lewin] down.' He would be a difficult act to follow, although both officers were exceptionally talented, but in different ways. Place was described later as, 'a worthy successor though with a different style.' (12)

In early March *Corunna* paid visits to Genoa in Italy and Villefranche in France, in company with HMS *Agincourt*, commanded by Captain D.H.F. Hetherington, who was Captain (D) of the 4th Destroyer Squadron. During this time Place recorded the only 'logging' of all his commands, with Sub Lieutenant F.A. Mallon being reprimanded for 'failing to ensure an adequate number of Holmes' lights.' At the end of March *Corunna* sailed to Gibraltar and then home to Chatham, arriving on 5 April. She spent the next five weeks in the dockyard, before sailing in early May to Portland. From there she sailed north to the mouth of the Humber, to undertake escort duties.

HMS *Corunna* had been selected as one of three ships to provide the escort for HMY *Britannia* as she carried the Queen and Duke of Edinburgh to Denmark for a state visit. On leaving *Corunna*, Lewin had been appointed as Executive Officer in *Britannia*; he had not wanted the appointment, but was ordered to the ship. When the Queen arrived on board on 18 May she saw Lewin and said to him (with a twinkle in her eye), 'Oh yes, Commander, you're the chap who didn't want to come to my yacht.' His attitude to the appointment did not, however, appear to hinder his future career prospects. (13) In the early evening, HMS *Corunna*, along with HMS *Duchess* (Captain N.H.G. Austen DSO, Senior Officer of the escort) and HMS *Diamond* (Captain M.G. Haworth DSC), accompanied *Britannia* on her journey east, sailing through some unpleasantly rough seas. Several of *Corunna's* company felt that she had been selected for the escort at the behest of her former Commanding Officer. This appears not to have been the case; it was originally intended that HMS *Salisbury* would be a member of the escort, but in March 1957 *Corunna* was selected after *Salisbury* had to enter dock for urgent mechanical repairs. The visitors arrived in Copenhagen on 21 May. Over the ensuing days there were a number of official events both on shore and on board the Royal Yacht, and Althea joined her husband in Copenhagen. In the evening of 21 May Place was one of many guests at a State Banquet hosted by the King and Queen of Denmark at Christiansborg Palace. Other guests included Professor Niels Bohr, the Nobel Prize winning physicist. The following day, Place attended a gala performance at the Royal Theatre, whilst Althea was invited to a supper dance hosted by the Royal Danish Navy; although they were together, invitations were not always joint. At a private lunch on 23 May, the Queen met Thomas Dinesen, one of only three Danes to have been awarded the Victoria Cross. He had been serving with the

Royal Highland Regiment of Canada in August 1918 in France when he was recommended for the award. On the same day, Godfrey and Althea received a tour of the Carlsberg breweries in Copenhagen, and in the evening he was a guest at the State Banquet hosted by the Queen in *Britannia*. On the final full day of the visit, Godfrey was able to attend functions with Althea, with lunch at the Naval Officers' Club and dinner hosted by HM Ambassador to Denmark.

The visit ended on 25 May, and *Britannia* departed in the company of her escort. However, Place's involvement with royal duties had not finished, as the escort accompanied *Britannia* to the Moray Firth, where the Queen spent two days reviewing the Home Fleet. As the flotilla arrived, the escort was passed to the 4th Destroyer Squadron, led by *Agincourt*, with *Alamein*, *Barossa* and *Corunna*. That evening, Place attended a dinner hosted for the Queen by Admiral Sir John Eccles in HMS *Ocean*. The next morning, divisions were held on the flight deck of HMS *Albion*, and later that day Place attended a reception in *Britannia*. This was followed by a fleet concert, written and produced by members of the Home Fleet for the Queen and presented by a cast of 170 to an audience of over 1,000 officers and men in HMS *Albion*'s hangar, which had been converted into an impromptu theatre. On the final day of the review the Queen spent time on board HMS *Ark Royal* observing flying operations before transferring to *Britannia* and departing with 4th Destroyer Squadron escort, including *Corunna*, to Lossiemouth for her onward journey to London.

Following the ten days of ceremonial duties, *Corunna* returned to training, and sailed from Lossiemouth to the west coast of Scotland. She spent a week undertaking firing practice, and spent 2 June at anchor in Loch Cairnbawn; this was the first time Place had returned since departing on 'Operation Source' some fourteen years earlier. *Corunna* returned to Rosyth in the middle of June and Place sat on a court martial for the first time; over the coming years he would sit on many, and later in his career was often President of the court. Later in June, *Corunna* sailed from Rosyth to the Dutch port of Den Helder, arriving on 19 June and staying for four days. On 24 June *Corunna* sailed through the Kiel Canal into the Baltic, and the next day arrived at the Danish port of Horsens for an official visit. The visit lasted five days, and when *Corunna* left she sailed north past the Jutland peninsula and took part in 'Exercise Fairwind' in the North Sea until 6 July, when she arrived at Londonderry. The following two weeks involved more exercises in the waters off the west of Scotland, and Place spent three days at Rothesay. The ship then sailed south to Chatham, arriving at the end of July, and remained in dry dock for all of August.

Place took leave in August and on his return took *Corunna* north. Initially, exercises were held off the west of Scotland, but later *Corunna* joined HMS *Bulwark* for exercises in the North Sea. After returning to Chatham *Corunna* sailed south and spent a week participating in trials off the south coast of Devon, before sailing to Spain. On 25 October the ship arrived at her namesake port, *La Corunna*, to pay a five-day visit. Place commemorated the Battle of Corunna, which took place in 1809 during the Peninsular War and was marked by the retreat of British troops from the French. As *Corunna* left Spain she embarked a passenger, Mr Bill Wyatt of Mooney Aircraft Inc., along with his aircraft which he had been forced to ditch off the coast of Spain. Place agreed to convey him and the aircraft back to England, an action that was later recognised by a personal thank you from the American Ambassador in London, Mr John Hay Whitney. *Corunna,* with *Agincourt,* arrived at the Pool of London on 28 November, and later that day the crew of *Corunna* had to rescue a man overboard in the River Thames. After a four-day visit, *Corunna* departed to Chatham where, on 18 November, Commander C.F. Gordon DSO, assumed command.

Chapter 11

Staff Matters: Promotion to Captain

In January 1958 Godfrey Place attended the Joint Services Staff Course (JSSC) at Latimer, Buckinghamshire. This six-month course trained the future commanders and staff officers of both British and foreign armed forces. Being tri-service, there were many visits to military establishments to allow participants to see what colleagues in other forces were doing. Another feature was time spent working in 'syndicates' of about eight people, invariably from different backgrounds, writing papers on a variety of topics which were then appraised by members of the directing staff. The six months spent at Latimer were summed up by one of Place's contemporaries as, 'a very gentlemanly existence.'(1) Place made a distinct impression, and it was recorded that, 'He is well above average in intelligence and adopts a bold and often unorthodox approach to his problems. A vigorous speaker.' His sense of duty had been clearly apparent to the directing staff, and he was noted as a good advertisement for the Royal Navy.

The half-yearly promotions list in June 1958 announced that Godfrey Place was to be promoted Captain on 31 December 1958; he would be just thirty-seven years old. At the same time, his next appointment was being decided, and it would involve a return to naval aviation.

In 1958 the Royal Navy had seven aircraft carriers operating fixed-wing aircraft. Naval aviation was now based around jet aircraft and was operating at a rather different tempo to that of just a few years earlier, when Place had served with 801 Squadron in Korea. Usually four or five aircraft carriers would be in commission at any one time, the remainder being in refit. The Captain of each carrier was responsible to the Flag Officer Aircraft Carriers (FOAC), a post held by either a Vice or Rear Admiral, who had his own staff, led by the Chief Staff Officer (CSO). As well as overseeing the Admiral's staff the CSO carried responsibility for drawing up plans for exercises and then presenting them to the Admiral for approval. Success in the appointment required an efficient and intelligent officer and one who could understand the issues facing the embarked squadrons as well as the Captain and crew of an aircraft carrier. In July 1958 Vice Admiral A.N.C. Bingley OBE was FOAC, and his CSO was Captain A.H.F. Sutton DSC*. Bingley (often called 'Baron Bingley') had served as a Fleet Air Arm observer in the Pacific during the war. He had a reputation for wanting things to be simplified; at times he found it difficult to adhere even to the norms of naval etiquette. Sutton was also an observer, who had been awarded the Distinguished Service Cross for his role in the attack on the Italian fleet at Taranto in November 1940. His appointment was coming to an end and a successor was required. The appointment was the responsibility of the Naval Secretary, Rear Admiral J.G. Hamilton CBE, who had identified a replacement for Captain Sutton. When Hamilton informed the officer in question (a naval aviator who had spent several years ashore) he had expected to be thanked for sending a dry-list officer to 'such a splendid appointment'. Instead the officer was far from pleased and 'nearly blew up with fury and resentment.' He informed Hamilton that he had readjusted his whole life, including 'embarking on a new wife,' and stated that 'he would not touch the job with a barge pole.' Since Bingley was soon to be replaced, discussions took place with his successor, Rear Admiral C.L.G. Evans CB, CBE, DSO, DSC, and it was decided that the best man for the job was Godfrey Place, whose achievements were summarised thus by Admiral Hamilton: 'He seems to have had a brilliant career so far during his short time as an aviator. I have seldom read such glowing 206s.'

Appointing Godfrey Place to the post, it was felt, would give him a position closely connected with practical flying but would not come between him and a sea command. He was to be appointed in the rank of Acting Captain.

Prior to taking up the appointment, Place was appointed to the Directorate of Plans in the Admiralty for about two months, commencing in August 1958. Following this, he spent most of October and the early part of November flying from RNAS Yeovilton. Most sorties involved flying locally, although there were some trips to RNAS Culdrose.

In order to take up his next appointment, Place flew to Gibraltar, on a commercial flight, to join HMS *Eagle*, Commanding Officer, Captain J.B. Frewen, on 17 November 1958. *Eagle* had been in dry dock at Gibraltar for two weeks, having been deployed in the Mediterranean since May. She had been busy, having provided support to a number of Arab countries following political turmoil in Iraq in July. *Eagle* was one of two 'Audacious' class aircraft carriers; she was launched in 1946 by Princess Elizabeth and commissioned in 1951. A large ship, she had a displacement of 43,000 tons, a complement (including aircrew) of 2,500 men and could carry 60 aircraft. Soon after Place joined, *Eagle* sailed to Malta, where she undertook combined operations with the aircraft carrier HMS *Victorious*. Following this, *Eagle* headed west and spent a few days at Gibraltar before sailing home to Devonport, arriving on 3 December. On 19 December Place left the ship for Christmas leave. (2)

During the Christmas period, Place's career again featured in the national newspapers. The 'Peterborough' column of the *Daily Telegraph* on 31 December reported his impending promotion under the headline, 'Captain (RN) at 37':

> At 37 Captain Godfrey Place VC has joined the relatively select company to achieve this rank in the late thirties. He achieves it at the same age as Lord Mountbatten, Captain in 1937. Place's career in the Navy has a legendary quality, submarine officer, pilot, navigating specialist and the VC, DSC and the Polish Virtuti Militaria to mark some of his exploits. Place was selected for promotion six months ago. In the meantime presumably an appropriate appointment has been found for him.

Place returned from leave on 12 January 1959 and on the following day Rear Admiral Evans assumed the position of FOAC. Charles Evans was in many ways a 'one off'; a highly experienced naval aviator, he flew with the Fleet Air Arm in the war and was jointly responsible for shooting down the first German aircraft in the conflict. He had later commanded HMS *Ocean* in the Korean War in the summer of 1952. A dapper officer, with a distinctive small beard, he was a very affable individual. One of the Royal Navy's real characters, he had married a Greek belly dancer during the war; she was a perfect foil for her husband and had been known to hurl an ashtray at him if upset by his behaviour at official dinners. Those who served with him described him as, 'charming, humorous and a consummate actor who was revered by all who worked for him.' Admiral Bingley left *Eagle* in traditional naval fashion, 'towed ashore' in his car by men from the ship. They pulled the car along the jetty at Devonport, and to make things a little harder Bingley instructed his driver to put the handbrake on. The car came to a standstill. 'Come on lads,' shouted Place, 'let's show the Admiral what we can do' – and the car slithered along the quayside for about thirty yards, before the towing party gave up and the Admiral was driven on his way. (3)

HMS *Eagle* left for the Mediterranean the next day and later undertook exercises off Malta, followed by an air defence exercise in the Gulf of Taranto alongside elements of the Italian Navy and Air Force. Once this was completed, there was an official visit to Naples, where Admiral Evans hosted a dinner party for guests from NATO and the Italian Navy. The guests included an American Admiral and his wife, the latter seated between Place and Captain Frewen. As the evening wore on she became rather inebriated, and both officers were the recipients of her amorous advances.(4) After departure from Naples, *Eagle* took part in exercises with the aircraft carrier HMS *Centaur.* Two weeks were then spent at Malta, during which Godfrey Place made the best use of his time and spent two days flying Meteors from RNAS Hal Far. *Eagle's* departure from Malta was delayed due to bad weather, when gales threatened to break the mooring lines and drive *Eagle* aground. The ship finally sailed to Gibraltar and then, in company of both *Victorious* and *Centaur,* took part in 'Exercise Dawn Breeze'. This lasted ten days and involved carrier-borne aircraft attacking targets in southern England that were defended by the RAF. During the exercise Admiral Evans and his staff transferred to HMS *Victorious;* they returned to *Eagle* on 23 March, and she sailed to Devonport.

It had been announced in January 1959 that the Queen would visit *Eagle* in April that year. As a dress rehearsal for the event *Eagle* embarked over 200 families early on the morning of 13 April and sailed for a day of exercises which allowed the guests to appreciate the operations of an aircraft carrier. Aircraft flew on and off the ship for nearly four hours, and in the early afternoon *Eagle* returned to Plymouth. The day was deemed a great success, and the recently promoted Vice Admiral Evans was quoted in *The Times* as being very much the man behind the idea. (5) Although this type of families' day may have been new to aircraft carriers, it was certainly not new to the Royal Navy. Place, when in command of HMS *Corunna*, had introduced just such an event. Age was no barrier, and amongst those who had visited *Corunna* was Place's son Charles, aged about eight, along with James Coles (also about eight), the son of Charles Coles, who had shared a room with Godfrey Place in Marlag.

HMS *Eagle* next sailed to Brest for a five-day visit and then returned to Portland, where the following week was spent rehearsing for the forthcoming royal visit. On 29 April the Queen and Prince Charles travelled from London to Weymouth by train and embarked in HMS *Eagle.* As guests of Admiral Evans, they spent some four hours watching displays by the ship's squadrons as well as touring the ship. The royal visitors were entertained to lunch by Admiral Evans before leaving the ship and returning to London. The next day, *Eagle* sailed to Devonport where she entered the dockyard for a major refit lasting four years. Place and other members of the Admiral's staff left the ship, and the flag was transferred to another ship. (6)

Admiral Evans' next flagship was HMS *Victorious*, Commanding Officer Captain C.P. Coke DSO. She had served in the war, her aircraft having taken part in attacks against the *Bismarck* in May 1941 and the *Tirpitz* in April 1944. After the war she underwent a major refit from 1950 to 1957. Smaller than *Eagle*, she had a displacement of 35,000 tons, a complement of 2,200 men and carried up to 36 aircraft. Admiral Evans and his staff flew on to *Victorious* on 5 May as she was sailing off the south coast of Devon. Place had made the most of the interval between flagships and managed to fly from RNAS Yeovilton before joining *Victorious*. During May the ship undertook exercises in the western approaches and in the waters off the west of Scotland, some in the company of HMS *Centaur*, before sailing to Spithead and then on to Rosyth. At Spithead *Victorious* was the host for 'Operation Shop Window', a display of the ship's operating capabilities to visitors from the Ministry of Supply and British aircraft constructors. Place missed this, and instead spent the time flying at RNAS Yeovilton.

HMS *Victorious* left Rosyth in early June for a five-day exercise with the RAF and Dutch and Danish forces, before sailing to Aarhus in Denmark, and from there on to Oslo, where the ship was visited by King Olaf. She returned to Portsmouth for a week of maintenance before sailing to America, in the company of the frigates HMS *Scarborough*, *Tenby* and *Salisbury* and RFA *Tidereach*. On 4 July, as she sailed near to the Azores, she was involved in the rescue of three American airmen. They had been forced to eject from their aircraft at 30,000 feet, and were located by a British merchant ship before being picked up by the USS *Camp*. A helicopter was sent from *Victorious* to transfer the navigator, as well as a rating from the *Camp* who was in need of medical attention, to the American air base on the Azores. (7) The first port of call in America for *Victorious* was Norfolk, Virginia, from where she took part in 'Exercise Riptide', cross-operating with two American aircraft carriers, USS *Saratoga* and *Essex*. One of the prime objectives of the visit was to demonstrate the capabilities of the new radar system, 984/CDS (Comprehensive Display System), fitted in *Victorious* which had been described by the First Sea Lord as 'the best in the world'. The radar system lived up to its description and achieved almost a ninety-five per cent detection rate. Place skilfully ensured that the exercises ran smoothly, and did so very calmly; he was noted by the Commander (Air) as having 'just the right touch' and being able to ensure that 'temperatures did not rise too much amongst the staff on the bridge when operations were on the edge.'

Following the joint exercises, *Victorious* sailed to Boston and then to New York, where she moored at Pier 90 next to RMS *Queen Elizabeth*. In America Place was joined by Althea, and they were able to spend time together visiting the sights and making friends with American colleagues. In early August *Victorious* left New York and sailed home to Portsmouth, where on 12 August

Captain Coke left the ship and Captain H.R.B. Janvrin DSC assumed command. After leave and a period of maintenance, *Victorious* sailed at the beginning of September to the inhospitable waters of the Norwegian Sea to undertake 'Exercises Blue Frost and Barefoot', where the ship and her squadrons operated in cold conditions. As the ship headed home to Portsmouth Admiral Evans and his staff flew off and landed at Lossiemouth.

Evans travelled to Singapore in October 1959 and flew his flag in HMS *Centaur*, serving with the Far East Fleet. This was one trip that Place did not make; instead he stayed in England, where he took leave and spent much of October flying Vampires and Venoms at RNAS Yeovilton. Evans returned later that month and, along with Place, rejoined *Victorious* at the end of October, when she sailed to the Mediterranean. In early December there was an official visit to Marseilles, then she returned to Portsmouth.

In January 1960 *Victorious* undertook trials in the English Channel of a new aircraft built by Blackburns, identified as NA39. The first test flight was made in April 1958, and originally carrier trials were to have commenced in October 1959. However, a few days before the intended start, one of the prototypes crashed in the New Forest. The first carrier landing was made on 19 January 1960, in an aircraft flown by Lieutenant Commander D.J. Whitehead AFC and Lieutenant Commander E.A. Anson, the latter having served with Place in 801 Squadron. Over the next few days the NA39 undertook more than thirty launches and landings from the ship. The trials were a success and led to the NA39 becoming the Blackburn Buccaneer; later deployed on several aircraft carriers, it served with the Royal Navy until 1978. (8)

After these trials *Victorious* sailed north to Icelandic waters for anti-submarine exercises and then to Hamburg for an official visit. Whilst there, Place met several Germans whose paths he had crossed in 1943. One was a naval officer, who recognised Place and introduced himself by saying, 'I think we have met before.' 'Yes,' replied Place, 'the last time we met you had me marched stark naked through the streets of Narvik after you caught me trying to put an explosive under the *Tirpitz*.' The man roared with laughter, but Place just looked at a colleague nearby with a wry expression, and no more was said. Another visitor to the ship was Admiral Hans Meyer, commander of the German Naval Staff College, who had been the Captain of the *Tirpitz* in 1943. He and Place met in *Victorious*, where they sat and talked for hours about their wartime experiences. (9) The trip to Hamburg was not all work, and Admiral Evans took his staff for a run ashore to a club on the Reeperbahn. After several drinks, Evans took over from the drummer of the band (the admiral was an accomplished drummer) and played enthusiastically whilst a Brazilian girl sang her way through a strip-tease in front of him. Unfazed by this, Place sat at a nearby table talking to an equally 'well oiled' American officer about the intricacies of operating aircraft carriers.

Victorious sailed from Hamburg to Devonport, where Admiral Evans and his staff left the ship and transferred to HMS *Ark Royal*. She was a sister ship of *Eagle*, although slightly newer, having first been commissioned in 1955 and having recently completed a sixteen-month refit. Evans and his staff joined *Ark Royal*, Commanding Officer, Captain P.J. Hill-Norton, on 24 February, but within a week there were further changes. Place acquired his third boss in less than fourteen months when Rear Admiral R.H. Smeeton MBE replaced Evans as FOAC. He had served as a Fleet Air Arm pilot in the war and prior to that with the RAF. More recently, he had commanded the aircraft carrier HMS *Albion* during 'Operation Musketeer'. *Ark Royal* sailed to the Mediterranean for exercises, in company with HMS *Albion*. After a visit to Palermo she sailed to Malta, and in mid-April Place left the ship, being replaced by Captain N.G. Hallett DSC. (10)

Godfrey Place had impressed Admiral Evans; they had obviously worked very well together and, despite their very different characters, had 'gelled'. Evans wrote of him:

A dedicated and intensely ambitious naval officer who has organised his career in order to give himself the widest possible professional experience ... I have never met an officer of his seniority with wider professional knowledge. I could not have wished for a better Chief of Staff.

He recommended that Godfrey Place should serve in the Admiralty, and noted that he was 'admirably suited to command a carrier.' His final comment was: 'I consider that he has set his sights on becoming First Sea Lord; he might make it.'

Place's next appointment, announced in December 1959, was to be at the Admiralty. Having left Ark *Royal* at Malta he returned to London and commenced his new job in April 1960, as Deputy Director of Air Warfare (DDAW). This was an appointment involving the planning of future requirements for naval aviation, both fixed-wing and helicopters. He and his family moved from West Camel and purchased a large flat in Barons Court, West London. A job 'driving a desk' in London was probably not what Place would have had relished. However, during the first six months of his appointment he again showed his ability, and his report from the Director of

Naval Airwarfare, Captain O.N. Bailey, recorded: 'An outstanding officer of great drive and personality. He has got a good grip on the equipment side of the job remarkably quickly.'

He was marked high on the assessment part of the report, but the second reporting officer (Fifth Sea Lord, Vice Admiral Sir Laurence Durlacher KCB, OBE, DSC) considered that he had been 'somewhat overmarked.'

Before long, Place became frustrated in the job and in September 1960 approached the Naval Secretary, Rear Admiral F.R Twiss DSC, to ascertain how long he would be based at the Admiralty. He was told it would be a full two years, after which it was hoped he would return to sea. Place tried, unsuccessfully, to talk him into an earlier relief of appointment, possibly August 1961. The Naval Secretary's minutes reveal that it was planned for Place possibly to assume command of the aircraft carrier HMS *Hermes* in December 1962, although he was not made aware of this. A note was also made that Place was 'not a member of the Navy Club'. The paths of these two officers would cross again on several occasions over the next ten years, invariably not to Place's advantage.

In April 1961 his colleague and great friend Commander Donald Cameron VC, died suddenly at the Royal Naval Hospital. A few months earlier there had been reports of a number of 'bogus VCs': people impersonating those who had been awarded the Victoria Cross, including one who died having successfully impersonated a deceased VC from the First World War for forty-five years. Shortly after this came to light, staff at a hospital rang Sir John Smythe VC, MC, Chairman of the VC & GC Association, to inform him that, 'Donald Cameron VC was seriously ill in hospital and they thought he would like to know.' Smyth recalled that, 'At once I phoned his friend Godfrey Place to ask if he would go and visit him, but he replied "but Cameron is perfectly well and sitting in the room with me at this minute."' (11)

Donald Cameron had asked for his body to be committed to the sea. C.P.O. Brian Davies was the gunnery instructor (GI) at *Dolphin* in April 1961. Earlier in his career he had served in HMS *Bonaventure* in the Far East during 1945, when she had acted as the depot ship for midget submarines operating against Japanese targets. This included 'Operation Struggle', the attack by XE3 on the Japanese ship *Takoa* in the Jahore Straits, following which Lieutenant I.E. Fraser and Able Seaman J.J. Magennis had both been awarded the Victoria Cross. Davies was rung by the Commander of HMS *Dolphin*, who informed him that Donald Cameron had died and was to be buried at sea, and that Brian Davies was to organise this. He was responsible for providing guards for the body as it lay in St Nicholas' Chapel at HMS *Dolphin*, before the committal. He remembered very clearly one episode. On

Wednesday, 12 April, at about 20.00, all four sentries had been fallen out and Brian Davies was about to lock the chapel, when a 'rather small man in civvies came up to the chapel.' Davies knew straight away that he was a naval officer. 'Are you locking up?' he asked, 'I would like to come in.' He went in and Davies stood outside. After about five minutes the man came out and said, 'Thank you very much, GI.' The committal took place the next day, Thursday, 13 April, and was attended by a number of VIPs. The body of the late Commander Donald Cameron VC was embarked in the submarine HMS *Thule*, Commanding Officer, Lieutenant M.J. Casserley, at 14.30. Brian Davies saw the man from the evening before, this time in naval uniform. He remembered seeing a VC ribbon and four rings on his uniform and thought, 'I know who you are.' Godfrey Place went on board the submarine for the committal, which took place about two hours later, when *Thule* was 4 miles south of Nab Tower; this was probably the only time Place went to sea in a submarine after 'Operation Source'. After the committal, Place approached Brian Davies and said, 'All very impressive GI. We haven't met, what is your name?' 'Davies' was the reply. 'Good,' replied Godfrey Place.

A few weeks later, Brian Davies was summoned, he knew not why, to the Admiralty for a Monday morning meeting. He travelled up from Portsmouth and on arrival was directed to a room where waiting for him was Godfrey Place, who said, 'I have been studying you. I have been appointed to 25th Escort Squadron, and we are commissioning *Yarmouth*. Would you like to come as my GI?' Brian Davies said, 'Yes', and in April 1962 he joined HMS *Yarmouth* at Devonport.

Whilst at the Admiralty, Place was able to maintain contact with pilots of the Fleet Air Arm when invited to be the Reviewing Officer for the passing out parade of No. 90 Royal Naval Course, in July 1961. Basic training for Fleet Air Arm pilots had moved from RAF Syerston to RAF Linton-on-Ouse in 1957. Place travelled to the airbase the day before the parade and that night dined with the seven pilots who were to receive their Wings from him the following day. (12)

Place's time at the Admiralty came to an end in September 1961, by which time he knew that his next appointment would be at sea, as Commanding Officer of the frigate HMS *Yarmouth*, and as Captain of the 6th Frigate Squadron, from April 1962. His successor as DDAW was Captain E.M. 'Winkle' Brown MBE, DSC, AFC, a highly distinguished pilot who in 1945 had made the first landing by a jet aircraft on to an aircraft carrier. At the end of the war he had led the 'enemy aircraft flight', a group of elite pilots who evaluated and flew captured German aircraft. In September 1961 there were a number of major decisions about to be made on the future of British naval aviation, with plans for new aircraft carriers about to be submitted for assessment. Far-reaching decisions were going to have to be made, and Place was pleased that his replacement was a man with such a tremendous knowledge of naval aviation, since he did not feel competent to make the decisions himself. Place told him, 'Winkle, I am glad you are taking over as I've had enough.' During the handover period, Place and Brown were invited to Elstree Studios, where they met the cast of Billy Budd, which was being filmed at the time. The film was directed and produced by Peter Ustinov who also acted in it, alongside Terence Stamp and David McCallum. Winkle Brown recalled Place appeared ill at ease at the studios, which was not unsurprising given that he had little time for those, regardless of who they were, who were full of their own self-importance.

Place was glad to leave the Admiralty, since his appointment had not been as successful as many of his previous ones. In October 1960 Captain D. Vincent-Jones DSC* had taken over as Director of Naval Airwarfare, Place's boss. He had served as an observer in the war and arrived at the Admiralty from an appointment as Naval Attaché in Buenos Aires. The two did not get on well. Vincent-Jones did not share Place's work ethic and did not give him the technical help needed to undertake his job. His reports on leaving the appointment cast light on some of these problems; they were mixed, and at times critical of Place. There was recognition of his 'burning zeal and great energy', but noted an 'unorthodox though effective approach to staff work … does not suffer fools gladly … a dynamic and aggressive individualist, with a strong spirit of adventure who is more suited to an environment of war than peace.' As had happened one year earlier, Admiral Sir Laurence Durlacher was the second reporting officer; he was again critical of Godfrey Place and on this occasion, rather than suggesting he had been overmarked, altered the marks down on the confidential report. He added:

> I am amongst the senior officers who are at times aggravated by Place. In spite of his many outstanding qualities enumerated in this report his weakness is an inability to see any other point of view than his own or to listen to any argument that conflicts with it.

In retrospect one might wonder if there was more than an element of professional jealousy now affecting Place's career; by September 1961 he was one of only two serving members of the Royal Navy who held the Victoria Cross, and within a year he would be the only one (Lieutenant Commander P.S.W. Roberts VC, DSC retired in July 1962). Certainly, Althea felt that the Victoria Cross was becoming a hindrance to Godfrey's career.

Place was keen to make the most of his next appointment, in command at sea. Before joining his new ship, he and his family moved to Corton Denham, Dorset, not far from RNAS Yeovilton. This was to be the family home for over thirty years, during which time he spent much of his leave undertaking home improvements. During October and November he spent time flying, and the last entry in his flying log was made on Friday, 10 November, when he flew a Vampire for about thirty-five minutes. Although his days of fixed-wing flying were drawing to a close, he was determined to learn to fly helicopters. He tried to join a helicopter course, which he described as, 'very difficult, but I haven't given up hope – shortage of instructors.' At the same time, he received notice from Admiral Twiss that there might be alterations to the organisation of Frigate Squadrons. This caused Place to reply, 'When someone starts re-organising the fleet, I always think it is time to reduce the staff of the Plans division.' It was typical of Godfrey Place to offer an honest opinion, but this may not have been the most tactful of responses to send to the Admiralty.

Chapter 12

Squadron Command

On 25 April 1962 Godfrey Place relieved Captain H.R. Hewlett as Commanding Officer of HMS *Yarmouth* and as Captain of the 6th Frigate Squadron at Devonport, comprising HMS *Yarmouth*, *Brighton* and *Llandaff*. (1) *Yarmouth* was a Type 12 frigate and had recently come out of refit, but had serious faults, not least in her radar systems. As a result, the decision was made to swap crews between HMS *Yarmouth* and her sister ship HMS *Rothesay*. The latter, under the command of Captain D Jermain DSC*, had been the command ship of the 20th Frigate Squadron, based in Londonderry. She arrived at Devonport on 4 May. Five days later Place assumed command of *Rothesay* and later that afternoon he addressed the lower decks. (2) Initial trials were undertaken in the Portland area before sailing to Portsmouth for the commissioning service on 18 May. After this, the next two months were spent in trials under the watchful eye of Flag Officer Sea Training at Portland.

Having satisfactorily completed sea training by the middle of July, *Rothesay* sailed to Portsmouth, where Place took two weeks' annual leave. The ship took part in Navy Days in early August, and he then led the squadron as they travelled to the Far East – a deployment which would last nearly a year. They sailed first to Gibraltar, where they joined the aircraft carriers HMS *Hermes* and *Centaur* and USS *Forrestal* and *Enterprise* for 'Exercise Riptide'. *Rothesay* undertook air defence exercises as well as acting as plane guard ship for the aircraft carriers. After a week of exercises, the squadron visited Gibraltar and then sailed into the Mediterranean. They transited the Suez Canal on the night of 22 August and sailed to Aden. It was just over forty years since Place had first visited this port, for which he still had little fondness or regard.

After leaving Aden, the squadron called at Colombo and, after a two day visit, encountered a torrential rain storm as they left harbour. On 7 September *Rothesay* arrived at Singapore, where the ship entered dry dock for a period of maintenance. The ship's ratings proceeded ashore to live in the relative comfort of HMS *Terror*, whilst most officers remained on board. HMS *Ark Royal* was the aircraft carrier assigned to the Far East fleet at this time, and at the end of September *Rothesay* proceeded to the South China Sea, off Pulau Tioman (a well frequented exercise area to the east of Malaya), in the company of *Ark Royal*. She acted as plane guard during a week of flying exercises, many of which took place at night. The ships then sailed to Hong Kong, and back to Singapore in early October, again undertaking flying exercises.

Amongst those who served in HMS *Rothesay* was the Gunnery Instructor C.P.O. Brian Davies who had first met Place in April 1961 at Portsmouth. On that first meeting, he had noted that Place was not very tall and, although this had been to his advantage in submarines, it caused problems in *Rothesay*. Davies recalled how uncomfortable Godfrey Place was at being shorter than anyone appearing in front of him on a disciplinary matter. He remembered in particular one incident when he was standing in for the bosun at the defaulter's list. Place came down to where the assembled members of the crew were to appear before him. He looked at the ground and then spoke sharply: 'Davies, report to my cabin, at once.' Davies did as requested, and on arrival his commanding officer's face was puce. He was asked, 'Chief where is my stool?' 'What stool, Sir?' 'What stool? The stool I stand on. No one is taller than me at the defaulter's list!!'

Rothesay, with other squadron members, accompanied *Ark Royal* as she sailed from Singapore, arriving at Aden in early November. After a week there they met HMS *Bulwark* (now a commando carrier) for flying and amphibious exercises as they headed south to Mombasa. On 21 November *Rothesay's* log recorded, '09.00 crossed line with King Neptune and court'. (3) The next day they arrived at Mombasa for a four-day visit. They sailed north from Mombasa with *Ark Royal*, and on the evening of 29 November a Sea Vixen made an emergency landing on *Ark Royal*. The aircraft was forced to ditch and the pilot was rescued by a Wessex helicopter from the aircraft carrier; this was the first night-time rescue by a Royal Navy helicopter embarked in aircraft carrier. The navigator was rescued by a sea boat launched from *Rothesay*.

At the beginning of December *Rothesay* was at Aden, where she was called upon to give assistance to a Greek merchant ship, the SS *Captantonis*, which had run aground on a reef off Perim Island in the western end of the Gulf of Aden. Her engines had failed in rough weather. Lieutenant Bruce-Jardyne remembered *Rothesay* being the first ship to the scene and commencing the salvage operation. Place was in his element leading his crew to salvage the ship. In order to get a tow on board, he took *Rothesay* very close to the rocks, having to cope with a fresh south-east wind and a choppy sea. He held *Rothesay* up against the wind until a tow had been passed, and then the crew started to free the *Captantonis*, after part of her cargo had been unloaded. Bruce-Jardyne recalled, 'It was an exhibition of outstanding ship handling in very adverse conditions, which impressed all the crew.' Two days later, the ship was afloat, and *Rothesay* sailed to Aden only to be informed that *Captantonis* had gone aground again, this time at Balfe Point, close to Perim Island. On returning to the scene, Place, along with four officers, crossed to the ship by whaler to assess the situation. Salvage commenced again, and *Rothesay* was joined by a Russian tug, the *Gorovnoy*. (4) After a further two days' work the ship was finally refloated, and *Rothesay* was ordered to pass the tow to the *Gorovnoy*, a move that was not very popular on board *Rothesay*. The crew were convinced that this would reduce their reward, but in fact all members of the crew received some salvage money. The actions of Place and his crew earned the ship a signal of congratulations from the Flag Officer, Middle East.

Next it was back to Singapore for Christmas, having briefly stopped at the island of Gan en route. Althea flew out to Singapore to join her husband after Christmas. By being away from home he had missed one of the coldest Christmas periods on record, during which Althea and their children had been in Grimsby; they were delayed on their return to Corton Denham as the village was cut off by snow for many days.

At the start of 1963 Place's title and responsibilities changed. The Royal Navy had decided to alter their fleet structure: frigate squadrons were to be replaced by escort squadrons, and the first to be commissioned was 25th Escort Squadron in January 1963. Commanded by Place, it comprised the frigates HMS *Rothesay*, *Blackpool* and *Brighton*, the aircraft direction frigate *Llandaff* and the destroyer *Cavendish*. The advantages of a mixed squadron were that, 'It would provide a thoroughly versatile and hard-hitting escort unit able to cope with any situations that arise.' (5) In the middle of February the new squadron, along with HMS *Hermes*, which had relieved *Ark Royal* as the aircraft carrier in the Far East, departed from Hong Kong to undertake exercises en route to Bangkok. After a five-day visit to Bangkok, they sailed to Singapore, and then on to the Langkawi exercise area, to the west of Malaya. Here the squadron was involved in 'Exercise Jet 63' with *Hermes* for ten days, before returning once more to Singapore.

Civil unrest was a not uncommon feature of life in Singapore during the 1950s and 1960s, fuelled by both political and racial tension. At times the Armed Forces were called on to provide 'assistance to the civil powers', and when HMS *Rothesay* was at Singapore she was asked to provide such assistance. Brian Davies remembered one such occasion, on a Sunday morning:

The rates formed up at the dockyard gate and the rioters were throwing stones, but it was stalemate. Out of the blue, the Captain arrived and went up to the Lieutenant in charge and said, 'either do something or get back on board.' At which point the men put on their gas masks and fired four grenades of gas, and then advanced towards the crowd and fired three warning shots over their heads. Suddenly one sailor dropped to the ground and there was concern that he had he been shot. Medical help was summoned and he was taken back to the ship. Immediately an enquiry took place and it was found that the man's gas mask did not fit. Captain Place sent for me and asked, 'how can this have occurred? Do the respirators work?' The man in question had in fact borrowed a gas mask and the Captain asked how this could have happened? I did not have an answer. The Captain sent for the man and asked, 'did you know that the mask was not yours?' 'Yes' he replied, and continued, 'I couldn't find my own so I took this one.' Captain Place then asked, 'Why did you not tell the Chief you had lost it?' There was no answer, to which the Captain replied, 'I think that says everything.'

In April and May *Rothesay* was involved with further naval aviation exercises, involving HMS *Hermes* and the Australian aircraft carrier, HMAS *Melbourne*. She paid visits to Manila and Hong Kong before returning with *Hermes* to Singapore. Place's time in the Far East with *Rothesay* was now drawing to a close. However, with a house in England in need of home improvements, Place had made the most of his time in Hong Kong and purchased a quantity of local hardwood for his dining room. Having acquired the wood at a very competitive price, he had to get it back home. Some of it was stored in his bathroom in *Rothesay*, but there was not room for it all. He approached the officers of HMS *Hermes*, where his former colleague from 801 Squadron, Commander A. J. Leahy DSC had just joined the ship as Commander (Air), and asked them to take some wood home for him in the aircraft hangar. They duly obliged.

Having been away for nearly ten months, the 25th Escort Squadron were keen to get home and left Singapore in early June and sailed across the Indian Ocean. *Rothesay* paid a visit to Cochin, India, where they undertook combined exercises with the Indian navy. During these the crew of *Rothesay* became frustrated with the inefficiency of their Indian colleagues. Brian Davies remembered being summoned by Place one afternoon:

The Captain's steward came to me and said, 'with Captain's compliments, he would like to see you.' I presented myself at the

Captain's cabin and was asked, 'Chief, what is the feeling on the lower deck?' I replied, 'Boredom, sheer boredom. When is something going to happen, Sir?' Captain Place replied, 'I've arranged that some of the ship's company are to go across to the carrier for a flight in a plane, and you, chief, will go first, by jackstay transfer.'

The squadron transited the Suez Canal on 21 June and sailed to Malta and then on to Gibraltar, before arriving at Portsmouth on 4 July, having been away for eleven months. The next month was spent taking leave and contributing to Navy Days at Portsmouth. Whilst at Portsmouth Godfrey Place again demonstrated his ability to take command of difficult situations. Two people were reported missing in a dinghy in Portsmouth harbour. There was a great deal of activity by a range of people attempting to locate the dinghy, much of it totally unfocussed and unproductive. Place was on the bridge at the time and could see a potential disaster unfolding. He asked the Officer of the Watch to pass him the microphone. Using the ship's tannoy, he announced, 'This is Captain Place of the warship *Rothesay*. Please keep quiet whilst I tell you exactly what to do in the harbour.' From that point he took over the command of the rescue operation.

Place's time in *Rothesay* was soon to end, but there were still deployments nearer to home. Come the end of August, *Rothesay* was at Devonport, serving with the Home Fleet and preparing to take part in a multi-national exercise in Torbay. 'Exercise Unison 63' involved a large number of Royal Navy ships and coincided with a conference of the Commonwealth navies hosted by Admiral of the Fleet Lord Louis Mountbatten at the Royal Naval College, Dartmouth. It was intended that conference delegates, including the Minister of Defence, would visit the assembled fleet; there was no room for error in ensuring that the exercises went to plan.

'Exercise Unison 63' commenced on Thursday, 5 September, and soon faced its first obstacle: Brixham trawlermen. These fishermen were not renowned for compromise and were concerned at the impact the exercise might have on their livelihoods, especially if ammunition was to land in the sprat shoaling grounds. An agreement was reached early on between the Royal Navy and the trawlermen: the former were to provide daily radio notice of any stretch of water to be used in the exercise, and the latter would be allowed to fish as normal, provided they moved out of an area where prior notice of exclusion had been given. On the first day there were clashes between the fishermen and the navy, eight trawlers having been ordered out of the area by gunboats. One fisherman remarked to the local press, 'It's not looking too good at the moment.' For the Royal Navy matters only got worse when two days later they lost six depth charges about eight miles off Brixham. The Admiralty reported that, 'they may not be particularly dangerous to fishermen', and there were no plans to retrieve them. This angered the fishermen, who were concerned at possible damage to the shoaling grounds. They were, however, soon delighted to hear that the decision had been reversed and the depth charges would be salvaged. At the end of the week, when the exercise had finished, a message was sent to Commander-in-Chief, Plymouth, from Ernie Passmore, owner of the trawler *Our Unity*: 'Please convey many thanks to all ships concerned in assisting fishing vessels to carry on their normal work.' (6)

The reason for this remarkable change of attitude was described by Rear Admiral D.C.E.F. Gibson DSC, Flag Officer Aircraft Carriers, who recalled:

> There was much trouble with the south coast fisherman because we spent a great deal of time steaming to and fro in their fishing area; this problem, a serious matter for both sides, was partially solved by Captain B.C.G. Place VC, DSC, who anchored close to shore and exercised hospitality and an understanding manner. (7)

Rothesay had anchored in Brixham harbour each night and had thrown some excellent parties for the fishermen, who probably found it difficult to keep up with Place. Being entertained in this way by a war hero and the only serving member of the Royal Navy holding the Victoria Cross certainly made a difference, and allowed the exercise to be completed after amicable relations were restored with the fishermen.

By now, Place was aware of his next appointment, as Commanding Officer of the Boys' Training Establishment, HMS *Ganges* at Shotley. He was aware that there were a number of problems at the establishment, not least bullying of the boys, who were aged fifteen when they joined. He took several men from *Rothesay* with him. One of those was Brian Davies, who recalled being invited to the Captain's cabin and being told, 'I am going to *Ganges*, we must stamp out the bullying.' To which Davies replied, 'Good luck to you, Sir.' Place then said, 'I think you would be the right man to come with me', to which Davies thought, 'better the devil you know.' Place assured Davies that if he came with him to *Ganges* his next draft (which would be his last) would be wherever he wanted. He was true to his word.

After 'Exercise Unison 63' *Rothes*ay sailed to the Polish port of Gydnia for an official visit, one of the first by the Royal Navy since the war. Although Place had served alongside the Polish Navy in 1941, and had strong links with them, Poland in 1963 was a very different country from that which

Borys Karnicki and others had left in 1939. *Rothesay* arrived at Gydnia on 16 September for a three-day visit, during which the ship was open to visitors. Lieutenant Bruce-Gardyne remembered:

> The crew were all horrified by the grim desolation of the city. There was absolutely nothing in the shops and the people appeared totally cowed by the oppressive regime. They flocked on board us when we were open to visitors and wanted to give us messages to take to their relatives in England. This was to such an extent that the authorities eventually frisked all visitors to see if they had hidden letters. We still managed to take short written notes to dozens of Poles who had either escaped or never returned after the war.

The visit was marked by the obvious desire of the political authorities to undermine the 'officer class' by demonstrating great hospitality to ratings. Ten ratings, including Davies, were flown to Warsaw, where they were interviewed on the radio. After a guided tour of the city they attended an evening reception. All those selected to travel were interviewed by Place before leaving, and Davies remembered him talking of his great affinity for the Poles, but adding, 'You do realise that the officer class are not accepted here, so you will be deputising for me.'

Back in Gydnia, Place and a number of officers were scheduled to attend a wreath laying ceremony at Malbork Commonwealth War Graves Cemetery. This held the graves of a number of RAF men who had died in captivity during the war, and it must have brought back poignant memories for Place of his time at Marlag. Lieutenant Bruce-Gardyne was the liaison officer for the visit and had to travel with the Polish Naval Political Commissar in charge of the visit. He recalled:

> We had embarked the Commander-in-Chief Portsmouth's band for this ceremony and had also trained up a guard of honour. We all departed for a long drive to the cemetery, mostly travelling in a bus but Godfrey was in a car with the local Polish Senior Naval Officer, and I and the Commissar in another car. We stopped for a final clean up just short of the town and when we set off again my car would not start. I then tried to stop other passing cars in an attempt to get us to the ceremony in time, to the Commissar's absolute fury. Eventually I managed to stop a lorry full of turnips and climbed on top and insisted we drove into the town. He, in disgust, got into the cab and I sat on top of the turnips with my sword – we arrived in time for the ceremony but

the Commissar was never seen again! Much to Godfrey's and my delight!

Rothesay sailed from Gydnia on 20 September to Hartlepool, where she undertook a two-day visit, before finally sailing home to Portsmouth. In October *Rothesay* entered the dockyard for refit and Place went on leave at home, where much of his time was spent working on the house at Corton Denham. There was much work to be done to create a home. Place, who had grown up as a self-confessed nomad, wanted to settle down one day in his own home. He had written to Althea in May 1943:

> I am very keen to have a house of our own fairly soon, after the war, because the word 'home' has a remarkable effect on me and the idea of living somewhere always with intervals of absence is appealing to a nomad like myself.

The choice of property had initially caused concern to friends locally; when Place told them that he was purchasing the Old Bakery, the response was invariably that they hoped it was not 'the old building up by the church'. It was. The house and gardens were in need of major work, but Place relished the prospect and and set about laying a new dining room floor with the Loleando and Mohouhoo wood purchased in Hong Kong. This job soon became a combined effort with Althea, since none of the local craftsmen he approached was willing to take on the job, claiming that the wood was too hard to work with. Place, who always thrived on a challenge, proved them wrong. The floor was laid successfully, and several parties were held there; it was so resilient and tough that even dancing in stiletto heels left no trace. Challenges also lay outside, where the garden, on the side of a hill, had to be terraced in order to be used satisfactorily. Here Place, again aided by Althea and the children, set about building walls and creating suitable beds. Charles became quite adept at mixing concrete for his father, and Althea searched out stone for the walls. Opposite the house, workmen had demolished a building, and she asked if she could take some stone for the walls. They agreed, and Althea spent the next three days transporting stone in her wheelbarrow; after the third day the workmen, who had believed she only wanted a little, had to tell her to stop.

On 12 December 1963 Commander R.S. Agar assumed command of HMS *Rothesay* and Place made his way to Suffolk for his next appointment.

Chapter 13

Wisdom is Strength: HMS *Ganges*

Godfrey Place was serving with the Far East Fleet in March 1963 when he was informed by the Naval Secretary, Rear Admiral J.O.C. Hayes OBE, that it was planned to appoint him to HMS *Ganges* later that year. Place was asked if he 'could confirm that you have no strong personal reasons against being considered for this appointment?' Writing from Singapore, later that month, he replied:

Yes Sir! I would be thrilled to go to *Ganges*. Having been – for a little while – Commander of a training ship, I have a number of definite ideas and, although I am not a professional trainer by experience, I have seen the output in most walks of the Navy. I have a small additional reason ... a son at Oundle which is not very far away.

At the same time he was concerned with possible handover dates, not least because of the impact on his family. He pointed out he would see very little of his children from April 1962 to the Christmas holidays of 1963 and requested: 'If it were at all possible to delay my going to *Ganges* until after Christmas so I can have some of their holidays among their friends, I would be very grateful.'

In May 1963 the appointment was confirmed. Admiral Hayes, writing to Admiral Sir Wilfrid Woods GBE, KCB, DSO, Commander-in-Chief, Portsmouth, summarised Godfrey Place's career. He noted the 'remarkable diversity of experience and success', but interestingly failed to mention the award of the Victoria Cross until the last line of the letter:

It is fair to add that an apparent intolerance has at times aggravated his seniors. Second Sea Lord [Admiral Sir Royston Wright] and I have known Godfrey Place since we trained him as a cadet just before the war. He can be an awkward customer, but by the very scope of his experience he must clearly be considered for fairly, (if not very) high places in the future ... I think 'the mums' of *Ganges* would quite like a V.C. too.

In his reply, Woods agreed that Godfrey Place would do very well at *Ganges* and added: 'It is sufficiently isolated to make it difficult for him to "aggravate his seniors" there!'

Admirals Hayes and Wright appear to have drawn on their memories of Godfrey Place gained when both were serving as lieutenants in HMS *Vindictive* in 1938. At that time Place had made an impression on them, not least by his habit of placing drawing pins on Lieutenant Hayes' seat before he entered the classroom to instruct the cadets.

The Royal Naval Training Establishment, Shotley was founded in 1905 for the training of boys joining the Royal Navy, and adopted the name HMS *Ganges* in 1927. The establishment lay at the eastern end of the Shotley Peninsula, with the River Orwell to the north and the River Stour to the south. As Admiral Woods had pointed out, it was a relatively isolated area, so much so that in the winter of 1962-63 HMS *Ganges* had been totally cut off by snow.

In 1963 boys entered *Ganges* at the age of fifteen and effectively signed up for ten years of service in the Royal Navy, excluding the year at *Ganges*. It was a large establishment, with up to 2000 boys under training at any one time. Place assumed command on 12 December 1963, relieving Captain C.P. Norman DSO, DSC, who, like Place, had served with the 10th Flotilla at Malta in 1942. Place was the first and only Commanding Officer of *Ganges* to hold the Victoria Cross, although he was not the first Victoria Cross holder to serve there. In 1948 his fellow midget submariner, Lieutenant Commander Donald Cameron VC, had been appointed as a Divisional Officer at *Ganges*. Boys summoned to see him because of some misdemeanour remembered how easy it was to distract him into talking about midget submarines and the *Tirpitz*, so much so that he would forget why the boy had been summoned in the first place. (1) There were other links with the Victoria Cross through two 'old boys' of the establishment. Able Seaman Albert McKenzie had received the Victoria Cross for his part in the attack on Zeebrugge in HMS *Vindictive* in 1918 and Able Seaman James Magennis received the award for the attack on the Japanese cruiser *Takoa* in 1945.

Every five weeks, 120 new recruits arrived at Ipswich railway station to be met by navy buses and taken to Shotley. Place was extremely interested to know the boys' first impressions of *Ganges*, so quite frequently he would act as one of the coach drivers, paying particular attention to what was said during the five-mile run to *Ganges*. Wearing a naval driver's livery, he deliberately did not display the medal ribbon of the Victoria Cross. On arrival at *Ganges*, boys spent their first four weeks in a part called the Annexe. Here they were inspected by the Captain. Before the Captain arrived, the officer in charge would tell the boys to, 'look straight at Captain Place and not at his medal ribbons.' Place was, as might be expected, always well turned out and took obvious pride in his uniform, something noted very early on by the new recruits. Boys were in awe of him, most knowing that he was the man who had helped sink the *Tirpitz*, as portrayed in the 1955 film *Above us the Waves.* Pete Wilson joined *Ganges* in January 1965 and remembered:

> Captain Place inspected us in the entry block, and told us what was ahead of us. He was smaller than me, very slightly built but with piercing eyes. He spoke to each of us in turn, around thirty of us. Suddenly he was in front of me and of course I desperately wanted to look at the VC but did not dare as he was staring at me. He asked why I joined, and I replied that my Dad was in the Royal Navy in the Second World War as a radar operator, to which he replied, 'my regards to him.' I was much chuffed to think that he knew my Dad, until I heard he gave the same reply to all recruits regarding their naval relatives. For a boy of fifteen to meet the man who sank the *Tirpitz* it was a very proud moment.

Place ran a tight ship in *Ganges*. The regime was tough and boys grew up very quickly. In 1963 there was still corporal punishment, with boys receiving canings or 'cuts' for misdemeanours, for example leaving the site without authority ('going over the wall'). Other punishments included (for lateness in the morning) being forced to run around the parade ground wearing only pyjamas and carrying a mattress on the back, regardless of the weather. Boys also remembered the steep steps down to the water's edge, known as 'faith, hope and charity', with an incline of sixty degrees. Running up and down these at speed was another punishment. In many ways the regime had similarities to that which Place experienced at Dartmouth some thirty years earlier. One aspect of life at *Ganges* which caused him considerable concern was bullying. Brian Davies joined *Ganges* as the Gunnery Instructor in December 1963 and remembered seeing officers carrying sticks, which they used on the boys. Place had told Davies that if he had any concerns about what he saw that he should report directly to him, and not to any other officer. His confrontation of bullying appeared to be successful, and within six weeks of his appointment Place had started to change the culture; officers no longer carried sticks.

Boys at *Ganges* received basic instruction in a range of areas, including seamanship, wireless training, touch-typing and shooting. Although they spent a year at the establishment, boys had actually signed up for ten years. Place personally felt uneasy about this, although on several occasions he had to justify the Royal Navy's position in public. Charles Place remembers his father being interviewed on local television about this question and recalls that he appeared most ill at ease when defending the navy's position.

An iconic feature of *Ganges* was the mast in the parade ground. It was 143 feet high and at the top was a small platform or button, where the 'button boy' would stand. The mast had been removed from the corvette HMS *Cordelia* and then erected at Shotley in 1907. Climbing the mast was a traditional and mandatory part of training. On Sundays boys would practise the climb, and many later looked back and recognised how this 'wrought fear, challenged strength and gave satisfaction.'

Swimming was compulsory, and all new boys had to pass a swimming test. This involved jumping into the pool wearing overalls and treading water for three minutes. Many new recruits experienced their first near-drowning since most were not used to swimming in anything more than their trunks. In the first weeks at the Annexe boys had to take part in a boxing match, being matched for size. They were told to come out fighting without reserve, having been warned that the more timid they were, the longer the fight would last. The food at *Ganges* was lacking in both quality and quantity; food parcels were welcomed by the boys and invariably shared between friends.

Twice a term, Divisional Officers had to plan outings for the boys in their Division. Lieutenant Dick Husk was appointed a Divisional Officer in 1963 and, rather than take boys camping, decided on a sailing trip. Knowing that *Ganges*' two sailing cutters had been refitted at Chatham, he proposed taking a team of fifty junior seamen to sail them home. There was one slight problem; the weekend trip was scheduled for mid-November. He called on Place to outline his plan, which was deemed to be entirely satisfactory, but as Husk left the office Place asked, 'You can read a weather forecast like anyone else?' The party set off by coach and arrived at Chatham on Friday evening to find a Force 8 gale blowing and a Force 10 forecast for Saturday, when they were due to sail. Husk decided to postpone the trip for a day and sailed on the Sunday morning, when conditions were almost perfect, the wind having moderated to Force 4. The party arrived safely at *Ganges*, having sailed 50 miles in about ten hours, and on arrival Husk was summoned to see the Captain. He made his way to Place's office, thinking he was about to be congratulated on a well executed trip. On entering the office he was asked: 'Husk – why did you not sail on Saturday?' He answered that a Force 10 had been blowing. Place replied, 'When you set out to do something – do it. Had you lost a couple of boys that would have been unfortunate but all part of the experience.'

Since 1905 the Captain of HMS *Ganges* had lived at Erwarton Hall, an imposing sixteenth century country house about two miles away. Anne Boleyn spent some of her childhood there, and legend has it that her heart was buried in the grounds after her execution. The property had been leased from the University of Oxford for many years and in 1959 it was offered for sale. After much debate, indecision and delay, the Admiralty purchased it in June 1962 for the sum of £11,000. (2) This led to questions being raised in the House of Commons by a retired naval officer, Commander Harry Pursey MP (Kingston upon Hull, East). He wished to know how many rooms were in the house and how far it was from HMS *Ganges* itself. Significant improvement works were undertaken the following year to make the house safe for occupation. When Godfrey Place and his family arrived in December 1963 work was still ongoing, so they lived in a house at Shotley, next door to the Commander. Amongst the improvements undertaken was the installation of fire escapes. As the building was 'listed', external fire escapes were out of the question, so a number of Davey escape harnesses were fitted. Once installed, they had to be tested, and Charles Place remembered how a boy from *Ganges* was sent over to make a test escape. His descent was somewhat clumsy and he managed to put a foot through one of the ancient windows. Considerable time was then spent locating the glass fragments, and restoration experts were then employed to repair the window.

When the family moved into Erwarton Hall it soon became apparent that it was rather isolated. Although it had its own grounds, some of which were turned over to tennis courts by Althea, Melanie Place found it lonely, especially as her brother and sister were away at school. She remembered her frustration boiling over one day when she argued with her father, saying, 'All I want is a dog.' He replied, 'I have been looking for one for you for the last month.' In the end, Godfrey Place acquired Prince, a one-year-old golden retriever who was being rehomed. Prince was very unruly and totally unsuitable as a pet, and it was left to Althea to take him across the water to training classes in Harwich. Eventually Prince settled down to become a much loved addition to the family.

A number of staff were assigned to Erwarton Hall, including a cook, steward and bosun. Often they appeared to have been thrown in at the deep end, with little if any qualifications or experience for the position. The cook may well have known how to peel potatoes on board an aircraft carrier but often had little idea about how to prepare meals for visitors such as the First Sea Lord. Place found it hard to cope with those whose standards did not come up to his own; staff were dismissed if they failed to produce food to the correct standard. Tony Kenber remembered one incident when visiting his uncle and aunt. They had just sat down for lunch and the steward brought a joint of beef into the dining room. The beef fell off the server on to the carpet in front of all the guests. Kenber recalled that his uncle went ballistic and instructed the steward to 'go and wipe the bloody thing off under the tap!' On more than one occasion Althea had to salvage a culinary disaster in the kitchen whilst her husband entertained hungry guests.

Erwarton Hall was on the running route for the boys, and John Lefaucheur remembered an occasion when he and a number of other boys were out on a run. Believing that they were out of sight, they walked past Erwarton Hall, only to be seen by Place as he left the property. He rang up the officer in charge, and on returning to *Ganges* they were ordered to run another circuit. Despite this, many years later Lefaucheur described Place as 'the last of the true naval officers.'

Place's appointment to *Ganges* meant he would not be far from Charles at Oundle School, although due to his naval commitments he only visited the school a few times as a parent. However, he did visit in his professional capacity, since amongst the duties of the Captain of HMS *Ganges* was the inspection of cadet forces in the eastern region, including Oundle, where Charles was a member of the Naval Cadet Force. Its members were, invariably, those with the least interest in military training. Charles remembered his father inspecting the Naval Cadet Force, being thoroughly unimpressed by what he found and subsequently sending a stern report to the staff member in charge. Place did not support the idea of cadet forces, believing them to be amateur organisations, and he felt keenly that there was only room for the full- time professional in the navy.

Discipline at HMS *Ganges* was strict, both at Shotley and 'over the water' at Harwich and Felixstowe, where there would be patrols by members of the regulating branch. It was only after three months that the boys were allowed to 'go ashore', and then only on a Sunday afternoon. Boys found out of the establishment without authority would be apprehended and punished. Charles recalled an incident when, aged about fifteen, he was returning home from a cadet camp held at Lossiemouth. He arrived at Harwich railway station late in the evening and was still wearing part of his uniform. He was stopped by regulators who believed he was a *Ganges* boy out without permission. He then explained that he was in fact the Captain's son; they had heard many excuses before but not that one! Fortunately, Althea was able to come across from Erwarton and resolve the issue.

Open days at *Ganges* were an opportunity to invite not only families and friends, but also guests from outside. Amongst those invited were members of the Naval Cadet Force at Oundle, who had received such a poor report from Place on his inspection. Charles Place remembered that the journey was stressful; the minibus broke down on the way and the master in charge lost his way. The party arrived just in time for the start of the official displays; again they had not made a good impression on the Captain of *Ganges*.

As Captain of *Ganges*, it fell to Place to present prizes to boys. Dennis Rigley received a signed copy of a book from him and remembered, 'a man of small stature but with an air of calmness about him.' Clive Matthews won the school prize and the communications efficiency prize in his year, and both were presented by Place. He remembered Place as a small man who 'always had time to talk to you' and was not at all fearsome. Clive's school prize was a book, *HM Destroyers*, signed by Godfrey Place. Nearly fifty years later he remembered receiving the book from the only man he had ever seen wearing a Victoria Cross. The book remained Clive's pride and joy, which he was keen to show off, since 'who else had a book signed by a very famous admiral?' Although boys may have been in awe of Place, it did not stop them giving him a nickname. Jim Worlding remembered that he was called 'Fishy' in his mess. Little did he or his colleagues know that this was Godfrey Place's nickname when he was at the Grange School some thirty-five years earlier. The origin of the name was unclear to Jim Worlding, but he suggested that, 'The midget submarines were called "tin fish", and it would have been unbelievable that a person called Place in a mini-sub did not get the name Fishy.'

David Evans joined *Ganges* in 1964 and remembered Place as quite short but of average build. He spoke very quietly, and boys often had to crane their necks in order to catch what he said. He remembered one Sunday afternoon being on duty at the main gate when Place unexpectedly appeared. He said, 'Excuse me Sir, but I know that's the Victoria Cross but what are all the other medals?' Place proceeded to point out the Distinguished Service Cross, the Polish Cross of Valour and other medals. 'All for blowing up the *Tirpitz*?' Place replied, 'Yes,' smiled, and went on his way.

At the end of the year, boys left *Ganges* and continued their training at other establishments in the Royal Navy. This might be another shore establishment or a sea-going posting. On leaving *Ganges* they received a card signed by the Captain wishing them the best for their future career. It provided guidance on the way they should behave, and pointed out that the 'most important thing to have learnt at *Ganges* is instant and cheerful obedience. The navy depends on it.' Another telling observation was, 'It is fairly easy to do your job when things are going right, it takes a man to produce the results when life appears black.' Many looked back on their time at *Ganges* with a mixture of gratitude and relief: gratitude for what they learnt and how it influenced their life in the Royal Navy and later; relief that they had only spent a year there and were moving on, usually to less austere establishments. Colin Davies moved to HMS *Mercury*, the signals training school, which compared to *Ganges* was like Butlins. However, those who had been at *Ganges* during Godfrey Place's appointment in command remembered that they had been trained by a war hero.

In October 1965 it was time for Place to leave *Ganges* to command the commando carrier HMS *Albion*. As he relinquished his command he was 'towed ashore' in a Seahawk aircraft that was maintained for training purposes at Shotley, an occasion which featured in the national press. His time at *Ganges* was recognised as a success; it was recorded that he had 'dealt successfully and without fuss with the problems of a very large entry in 1964, combined with renovation works to the school buildings.' Interestingly, Admiral Sir Wilfrid Woods, who had been somewhat critical of him prior to his appointment, wrote positively, noting:

An extremely able officer and an outstanding leader with a refreshing and wide ranging mind. 'Eager' without being too much of a 'beaver.'

This time senior officers did not feel the need to mark down the scores in his confidential report.

Chapter 14

Strongly, Trustworthy, Happily: Command of *HMS Albion*

Godfrey Place and his family left Erwarton Hall in late 1965 and moved back home to Corton Denham, where they spent Christmas, a celebration that he always enjoyed but one which could be uncomfortable for the family. Place insisted that everything to do with Christmas had to be just right; festive decorations had to be exact, and this pursuit of excellence caused inevitable friction with the rest of the family, who wished to have a more relaxed occasion. Early in 1966, he flew to Hong Kong to assume command of HMS *Albion*. Often called 'The Old Grey Ghost', *Albion* was a 'Centaur' class aircraft carrier, laid down in 1944 but not launched until 1947. Post-war financial constraints delayed her commissioning until 1953. Place had encountered *Albion* earlier in his career; she was one of three fixed-wing aircraft carriers in 'Operation Musketeer' in November 1956 and had been the flagship for the Fleet Review at Invergordon in May 1957. *Albion* served as a fixed-wing aircraft carrier until January 1961, when she entered an eighteen-month refit at Portsmouth and was converted to a Landing Platform Helicopter (LPH), more commonly referred to as a 'commando carrier'. During the refit the catapults and arrestor wires were removed and additional mess decks were provided for the embarked commando; some of her armaments were also removed, allowing four landing craft (LCVPs) to be installed. *Albion* recommissioned, after the refit, in August 1962. (1)

It was early in 1965 that Place had discussed his next appointment with the Naval Secretary, Rear Admiral W.D. O'Brien DSC, when he visited HMS *Ganges*. The likelihood of command of an aircraft carrier was mentioned, and Place later wrote to the Naval Secretary: 'I would prefer a fixed wing, but I always enjoy wherever I am sent and wouldn't at all wish to try and pick jobs for myself.'

In July 1965 he was informed that his appointment as Commanding Officer of HMS *Albion* had been approved; it was an appointment that would bring plenty of adventure and excitement. Three months earlier, *Albion* arrived in the Far East under the command of Captain J.H. Adams MVO, relieving her sister ship HMS *Bulwark*. Through her amphibious capabilities she supported troops involved in the confrontation with Indonesia on the island of Borneo. HMS *Albion* spent Christmas at Singapore and sailed on New Year's Day to Hong Kong, arriving on 5 January 1966. Place boarded *Albion* at 09.00 on 12 January; later that day he wrote in the ship's log:

> 14.55 Rear Admiral J.H. Adams MVO left ship. Captain B.C.G. Place VC, DSC, assumed command. (2)

Admiral Adams had commanded *Albion* for two years and his next appointment was to be Assistant Chief of the Naval Staff (Policy) at the Admiralty. This was an appointment that was always highly sought after; if undertaken well it could be a stepping stone to higher things. In contrast, failure might be considered a 'hanging offence'. The issue of future naval aviation was to dominate Adams' time at the Admiralty, marked by the resignation of the First Sea Lord in response to the Defence White paper of 1966.

After Place had paid a number of official calls in Hong Kong he took *Albion* to sea. On 15 January she sailed to Singapore in the company of HMAS *Vendetta* and arrived three days later, having undertaken exercises en route. Place's first approach to Singapore Naval Base in command of *Albion* was undertaken in torrential rain and zero visibility due to a tropical storm but, despite these distractions, was completed without incident. At Singapore, *Albion* embarked men of 2nd Battalion The Royal Green Jackets, who had already endured an uncomfortable train journey from Penang to Singapore. On 21 January *Albion* arrived off Labuan, an island to the north-east of Brunei. Two days later she sailed to Tawau on the south-east of Sabah (part of Malaysia), where the troops were ferried ashore, both by landing craft and by Wessex helicopters of 848 Squadron, to bases deep within the jungle. They relieved men of the 1st Battalion The Scots Guards, and the roulement was completed in two and a half hours; the helicopters lifted over 900 men and 62,000lbs of stores in that time. The Commanding Officer of the Royal Green Jackets, Lieutenant Colonel E.N.W. Bramall MC,[1] recalled the operation as one of the slickest he had ever seen. During his time on *Albion*, he recalled, his men were well looked after and his officers were very impressed by the competitive price of gin in the wardroom. He encountered Godfrey Place briefly on the passage and was struck by how considerate he was.

---

1. Later Field Marshall The Lord Bramall KG, GCB, OBE, MC, Chief of the Defence Staff 1982-1985.

The confrontation in Borneo had started in December 1962, when British troops were urgently deployed to Brunei to counter an incursion by insurgents from neighbouring Indonesia. The British forces included Royal Marine commandos landed from HMS *Albion*, at the request of the Sultan of Brunei. Over the ensuing years there had been continued jungle fighting, much of which took place close to the border and involved, at times, incursions into Indonesian territory. Since the start of the confrontation, the Royal Navy, through the commando carriers, had played a critical role in providing helicopter support to troops in Sarawak and Sabah, being able to move troops in a matter of hours, as against at least a day by boat and on foot.

After the roulement, *Albion* sailed to Singapore, arriving on 28 January. Whilst 848's helicopters flew off to RNAS Sembawang in Singapore to continue training, Place took the opportunity to fly with them, and 848 Squadron log records: 'Flying in this time included Wessex familiarisations for the new Captain.' After nearly two weeks alongside, the helicopters rejoined *Albion* and she sailed to the Labuan area in the company of HMS *Duchess* and *Anchorite* to take part in 'Exercise Flying Foot'. *Albion* had embarked 40 Commando Royal Marines and was flying the flag of Commodore Amphibious Forces (COMAF), Commodore H.L. Lloyd DSC. On 14 February troops were landed by helicopter at Kota Belud in Sarawak. Place and Commodore Lloyd landed by helicopter in the afternoon and spent time meeting leaders of the local Dayaks, being entertained in traditional long houses. The troops re-embarked four days later, and *Albion*, along with the other ships, departed to Singapore. As might be expected, Place had made an impression on his visitors, and on returning to Singapore *Albion* received a signal from COMAF: 'I continue to be impressed by *Albion*'s efficiency and thoroughly enjoyed my visit.' Another visitor to *Albion* at this time was the Commander-in-Chief, Far East Fleet, Vice Admiral Sir Frank Twiss KCB, DSC, no great supporter of Godfrey Place. Twiss had the reputation of being 'somewhat strange' in his way of thinking and acting; many suggested that this was a result of his time as a prisoner of war of the Japanese following the sinking of HMS *Exeter* in 1942.

Despite being nearly 7,000 miles from home, Place was again in the news; his appointment to *Albion* featured in the national newspapers. On 14 February the *Daily Telegraph* carried a picture of him on the bridge of *Albion*, and reported:

Captain B.C.G. Place, the only holder of the Victoria Cross still serving in the Royal Navy on the bridge of the Commando Carrier HMS *Albion*, 23,000 tons of which he has taken over the command of in the Far East.

This was ironic, since the front page of the same edition carried a headline announcing the likely axing of aircraft carriers. The Defence White Paper produced by Denis Healey in February 1966 indicated that the proposed new aircraft carrier, CVA-01, was to be cancelled. The result was turmoil in the Admiralty and the resignation of the First Sea Lord, something which directly affected Place the following year. The scrapping of CVA-01 followed a decision in 1965 to cancel the proposed multi-role aircraft for the RAF, the TSR2, and purchase the American F-111 instead. The news would have been poorly received by Godfrey Place, who had not only seen the importance of aircraft carriers during his career, but was also a strong supporter of the British designed TSR2. It was also announced that British forces would withdraw from Aden following the country's independence – a decision that would directly impact on Place in his new command.

Soon after the announcement of the Defence White Paper, Prime Minister Harold Wilson announced that there would be a general election on 31 March. His majority was only four following the election in 1964, and he hoped to increase it. Althea had planned to visit Singapore and spend time with her husband, so left the Old Bakery in the capable hands of Andrea, Charles and Melanie. Charles remembered that one day they found a number of 'Vote Conservative' posters had been erected in the garden. The children presumed their father would have agreed, but they were less than impressed and not only removed the posters but replaced them with some supporting the Labour Party.

HMS *Albion* spent all March in dry dock undergoing maintenance, and during this period many of the crew moved ashore and were accommodated in HMS *Terror*. Place took leave and was joined by Althea. He also spent more time flying with 848 Squadron, under the instruction of Lieutenant Holcroft. Several officers joined the ship at Singapore, including a new Air Engineering Officer, Commander D.G. 'Pug' Mather. Place knew Mather from their time in the Fleet Air Arm; they had trained together in 23RN Course at Syerston and with 736 Squadron at RNAS Culdrose before serving with 801 Squadron in HMS *Glory*. Mather had been shot down in January 1953 and his obituary was placed in the Naval List for 1953, although he had actually been taken prisoner. He endured appalling conditions in a North Korean prison, being kept in a cell only five feet high and tortured by his captors. In August 1953 he was one of a small number of prisoners to be repatriated and later resumed his career with the Royal Navy.

Having left dry dock in early April, *Albion* undertook preparations for her next deployment. On 19 April helicopters of 848 Squadron rejoined the ship and the next day she sailed for Labuan in the company of HMS *Ajax* and

Anchorite. Albion returned to Singapore, embarked 40 Commando and sailed to Kuching Bay, Sarawak, where troops were landed to relieve 42 Commando. In May *Albion* sailed to Kobe in Japan for an official visit that lasted eight days. The visit coincided with the arrival of typhoon Imra, which brought two days of extremely wet and windy weather and blew the cherry blossom off the trees. A cocktail party on board *Albion* was noted to be a 'chilly ordeal' due to the unusually cold and wet weather. *Albion* was, however, a major attraction, and despite the unfavourable conditions some 4,000 visitors came on board when she was open to the public. With the round of official engagements completed, *Albion* departed for exercises off the coast of Borneo, before returning to Singapore in early June.

The next two weeks were spent preparing for 'Exercise Longhop', which took place in the area near Pulau Tiomen, off the east coast of the Malayan peninsula. The Flag Officer Second in Command, Far East Fleet, Rear Admiral C. P. Mills CBE, DSC, flew his flag in *Albion*. 'Exercise Longhop' lasted ten days, and *Albion* then returned to Singapore, where the newly appointed COMAF, Commodore D.A. Dunbar-Nasmith DSC, visited Place. The two knew each other from their days at Dartmouth; Place was one term behind the Commodore. His father, Admiral Sir Martin Dunbar-Nasmith VC, had been part of the inspection team of the Royal Naval College, Dartmouth in 1935, soon after Place had joined. In middle of July *Albion* sailed to Hong Kong and then returned to Singapore via Labuan. By this time the Indonesian confrontation had ended, a ceasefire having been signed at the end of May.

Albion was soon to leave the Far East, and on 9 August Place entertained Vice Admiral Sir Frank Twiss and his wife at a farewell dinner on board. Two days later, *Albion* sailed with HMS *Salisbury* to the island of Gan and then on to Aden and through the Suez Canal. She rendezvoused with *Bulwark* in the Red Sea, allowing stores to be transferred, and Place flew to *Bulwark* to pay a visit to her Commanding Officer, Captain D.B. Law DSC. *Albion* had been away from home for nearly eighteen months, and the crew did not wish to dawdle. It was noted that, 'A full power trial was not carried out in the Suez Canal, but no time was lost on the way home.' *Albion* reached Malta on 31 August and after a brief stop sailed to Gibraltar and then home, arriving in Plymouth Sound on 7 September. Helicopters of 848 Squadron flew off to their parent air station at RNAS Culdrose, and *Albion* sailed to Portsmouth, arriving the following day. The ship was to undergo a refit and, following removal of ammunition and stores, she entered dry dock in early November. She remained in dry dock until February 1967, when she was refloated and moved to Middle Slip Jetty.

The commissioning service for *Albion* was held on Thursday, 6 April 1967, a grey and overcast day befitting the 'Old Grey Ghost'. Sir Norman Tailyour KCB, DSO*, Commandant General, Royal Marines, was the guest of honour; he had served with Godfrey Place in HMS *Theseus* when he commanded 45 Commando.(3) In true naval tradition, Althea cut the commissioning cake, watched by her husband. Four days later, helicopters of 848 Squadron flew back to *Albion* from RNAS Culdrose, and the rest of the month was spent undertaking trials, mostly at Spithead; she was starting to take shape again as a commando carrier. Lieutenant Commander R.D.D. 'Derek' Bamford joined *Albion* as first lieutenant in April and on arrival visited Godfrey Place who told him: 'You are as safe as houses ... I fired your predecessor and if I fire you then the Admiralty will come down on me like a ton of bricks.'

On 1 May *Albion* departed to Liverpool, sailing through the rough Irish Sea, having embarked Commander-in-Chief Plymouth, Vice Admiral Sir A.A. Fitzroy Talbot KBE, CB, DSO*. The arrival of *Albion* made front-page headlines in the *Liverpool Echo* ('Navy Puts on a Pierhead Spectacular'); as the ship arrived, seventeen Wessex helicopters were flying overhead. The visit was to commemorate the Battle of the Atlantic, and *Albion* arrived at Princes Pier on 5 May. Over the next three days there were a number of official engagements, and Place attended the memorial service at Liverpool Cathedral on 7 May. The ship was open to visitors, who had to contend with heavy rains that soaked the flight deck, making conditions underfoot somewhat treacherous. Place also received one special visitor: Ian Fraser VC, Commanding Officer of XE3, who lived nearby in Wallasey and came on board at the invitation of the Captain. (4)

Albion left Liverpool and sailed south to Portland and continued her work up, under the watchful eye of the Flag Officer Sea Training. As part of the programme *Albion* undertook a degaussing run off the south coast which entailed steaming at speed through a measured distance. On the appointed day it was foggy and there were no visible landmarks on land. Derek Bamford remembered that the ship sailed quite close to the coast in rather shallow water. All the team were up on the bridge with Place, who took the more junior officers through the exercise. After a couple of runs the fog lifted and landmarks became visible, at which point Place said, 'Right, over to you, you can finish,' and left the bridge. Derek Bamford felt this clearly demonstrated Place's standing as a Commanding Officer; a less able or experienced one would not even have started the exercise in those conditions, let alone handed over when he did.

It was not only his officers who had great respect for Place. Mike McAllister, a junior seaman in *Albion*, recalled:

Captain Place commanded great respect from his junior officers and subordinate ranks alike. He was what we called 'an officer and a gentleman'. Captain Place was always smartly turned out, as smart as a guardsman every single day. He set the example above normal naval training and discipline. If he asked you to do something, he actually said 'Thank you' afterwards. This made a tremendous difference and was picked up very quickly by everyone on board. You weren't ordered like the orders given by younger inexperienced officers. When these officers ordered young sailors, the sailors took their time deliberately. Whenever any major event was imminent on board *Albion*, he always planned well in advance and rehearsed the event thoroughly with his officers. I often saw him in the amphibious operations room with various commanders of each section and the brief was checked and double checked before we went into action on every occasion. He was of shortish build but with dark eyes of steel and bushy eyebrows, yet he commanded so much respect. He seemed to have his fingers on every pulse and always knew what was going on. We saw him as the loneliest man on the ship but would do anything for him. He often used to appear on the bridge in the middle watch unexpectedly (2359-0400) and every look-out would be tested by him as to what he could see through the binoculars.

There were further exercises in the English Channel and South West approaches, followed by a three-day visit to Plymouth. Having embarked 41 Commando and 145 Battery Royal Artillery, *Albion* sailed north to the Bristol Channel and undertook 'Exercise Dry Fly' off Lundy. By 26 May *Albion* was in the waters near Mull and commenced amphibious exercises, landing marines by LCVP. Early the next day, *Albion* launched a search and rescue mission for the Israeli submarine *Leviathan* that had reported two men washed overboard whilst off the coast near Stranraer. Helicopters were scrambled and spent over two hours searching the area, but the mission was unsuccessful. 'Exercise Dry Fly' continued over the following four days at Red Bay off the coast of Northern Ireland. However, on 31 May *Albion* received a number of urgent signals that led to a rapid change in the deployment, taking her and her Commanding Officer to a potential conflict zone in West Africa.

Nigeria had gained independence from Britain in October 1960, but this was followed by periods of political unrest and, in 1966, a series of military coups. The country had three major tribal groups: the Hausa in the north, the Yoruba in the west and the Ibo in the east. Following tribal clashes and increasing tension between the federal and regional governments, the eastern region, under the leadership of Colonel Ojukwu, served intention to declare independence in 1967. The Ministry of Defence had kept a watching brief on developments and by March 1967 had formed two plans for the possible evacuation of British citizens from Nigeria; codenamed 'Allgood' and 'Credence', both initially involved the securing of airfields at Kano and Lagos by means of a parachute assault. Once secured, the airfields would allow transport aircraft to evacuate citizens either to Malta or directly to Britain. Both plans required a significant naval contribution and envisaged the deployment of either a strike carrier or a commando carrier. Plans for evacuation of as many as 21,000 British citizens from Nigeria were formalised in the middle of April, and it was noted that up to 4,300 were based in the eastern region, mostly employed in the oil industry. As tensions rose in Nigeria, the Defence Operations Executive of the Ministry of Defence identified HMS *Albion* as the nearest deployable carrier. She was alongside in Portsmouth at that time, about to depart for Liverpool, and it was estimated that she could reach the coast of Nigeria within twelve days. (5)

On 31 May Colonel Ojukwu informed the world that eastern Nigeria was declaring independence, effective from midnight, and the new state of Biafra came into existence. Some 3,000 miles way, Godfrey Place and the crew of *Albion* had to rapidly plan for a deployment to the Atlantic. At 08.00 'Exercise Dry Fly' was in progress, commandos were landing by helicopters to assault gun emplacements at Red Bay. At 14.45 a signal was received ordering *Albion* to proceed to Gibraltar at full speed. The Captain's secretary rushed to flying control and asked for Commander (Air) to arrange for him to be sent ashore urgently to inform the Commando that they had to embark immediately. All troops had returned to *Albion* by 18.00, and she sailed south. (6) By 05.00, 1 June she was off the coast of Cornwall and a helicopter shuttle to and from RNAS Culdrose took place, allowing *Albion* to embark more helicopters as well as extra stores. The real possibility of having to evacuate civilians was apparent in the material embarked; Derek Bamford remembered that 5,000 Tampax were driven down from Scotland to Culdrose before being loaded by helicopter. He was responsible for storage of the extra material and remembered it as 'a bit of a nightmare'. The rapid deployment of *Albion* curtailed the ship's ability to fully work up after her refit. Place later wrote that she had only fared so well over the coming seven months because a large number of officers and men in key positions had returned to the ship in April 1967 from the previous commission.

The crew of *Albion* were unsure where they were going, although some believed that as they were on a war footing they would be deployed to the Middle East. Tensions were rising in this area of the world. In the middle of

May President Nasser had mobilised all Egyptian reserve forces, a move that was followed by mobilisation of Israeli reserves. On 23 May Nasser closed the Straits of Tiran to Israeli ships, blocking their use of the Gulf of Aqaba and the port of Eilat. This move was taken as an act of war by the Israelis, and tensions were further increased by Nasser declaring that the Suez Canal would be blockaded if any foreign powers attempted to interfere in the area. By the beginning of June it appeared not to be a question of whether war would break out, but when.

HMS *Albion* arrived at Gibraltar at 01.00 on 3 June and took on more stores and fuel, the operation carried out partly under the dockyard's floodlights. More pilots from 848 Squadron joined the ship; some had said goodbye to their colleagues at RNAS Culdrose some three days previously, only to find that they were flown down to Gibraltar. Four helicopters landed on *Albion*, making a total of twenty-two embarked. *Albion* left Gibraltar and initially sailed south east, but once out of sight of land she turned and sailed along the north coast of Africa to enter the Atlantic again. Luck had been on the side of *Albion*; her brief visit to Gibraltar had taken place just a few days before further Anglo–Spanish talks were due to take place regarding the future of the colony. Over the next five days A*lbion* sailed south at 20 knots to arrive on 8 June at a position 5 degrees north of the equator, some 150 miles from the Nigerian coast. Place gave orders for *Albion* to avoid all ships by at least twelve miles, and helicopters were not permitted to fly. (7)

Although *Albion's* mission was classified as secret, her departure from home waters had not gone unnoticed. The Ministry of Defence were aware that publicity surrounding her departure could easily put at risk British personnel in Nigeria and might also inflame the situation in the Middle East. Although they were willing to admit that *Albion* had left Scotland, there was to be official 'stonewalling' regarding her destination. Both national and regional newspapers attempted to report on *Albion's* progress. On 1 June 1967 *The Times* reported that '*Albion* sails on secret mission … commanded by Captain Basil Place who won the VC for his wartime exploits with midget submarines.' On the same day, the *Daily Telegraph* reported, 'The Commando carrier *Albion* 23,000 tons sailed for the Red Sea via the Cape of Good Hope' and that she had been ordered to reinforce British forces south of Suez. The paper stated that a decision had been made that *Albion* would not pass through the Suez Canal so as not to inflame the situation in the Middle East. On 3 June the *Daily Express* reported that *Albion* was in the Atlantic. In response to these and other stories, the Ministry of Defence realised that their 'stonewalling' would no longer be appropriate and released a short statement on 5 June:

The move of *Albion* has no connection with events in the Middle East or the Mediterranean. She has sailed as a precautionary measure to be available in the Atlantic.

Off the coast of Nigeria, Place oversaw the finalisation of the evacuation plan; this was to involve the initial establishment of bases at Port Harcourt and Calabar which would also serve as fuel dumps, allowing helicopters to fly up country if necessary. *Albion*'s LCVPs would be used to transfer people from the coast out to the ship. On 10 June Place informed the Ministry of Defence of the evacuation strategy, and it was estimated that within two hours they would be able to start evacuating 200 people per hour. On board, the crew were making preparation for new arrivals; *Albion*'s hangar was converted into accommodation space with about 500 camp beds.

The British government were keen not to become involved in Nigeria's internal affairs and, aware of newspaper reports about *Albion*'s departure, informed both General Gowon, the Head of State of Nigeria, and Colonel Ojukwu of *Albion*'s presence, advising that she was there solely to allow evacuation of British citizens, if needed. Over the following days *Albion* steamed at about 5 knots off the coast of Nigeria, well out of sight. Although the Ministry of Defence had decided that Place would be the Commander of 'Operation Credence' if it were to occur, he would only assume the title of COMBRITSNIG (Commander British Forces Nigeria) once the operation commenced. Civilians were already leaving Nigeria, by chartered aircraft and civilian ships from Port Harcourt, and despite the rhetoric from both sides there was no fighting as yet. (8)

Boredom was starting to set in on board *Albion*, and Place obtained permission for helicopters to fly, but only to a height of some 50 feet. The isolation was also broken to some degree by the arrival of RFA *Tidespring* with stores and much sought-after mail. The flight deck of *Albion* at times resembled a holiday camp, as the crew made the most of the tropical conditions, fishing being a favourite pastime. Down below, the heat was causing problems, especially in the boiler rooms where crew had to wrap their hands in cloths before attempting to climb the ladders.

The secrecy of the mission also affected friends and relatives back home. They read a number of stories in the newspapers, but the official line from the Royal Navy was that 'all are safe and well'. In retrospect, it was felt that the Ministry of Defence did not handle the situation well but hopefully learnt a lot for the next time. At home in Corton Denham, Melanie Place, now thirteen years old, had been attending school as a day girl. It was decided that she should board at nearby Sherborne School in the light of the uncertainty in the family with her father away. Melanie was most unhappy about this; she had seen both her sister and brother attend boarding schools and knew just how unhappy they had been. She was very upset, not least because it meant separation from the family dog Prince, who had now settled down in his new home. Sending his daughters to boarding school was at odds with what Godfrey Place had believed when he was first married. In a letter from Marlag in 1944 he wrote: 'I think there ought to be laws against boarding schools for girls.' However, he had yet to realise the impact long periods away from home would have on family dynamics and the pressures this would place on Althea.

By 23 June it was becoming difficult to maintain *Albion* in her waiting position. It was suggested that if she were to remain there for any length of time she should have some time alongside, perhaps at the Azores. Similarly, if she were to stay in the Atlantic past the middle of July this would prevent her planned departure in September to cover the withdrawal from Aden. Later that day, it was decided that *Albion* should return home, and two days later she sailed north to Gibraltar arriving on 1 July, when leave was granted. She had been at sea for a month. The Royal Marines made the most of their time ashore, leaving a wake of devastation, before *Albion* sailed home to arrive at Plymouth on 5 July.

Albion's arrival at Plymouth allowed helicopters of 848 Squadron to fly to RNAS Culdrose, and *Albion* was to enter Devonport to allow the rest of the squadron to disembark. On arrival there was heavy weather, and the Queen's Harbour Master wanted *Albion* to stand off for a day before entering harbour. Place was not inclined to take this advice and was determined that he would get the ship alongside that day. The approach was somewhat challenging, but *Albion* moored alongside without event. Having successfully brought her home, Place left his ship saying, 'Now I can get to my daughter's 21st birthday party.' Two days later, *Albion* departed for Portsmouth, arriving on 8 July. Her deployment was still secret, and when Place was interviewed by *Navy News* he responded: 'I am not allowed to reveal my orders yet. The mystery which seems to have been building up around our movements will have to remain for the time being.' (9) The mystery remained for some time, and the Commission book covering 1967 to 1968 had scant coverage of the operation.

The remainder of July and all of August were spent at Portsmouth. Place took leave in early August, and later that month the ship was open for Navy Days. He also organised an unusual entertainment for the ship's company by extending an invitation to Billy Smart's circus. The circus duly arrived and performed, with high wires rigged across the flight deck and elephants strolling along the quayside not far from HMS *Victory*.

In early September *Albion* prepared to depart for the Middle East, via the Cape, the Suez Canal having been closed following the Six Day War in June. She left Portsmouth on 7 September, and on the previous day Place had entertained five holders of the Victoria Cross and three holders of the George Cross for lunch, including Brigadier the Rt Hon. Sir John Smyth VC, MC, Mr Robert Cain VC and Mrs Odette Hallowes GC.[2] The occasion was noted in *The Times*, which under the title of 'Flag rank of lonely VC' reported Place's forthcoming promotion to Rear Admiral and stated that he was, 'The only serving officer holding the Victoria Cross in any of the three services.' (10) The paper was forced to apologise two days later when it was drawn to their attention that Lieutenant Colonel P.A. Porteous VC was still serving with the Royal Artillery; he had won the Victoria Cross for his part in the raid on Dieppe in August 1942.[3]

Having sailed from Portsmouth, *Albion* arrived at Devonport where 848 Squadron embarked from RNAS Culdrose. The ship then proceeded to take part in 'Exercise Last Fling' off the south coast of Devon with 41 Commando.

On 13 September *Albion* sailed south, on her way to South Africa. The ship crossed the equator on 20 September and C.P.O. P.G. 'Bill' Clarke was to play King Neptune in the ceremony of 'crossing the line.' He was in charge of the aircraft workshop and had met Godfrey Place on several occasions on Captain's rounds, during which he was always interested to know what was going on in the workshop, although he came across as rather reserved. The day before the ceremony, Bill Clarke was invited to the Captain's cabin. Place knew full well that as Commanding Officer he could expect to be put in the pool, but told Bill Clarke that he needed warning when he was about to be thrown in. Although not afraid of water, he did not like the idea of going in unexpectedly. A plan was hatched. King Neptune would say, 'I now award you the Royal Barge', and at the same time he would stomach-butt the Captain and push him into the pool. The plan worked well, and the ceremony went off without a hitch.

The ship passed the Cape of Good Hope late on 26 September and early

---

2. The others attending were: Major General Sir Henry Foote VC, Rev. Harold Woolley VC, Lieutenant Colonel R.L. Haine VC, Air Marshall Sir Lawrence Sinclair GC and Miss Dorothy Thomas GC.
3. At that time there were two other serving members of the Army who had been awarded the Victoria Cross: William Speakman VC, who received the award in 1951 for action in Korea, and Rambahdur Limbu VC, who was awarded the Victoria Cross for gallantry in operations in Indonesia in November 1965.

on 29 September arrived at Durban, to be greeted by the 'Lady in White' (Mrs Perla Siedle Gibson), who sang for the ship from the jetty. The arrival of *Albion* was the first occasion that a ship of her size of the Royal Navy had visited Durban since 1959. Over the ensuing six days Place had a somewhat strenuous time, making a number of official calls as well as playing host to many visitors, including the Mayor of Durban and several Members of Parliament. The ship's activities included being open to visitors and hosting a children's party.

The visit by *Albion* had led to heated questions in the House of Commons in May 1967, when Willie Hamilton MP demanded that the visit be banned, suggesting it was 'tantamount to condoning apartheid.' David Winnick MP enquired what would happen to members of the ship's crew who might be liable to discrimination during the visit, and was informed that any who might be affected would be given the opportunity to withdraw before the visit. In fact, there were two or three coloured members of the ship's crew at the time. The visit was a success, although the detractors in Westminster did not appear to read the *Durban Herald*, which reported that amongst their numerous activities, several members of the ship's crew donated blood to the local transfusion service. HMS *Albion* sailed on 4 October in high winds and, at Place's invitation, the 'Lady in White' sang from the flight deck as the ship left harbour; she was then flown ashore by helicopter.

Albion sailed north and when passing Mombasa made a special delivery. The Resident Naval Officer had asked *Albion* to transport a brand new Mercedes car for him from England. It had been loaded at Portsmouth and would be carried gratis, but the owner had to accept possible delay or damage. Originally it had been planned for *Albion* to visit Mombasa and unload the car. However, with the ever changing situation in Aden, the visit was cancelled. As the ship was passing Mombasa, the car was hoisted by helicopter on to a small freighter for delivery. During the operation the load started to swing, and to ensure the safety of the helicopter the car had to be jettisoned into the sea, provoking a huge cheer from the watching crowd assembled on the flight deck.

Aden, a barren and uninviting land, lies at the southern entrance to the Red Sea and is made up of two peninsulas encircling a natural harbour. It was acquired by the East India Company in 1839 as a base for refuelling ships and nearly twenty years later became part of the British Empire. Its strategic importance was enhanced by the opening of the Suez Canal in 1869. From 1937 to 1963 it had been a Crown Colony and in 1963 it became part of the Federation of South Arabia, under British protection. Aden was never a popular port of call; in 1908 Frederick Treves, on his passage to Uganda, had described it as 'the fag end of the world' (11), and ships of the

Royal Navy usually called at Aden for the shortest time possible. Since the early 1960s there had been political unrest, with the Federation government coming under attack by two terrorist organisations, the Front for the Liberation of Southern Yemen (FLOSY) and the National Liberation Front (NLF), both receiving support from neighbouring Yemen, which itself received aid from Egypt. British troops had been sent to the colony to counter the terrorists, both in Aden and in surrounding desert areas of the Radfan. Having indicated in 1966 that Britain would no longer support bases in Aden after independence, the time for British forces was limited. In July 1967 the Foreign Secretary announced that there would be complete withdrawal by January 1968, and that a naval task force including a commando carrier or aircraft carrier would stand off Aden for six months after independence.

The withdrawal of all British forces from Aden was given the codename 'Operation Magister', in which the Royal Navy played a critical role. Withdrawal of personnel and stores was to be by sea and by air, leading up to a final exit on 'W Day'. As the RAF departed from their base at Khormaksar, it would be left to the Royal Navy to provide air support over Aden and oversee the final departure. Although the rundown was planned to take place over several weeks, there was a contingency plan for rapid evacuation of British forces if the political situation demanded. Planning had been in progress for many months but became more difficult following the Six Day War, which closed the Suez Canal and limited the number of 'friendly' ports that could be used by ships of the Royal Navy operating in the Middle East. (12)

Security in Aden had deteriorated during 1967, the terrorists being spurred on by knowledge of the impending British withdrawal, amid what was described as the 'apparent apathy with which murders of British servicemen were accepted by the authorities.' In addition, the Six Day War had added to the instability in the region. It was against this background that on 20 June there was a mutiny by members of the newly formed South Aden Police which left twenty-two British soldiers dead. The repercussions were considerable, and troops were forced to withdraw from the Crater area of Aden. At that time the Royal Northumberland Fusiliers were due to be withdrawn from Aden and replaced by 1st Battalion The Argyll and Sutherland Highlanders. The latter took over responsibility for Crater on 25 June, and their Commanding Officer, Lieutenant Colonel C.C. 'Mad Mitch' Mitchell, was ordered to 'play it cool'. In a well publicised operation, Mitchell led his troops into Crater on the night of 3 July, with Pipe Major Robson playing the Regimental Charge at their head. The area was retaken and order restored, making Mitchell a household name in Britain. However, the tactics employed led to criticism by senior officers, and repercussions continued for several years. (13)

Having sailed at full power from Durban, HMS *Albion* arrived in off Aden in the company of HMS *Phoebe* and RFA *Lyness* on 11 October. She rendezvoused with her sister ship *Bulwark*, which had transported 42 Commando from Singapore before landing them at Aden; responsibility for looking after the commandos now lay with *Albion*. Over the next seven weeks all their requirements, from ammunition to ice cream, would be provided by helicopters of 848 Squadron. The squadron also assumed responsibility from the RAF for internal security over Aden, and Godfrey Place later wrote: 'All pilots (except me!) had at least one up country flight in the left-hand seat of an RAF Wessex.' (14)

Despite overseeing the early phases of the withdrawal, Place found time to fly, and in the first week of November the squadron helicopter instructor flew with him on several occasions to teach him circuits and landings in a Wessex, with the aim that he could land himself on board HMS *Eagle;* whether he undertook such a landing is not recorded.

Place assumed the role of Senior Officer Present Afloat (SOPA), Aden on 24 October, a position he held until 6 November. Amongst those who visited him on board *Albion* was the High Commissioner, Sir Humphrey Trevelyan GCMG, CIE, OBE. A highly experienced diplomat, he had originally joined the Indian Civil Service. His knowledge of the Middle East was unsurpassed, having previously served as Ambassador to Egypt in 1956 and Kuwait in 1961. He had been brought out of retirement to oversee the last months of British rule in Aden. As SOPA, Aden, Place also spent some time visiting ships of the gathering task force, including the Landing Ships (LSLs and LSTs). He noted a problem, observing that, 'Merchant Navy officers have an independence of mind that clouds their co-operation with the Services unless they feel intimately involved.' These ships were managed for the Ministry of Transport by the British India Steam Navigation Company. Place believed that they should be under naval control from the very start of an operation. In his report in December 1967 he suggested that they should be part of the RFA, a move which took place in 1970. (15)

Place frequently visited Aden on official duties, and recorded the obvious tensions on land, so much so that almost every hour saw a different prediction of events. By contrast, *Albion* was much calmer, although the crew could see fighting in Aden and surrounding areas, especially at night when gunfire was clearly visible. Place would often travel ashore, or to other ships, by means of the recently acquired Fairey Huntress, a 36-foot fast motor boat. It was new to the Royal Navy, Place was keen to try it out and whenever possible he would drive himself. On one occasion, when collecting guests for a dinner party, he took the helm. With the rest of the crew on board, suitably dressed in tropical whites, he pushed the throttle forward and the boat shot off with such acceleration that the stoker was thrown over the stern into the sea. The boat was also used for water ski-ing, a sport that Place learnt rather late in his career, but one that he enjoyed immensely, despite injuring his hand. His enjoyment was such that stories even circulated of him being towed behind *Albion* on skis.

HMS *Eagle,* Commanding Officer, Captain J.E. Pope, arrived in the Aden area on 4 November, having sailed from Singapore, flying the flag of Flag Officer Second in Command, Far East Fleet, Rear Admiral E.B. Ashmore CB, DSC, who was to be in command of the Royal Navy force, designated Task Force 318. On his arrival, Place flew to *Eagle* and briefed Admiral Ashmore on the situation at a working breakfast. Within two days it was realised that the communications in *Eagle* were not adequate for the joint sea, land and air operations, and Ashmore transferred his flag to the assault ship HMS *Fearless,* Commanding Officer, Captain M.W.B. Kerr DSC. No sooner had this taken place than he was woken early on 6 November to be given a telegram; his daughter had been killed in the Hither Green Railway disaster the night before. After meeting the Commander-in-Chief, Middle East Command, Admiral Sir Michael Le Fanu KCB, DSC, he was advised to travel home as soon as possible. There was thus need for a replacement, and the job fell to Godfrey Place, who was described by Ashmore as 'perfectly capable of taking charge of the force in the circumstances then prevailing.' (16)

Place transferred from *Albion* to *Fearless* on 7 November and assumed the duties of Commander of Task Force 318. In this role he was promoted, temporarily, to the local rank of Commodore, and the ship's log recorded: '08.00 Hoist Commodore Place's broad pennant.' (17)

At the beginning of November the Defence Secretary had announced that the date for withdrawal was to be moved forward to the end of November, a decision that caused an increase in the number of terrorist attacks. Remembrance Day was marked by a further escalation in violence against British servicemen; Marine Blackman was severely wounded and became the last British casualty in Aden. Place remained as Task Force commander until 13 November, when Admiral Ashmore returned, having spent only six days away from Aden on what some considered a very short period of compassionate leave. This caused some to question Ashmore's confidence in

Place, but Ashmore was, like Place, an officer with determination and a strong sense of duty to the Royal Navy, who would have wished to successfully complete the work of Task Force 318.

Whilst Place was in *Fearless*, the RAF Hospital at Khormaksar Beach was closed and twenty-two of the staff were withdrawn to *Albion*. The group included two nursing sisters, who remained on board until she reached Singapore. They not only undertook their normal medical duties, but played an important role in the mixing of the ship's Christmas cake. The Executive Officer of *Albion*, Commander D.J. Farquharson, was temporarily appointed as Commanding Officer in the absence of Place, but without any advancement of rank. On his return to *Albion*, Place, with his usual attention to detail, reviewed and annotated the ship's log for the days that he had been away, correcting where an entry of 'Captain' to 'Commanding Officer', when referring to the appointment held by Commander Farquharson over the period. (18)

To mark the withdrawal from Aden a fleet review was held on 25 November. The twenty-four ships of the task force were inspected by the High Commissioner, who sailed in HMS *Appleton*, accompanied by Commander-in-Chief, Middle East and Admiral Ashmore. The crew of *Albion* mounted 'Position Alpha' at 11.30 as *Appleton* sailed past, and this was followed by a flypast made up of nine Buccaneers and Sea Vixens from HMS *Eagle*, along with twenty-four helicopters, of which nineteen were from 848 Squadron. They received a congratulatory signal from Ashmore: 'Congratulations on your fly past for the High Commissioner. It was punctual, accurate and impressive. A splendid demonstration and typical of the Fleet Air Arm.'

The scale of 'Operation Magister' became obvious from the weekly reports sent to Commander-in-Chief, Middle East Command. At the end of October there were 9,000 personnel remaining, and by 20 November this had almost halved to 4,900. (19) Many had been flown out in RAF aircraft, although this was not without risk; one aircraft had been shot at as it flew over Egypt on the journey home. The final withdrawal commenced on the night of 25 November, and over the following two days men and equipment left Aden by aircraft and by landing craft to ships of the task force. The High Commissioner departed by RAF transport early on 28 November, with the Royal Marine band playing *Fings Ain't Wot They Used to Be*. He was later to remark that, 'we left without glory, but without disaster.' In preparation for the handover of Aden to South Yemen, *Albion* sailed from Aden harbour later that evening to a position five miles north-east of Khormaksar, where she anchored in preparation for the final withdrawal or

'W-Day'. Members of the press arrived on board to cover the final hours of British rule; they appear to have hit a nerve with Place, who later wrote that, compared with foreign journalists, the British reporters were, 'poorly informed, less courteous and invariably looking for a story about something going wrong.' (20)

W-Day arrived, and, as planned, the helicopter transfers started early and were soon ahead of schedule; at 12.45 *Albion* moved to 'assault stations'. The final evacuation point in Aden was the twelfth green of Khormaksar golf course, and at 14.50 the last 120 men of 42 Commando were withdrawn; at 14.55 *Albion's* log recorded, 'All troops airborne'. (21) The last British serviceman to leave, Lieutenant Colonel T.D. Morgan MC, arrived on board *Albion* at 15.19. During W-Day 848 Squadron had embarked 711 passengers and 112,000lbs of stores. British sovereignty was now officially represented solely by the White Ensign flying in HMS *Albion*. Just before midnight she weighed anchor and, in the company of *Tidespring, Ajax*, and *Barossa*, sailed out of territorial waters. Aden was now the capital of the People's Republic of South Yemen.

Godfrey Place's own feelings about Aden were summarised at the end of his report to Admiral Ashmore:

> I first visited Aden when I was four months old, nearly 46 years ago, and have been there many times since. But like most I talked to on W-Day I felt no particular joy or regret that the British had left: I think most were glad to have finished this phase of the commission, and be a step nearer another country, more civilized peaceful fertile and prosperous. These things Aden will never be. (22)

Albion had spent forty-five days in the Aden area during which time she had demonstrated herself as 'indispensable' to the Task Force Commander. She had undertaken many roles, not least that of a hotel. Place recalled that many people ended up spending a night on board, either as they left Aden or joined other ships; *Albion* had mess bills for 350 officers above her normal complement. There had, however, been good news in the wardroom in October, when a syndicate of members won £12,000 on the football pools.

Having left the territorial waters of the People's Republic of South Yemen, *Albion* remained in the area for a further week, as part of contingency planning. There was no apparent cause for concern, and on 7 December the ship proceeded towards Singapore. She arrived early on 16 December, having been at sea for seventy-three days. On arrival, a fifteen-gun salute was fired for Commander-in-Chief, Far Eastern Fleet, Vice Admiral Sir William O'Brien KCB, DSC, but plans for manning the ship at 'Position Alpha' had to be cancelled due to a tropical storm. Place had to forgo this ceremony on the last occasion he commanded one of Her Majesty's ships entering harbour. (23) Within two hours of securing alongside at Singapore Naval Base, 42 Commando disembarked. Place's time in command was fast coming to an end, and his successor, Captain M.S.Ollivant MBE, DSC, called on him on 21 December.

Saturday, 23 December 1967 was the last day of Place's command of *Albion;* it was also the last day that a member of the Royal Navy holding the Victoria Cross was appointed to a warship. He held a dinner party for a number of guests in the evening, and at 23.00 his guests left. The ship's log recorded: '23.55, Captain Place (VC) leaves ship.' *(24)* As might be expected, his departure was very low key, there was no ceremony of towing him ashore; he left quietly, with typical modesty. Captain Ollivant arrived at 09.00 on 24 December and assumed command of the 'Old Grey Ghost'.

It was somewhat fitting that Place's appointment in *Albion* had ended in Singapore. His contribution to *Albion's* commissioning book (1964-66) read:

> A warship is still the most complex and interlocked organisation of different professional skills in any walk of life – and a commando ship more so than most others. The inter-reliance between so many men of such varied expertise makes for a comradeship that we should remember for long times: a comradeship that has made possible the two remarks I heard, that I personally shall remember most about this ship. '*Albion* to me is the most useful ship on the station' and – from someone in the Naval Base – 'it's always fun when *Albion*'s in Singapore – they do things.' (25)

It was not possible for Place to fly home to Britain in time for Christmas with his family; for them it would be the last Christmas when he was away on duty. He spent Christmas in Singapore as guest of Admiral O'Brien. They were old friends, O'Brien having been responsible for appointing Place to *Albion*. He remembered Godfrey Place as one of the most determined men he had ever encountered and who demonstrated this trait in everything he undertook. At Admiralty House in Singapore there was a water chute which projected people, in a sitting position, into the pool. Place decided that it should be quite possible to slide down the chute standing upright, and attempted to do so. However, he tipped over backwards and, as he entered the water, cracked the back of his head on the end of the chute, knocking himself out and having to be rescued from the water. As soon as he had recovered consciousness, he got up, strode back towards the slide muttering, 'It must be possible!', and had to be restrained from further attempts.

After Christmas, Godfrey Place said farewell to friends in Singapore and returned home to his family, to promotion and to his final appointment in the Royal Navy.

Chapter 15

Flying the Flag

On 7 January 1968 Godfrey Place was promoted. Rear Admiral B.C.G. Place VC, DSC was to be the next Admiral Commanding Reserves and Director General of Naval Recruiting. Place had been ambitious throughout his career, a trait identified by his colleagues early on, and he was the first member of Hood term to reach the rank of Lieutenant Commander (1950), Commander (1952), Captain (1958) and now Rear Admiral. However, this latest promotion had not been plain sailing.

The process had lasted almost nine months, longer than might have been expected. In April 1967 Place was notified that he was on the short list for promotion and in a letter of 26 July he received news that he had been selected for promotion, effective January 1968. At this time the First Sea Lord was Admiral Sir Varyl Begg GCB, DSO, DSC. He had succeeded Sir David Luce GCB, DSO*, who had resigned in the wake of the Defence White Paper of 1966. Begg, who like Place did not suffer fools gladly, wished Place to be appointed as Admiral Commanding Reserves, a decision made known in a letter of 11 August. This news was not received at all well; initially, Place did not wish to accept the post. On 15 August he advised the Naval Secretary, Rear Admiral J.G.B. Cooke CB, DSC, that he 'would rather leave the navy than be Admiral Commanding Reserves.'

His reluctance was for several reasons. He was worried about the financial demands of the job, especially succeeding Rear Admiral Geoffrey Carew-Hunt, who he had succeeded before, as Executive Officer in HMS *Theseus*, an experience he had found expensive. Then there was the matter of leave; Place was concerned that he would be going straight from one job to another and wished to take some leave. On checking with the Master-at-arms, 'the man who keeps a record of all these things', he was assured he was due twenty-six days leave, and since he would leave HMS *Albion* in Singapore he wished to have time to say goodbye to friends out there. The very idea of working with reserves did not go down well; Place wrote that Althea had been very 'boot-faced' about his last job with the reserves (when on the staff of Flag Officer Flying Training, 1953-55). He also had reservations about the reserves themselves, perhaps from the days of 'Operation Source', when some of his RNVR colleagues had not lived up to expectations. He had certainly expressed the opinion to his family that he felt there was only room for full-time professionals in the Royal Navy.

Place was rightly concerned about where this appointment would take him. Although some of his predecessors had gained promotion from Admiral Commanding Reserves, many had not; was he being placed in a career 'cul-de-sac'? Finally, a man who throughout his thirty-three year naval career had relished the excitement of action at sea, be it below, above or on the waves, was unlikely to have been enamoured of the prospect of responsibility for primarily land-based reservists.

The post of Admiral Commanding Reserves reported to the Second Sea Lord, and on 1 August 1967 Vice Admiral Sir Frank Twiss took over the post, an appointment that Place would have been painfully aware of. Their professional relationship had been poor ever since Place served at the Admiralty in 1961, when Twiss was the Naval Secretary. With the First Sea Lord unavailable, Place felt he needed to discuss his appointment with another senior officer; it was obvious that approaching the newly arrived Second Sea Lord would be futile. Instead, on 16 August he flew by helicopter to Plymouth to seek advice from the Commander-in-Chief, Plymouth, Vice Admiral Charles Mills CB, CBE, DSC. Place knew him from his time with *Albion* in the Far East. He told Mills that he was 'unqualified for the job' and worried about the costs of entertaining, but was reassured by the observation that, 'the cost of a job is largely what an incumbent makes of it.' A week later Place spoke with the Naval Secretary and implicitly accepted the post. However, the saga was far from over, since Twiss had got wind of Place's reluctance, informed the Naval Secretary that he had not formally agreed to the nomination and, as of 31 August 1967, was minded to wait until the July 1968 promotion list to obtain a relief for Admiral Carew-Hunt. He had already contacted the latter who was willing to extend his appointment for six months, if needed. It was left to the Naval Secretary to remind the Second Sea Lord that, in fact, the appointment of Godfrey Place as Admiral Commanding Reserves had already been approved by the First Sea Lord and by the Secretary of State; the only reason it had not been publicised was due to uncertainty over the timing of handover of command of *Albion* to Captain Ollivant. On 1 September, just a few days before *Albion* was to sail to South Africa and the Middle East, Place wrote to the Naval Secretary about the situation, 'The whole thing fills me with abject gloom.'

To try to resolve the issue, the Naval Secretary arranged for the First and Second Sea Lords to meet on 4 September; the matter was urgent since *Albion* would be sailing on 7 September. The Second Sea Lord had not, at this point, absolutely said 'No' to Place, but if he was adamant in his objection, the Naval Secretary had two options: Place could be appointed as Flag Officer, Gibraltar in February 1968, or as Admiral Superintendent, Portsmouth in April 1968. The possibility of his appointment as Flag Officer Aircraft Carriers, a post that Godfrey Place would have relished, was, however, ruled out. The Second Sea Lord stated that he preferred not to appoint Place, but did not say his appointment was unacceptable. He had his own man in mind for the post, and suggested that Place be appointed as Assistant Chief of the Naval Staff (ACNS), either (W) Warfare or (O) Operations. Finally, on 6 September Place wrote to the Naval Secretary stating that he did not want to make a fuss and, although not over-enthusiastic about it, he would accept the appointment. A saga that had lasted over six weeks and involved the two most senior officers in the Royal Navy was now finally resolved.

News of the promotion led to a flurry of congratulatory letters from colleagues, friends and family. The First Sea Lord wrote a letter of congratulation, and a pilot who had served with Place in 801 Squadron some fifteen years earlier wrote, 'I always remembered you saying late one "Follies night" that you were going to be an Admiral. I always believed you.' Place also received a letter from Peter Philip, the Commanding Officer of the passage crew for X7 in 'Operation Source'. He had returned to South Africa before the end of the war and in 1967 was working in the South African Embassy in Vienna. He wrote,

> It is a far cry from the days when an Admiral seemed to you (as he still does to me) to be a distant and superior being scarcely distinguishable from the Almighty.

Place assumed the duties of Admiral Commanding Reserves and Director General Naval Recruiting in February 1968. Rather than move from Corton Denham, he decided to rent a flat in London, in Bishops Park Mansions in Fulham. To do so, he needed a reference from his employer and requested one from the Naval Secretary, Rear Admiral D.A. Dunbar-Nasmith, saying, 'I am loath to heckle 2SL'; it was obvious that his relationship with the Second Sea Lord remained tricky.

Place relieved Rear Admiral Geoffrey Carew-Hunt CB, described by one of his staff as 'an outrageous rascal – a big man who was charming and almost worshipped by the RNR.' Place was very different, a quiet and sincere man, but still much admired by the RNR. He was noted as an Admiral who was readily approachable, but who could also be looked up to with respect and admiration.

The Admiral Commanding Reserves was based in the Old Admiralty Building, but he flew his flag in HMS *Discovery,* the ship that had been sailed to the Antarctic by Captain Robert Scott in 1901-05 and was moored at the Victoria embankment. In 1967 the naval reserves were somewhat different from those which Place had worked with in 1953. The RNVR (founded in 1903) had been merged with the Royal Naval Reserve in 1958, and the new organisation was named the Royal Naval Reserve (RNR). In 1968 the RNR was made up of eleven divisions distributed across the country, each with a captain in command. The reserve was somewhat old fashioned; certainly, the captains were invariably well off and tended to live rather royally when undertaking their duties with the Royal Navy. As a result, Place's concerns about the cost of the job were probably unfounded. However, he was never a fan of the reservists and retained his belief that the navy should be a totally full-time professional service.

The post involved a considerable amount of travel, visiting divisions around the country on drill nights. There was an official car for the Admiral, a Black Humber Hawk, and a driver. In March 1968 Wren Sally Saunders was drafted to London to serve as Place's driver. She recalled that on first meeting him she was struck by how short he was. Before too long, it appeared that her draft was going to be quite short-lived since she believed that Place wanted a Marine as driver. However, after a couple of months the appointment was made permanent; Sally Saunders believed this was due in part to a particular journey to Southampton. Place was invited to a meeting of Master Mariners on board a liner. They were late leaving London, and she remembered driving at breakneck speed whilst Place changed into his uniform in the back of the car. They arrived on time, with the Admiral suitably attired. Place developed a good relationship with his driver, and on long journeys he would do some of the driving. As a flag officer he was entitled to fly his flag from the car, but he invariably told Sally Saunders to cover the flag so as to create an element of surprise when they were visiting an establishment.

Travelling around the country, Place again found himself in the press, both local and national. Most stories led by describing him as the only serving naval officer with the Victoria Cross and gave a brief resumé of the exploits of 'Operation Source', before describing why he was visiting. The RNR were proud that their Admiral held the Victoria Cross, and this helped in his other role, namely Director General of Naval Recruiting. A Victoria Cross holder visiting sea cadets and new recruits would undoubtedly have been a great 'plus' for the service.

Not long after taking up his appointment, Place was invited to the fiftieth anniversary celebration of the Zeebrugge raid, which had taken place on 23

April 1918. The celebrations were held at the Belgian port where HMS *Vindictive* and others had taken part in a raid that led to the award of eight Victoria Crosses, two posthumously. *Vindictive* was destroyed, and it was her successor which served as a training ship for cadets from Royal Naval College, Dartmouth; its crew had included Cadet B.C.G. Place from September 1938 to April 1939.

Since 1945 Godfrey Place had spoken only sparingly of 'Operation Source'; this was typical of his modesty as well as his desire to move on to the next challenge. He had said a little about the attack on the *Tirpitz* when serving with 801 Squadron, but only after being pushed. When in command of HMS *Rothesay* he had been asked by his Gunnery Instructor, C.P.O Brian Davies, whether he would talk about 'Operation Source' to the junior seamen on board. His reply was straight forward: 'Some things are best forgotten about.' However, as Admiral Commanding Reserves he did speak a little more about his wartime exploits. On a visit to Jersey in 1969 he told the story of 'Operation Source' to an audience of seventy sea cadets. The local press reported that he told the story, 'Unemotionally and factually, as if he were telling of some event which he had happened to hear about.' The report noted how, 'This very detachment and calmness added greatly to the excitement of the exploit.'

Place was an active supporter of the Victoria Cross and George Cross Assocation, having attended almost all its reunions (held every two years) since its formation. In July 1968 the meeting involved lunch at Chelsea Barracks, followed by a reception hosted by the Queen at Buckingham Palace. Place lent his car to the Chairman of the Association, Brigadier the Rt Hon. Sir John Smyth VC, MC, and Sally Saunders remembered the great thrill of leading the procession to Buckingham Palace, where she took tea downstairs with the other drivers. Smyth later thanked her and presented her with a signed copy of his book, *The Story of the George* Cross.

The Admiral Commanding Reserves would also visit the annual RNR training exercises, normally held abroad. In 1969 they were in Gibraltar, and Place visited the numerous minesweepers taking part. On board one vessel he met Sub Lieutenant Cerwyl Jones, who was on the bridge when Place breezed in 'like a hurricane'. Jones remembered that he appeared 'fit and pugnacious,' and he asked, 'Where are we?' Jones, pointing to a chart, told him, 'Three minutes ago we were here'. The reply from Godfrey Place was typically straightforward: 'I want to know where we are now.'

In the spring of 1969 the Admiralty entered one of its twice yearly rounds of selection for promotion, and in April the Second Sea Lord provided his summary of Place's service:

He has been an energetic and forceful Admiral Commanding Reserves and Director General of Naval Recruiting; he is full of ideas, knows his own mind and is not backward in giving his views.

But he is not everyone's cup of tea, because in many ways he is not a comfortable bedfellow – he is a little abrupt, a little brusque and a little 'unconventionally press-on'.

At the end of the report, it was considered that Godfrey Place was deserving of consideration for promotion to Vice Admiral, noting that there was, 'a good deal of vigorous life left in Place.'

In July 1969 Godfrey Place heard news that, although not unexpected, was not what he would have hoped for. The Naval Secretary advised him that it was unlikely that the First Sea Lord would be able to offer him another appointment, and asked if he would remain as Admiral Commanding Reserves until July 1970. Less than two weeks later, he received confirmation in a letter from the First Sea Lord, Admiral Sir Michael Le Fanu, that he would not be promoted, and that he would be placed on the retired list the following year.

A glittering naval career was coming to an end; despite being the first member of Hood term to reach flag rank, Godfrey Place's naval career would not advance any further. At about this time, one officer who would be promoted was Rear Admiral T.T. Lewin DSC, whom Godfrey Place had relieved in command of HMS *Corunna* in 1957. Terence Lewin had joined the Royal Navy in 1939 as a 'Special Entry', and his career would culminate in his appointment as Chief of the Defence Staff 1979-82, during which time Britain would send a task force headed by two aircraft carriers to recapture the Falkland Islands following their invasion by Argentina.

In the New Years Honours list of 1970 there was the announcement of the award of the Companion of the Most Honourable Order of the Bath (CB) to Godfrey Place. Letters of congratulations poured in from home and abroad; Lord Mountbatten of Burma wrote, 'how nice to have two red ribbons together.' Place replied to almost all the letters he received; in his reply to an American colleague he described the award of honours as a 'curiously English process'. There was a letter from Aunt Maisie, always keen to know how his career was progressing, but her P.S. ('Do you know what your next job is?') might have been rather difficult to answer.

Place's retirement did not go unmarked or unnoticed; he was not going to be able to slip ashore quietly, as he had done from HMS *Albion* in Singapore. On 28 April 1970 a dinner was held for him in HMS *President*, home of the London division of the RNR. Shorty before midnight, he was piped into his barge for the trip to Westminster Pier. When he arrived, nearly one hundred officers and men (including Wrens) waylaid him, fixed tow ropes to his car and towed him up the Embankment, around Parliament Square and into the Old Admiralty Building. The police were 'in on the act', despite having been given very little warning, and controlled both the traffic lights and other traffic to ensure that the tow went without a hitch. Place received three rousing cheers in the forecourt of the Old Admiralty Building in the early hours of the morning, as the Royal Navy said goodbye to an man who had served for thirty-five years, and whose courage, determination and sense of duty had marked him out as a most exceptional officer.

Although Place had tried to ensure that he was placed on the retired list on 19 July 1970, his birthday, he was unable to do so, and so retired from the Royal Navy on 30 June 1970, three weeks short of his forty-ninth birthday. As the Second Sea Lord had noted, 'there was a good deal of vigorous service' left in him, and this would be apparent as he embarked on a new career.

Chapter 16

Retirement – of Sorts

The Royal Navy had been Godfrey Place's life for over thirty-five years, and retirement was not going to be an easy transition for him. He was not yet fifty, and for a man whose career had been characterised by duty, service and excitement, life without drawing the 'Queen's shilling' would be very different. However, he had always relished a challenge, and there were to be plenty over the coming years.

In 1970 Place was appointed as Personnel Director of the shipping company Cunard in London, but he lost the job when Cunard was taken over by Trafalgar House in 1971. He had already ventured into a number of businesses near to Corton Denham; one had involved boat-building and another the rental of tents and marquees. Neither had been a success and both soon folded. He had also worked from home as an Inspector for the Department of the Environment.

It was in 1971 that Godfrey and Althea purchased the saddlers 'Mabers' in Sherborne High Street, a business they would own and run for the next seventeen years. Althea had always had a great interest in equestrian affairs and had spent her time between leaving school and joining the WRNS working with horses and riding with the Brocklesby Hunt. Place immersed himself in the new venture and learnt how to make and repair saddles; it was typical of him that he wished to know not only how they were made but also how to do it himself. The shop was one of three that he and Althea came to own. Place played a full part in the running of the shop, and responded as its emphasis moved from saddlery towards the sale and repair of leather goods. Tony Kenber remembered very clearly his uncle selling a red leather handbag to a customer, something that Place had probably never envisaged doing during his days in the Royal Navy. However, the limits of his financial ability became apparent, not for the first time. Dealing with money had always been a challenge; in 1943, when meeting his future father-in-law, he was asked how much he had saved. As he said, 'I did a little hasty arithmetic and gave an answer based on fifty-two months per year.' Whilst working at Mabers he would happily spend several hours at home in the evening repairing a handbag and then charge a small fee, instead of trying to sell the customer a new bag. He thought nothing of asking a staff member to work extra hours, but did not consider the need to pay them for it. Fortunately, Althea's business acumen, undoubtedly derived from her family's business background, was put to good use and ensured that Mabers became a flourishing concern.

Although he was no longer working in London, Place retained the property in Bishops Park Mansions, having purchased the flat after he left the Royal Navy. Charles lived in the flat whilst at university and rented rooms to fellow students, both male and female. Place would stay in the flat when visiting London, and on one occasion announced he would be coming at the weekend. Charles let it be known that he would be away for the weekend, but had told his female flatmate that his father would be visiting. When Place learnt that the other occupant of the flat that weekend was a young lady, he decided that his trip was best postponed.

In 1974 Place was appointed by the Lord Chancellor, the Rt. Hon. Lord Elwyn Jones, to be the Lay Observer to the Law society. This was an entirely new position, created under Section 45 of the Solicitor's Act 1974. The role, set out in statute, was to:

Examine any written allegation made by or on behalf of a member of the public concerning the Society's treatment of a complaint about a solicitor or an employee of a solicitor made to the Society by that member of the public or on his behalf.

He commenced the job in February 1975 and had an office in the Royal Courts of Justice in the Strand. His appointment was featured in the national press, and reports referred to his gallantry in the war, although interestingly none picked up on his family's association with the legal profession. (1) At the end of each year he had to produce a report for the Lord Chancellor.

Over the three years that he was in post he received an average of 300 items of correspondence per annum, of which about half were deemed appropriate for investigation. Typically of his efficient modus operandi, the vast majority were addressed within the year. In about five per cent of cases he found that the Law Society had been less than adequate in handling the complaint and asked them to reconsider their actions, and in a very few cases he was openly critical of them. By the end of his first year he concluded that the three basic reasons for complaints about solicitors were delays, cost and incomplete explanations, and urged that these be addressed. In his third report in 1978 he did not hide his frustration at the continuing recurrence of similar complaints. (2)

Place noted that often people's first encounter with the law was when they were faced with a solicitor, and early in his tenure as Lay Observer he suggested that law should be taught as a compulsory subject at school, commenting that, 'Until there is a more complete understanding, many an individual's recourse to law will be a traumatic experience in which a sense of injustice will prevail.' In 1978 he made it clear that he would not be seeking to extend his term of office, a decision undoubtedly influenced by health problems.

Thirty years on from 'Operation Source', there remained speculation about the fate of X5, commanded by Henty Henty-Creer. In 1974 Place became a patron of an expedition which attempted to locate X5 in Kaa fjord. The expedition was led by Peter Cornish, an experienced sub-aqua diver who in 1973 had led a team which recovered the midget submarine XE8 from Weymouth Bay. The same year, he had been on a diving expedition in the north of Norway, attempting to locate a RAF Halifax bomber lost in April 1942 in a raid on the *Tirpitz* at Trondheim. Whilst there he visited Kaa fjord and undertook some initial assessments. The following year, in June 1974, a team of more than twenty divers set off to Kaa fjord to try to locate X5. They found part of what they believed to be a midget submarine, and although it was raised from the floor of the fjord no attempt was made to recover it. Two years later, the team, again led by Peter Cornish, returned to Kaa fjord and were joined by divers from the Royal Engineers, led by Lieutenant Colonel Graham Owens. Over three weeks in July and August the team mapped the floor of the fjord, using side-array sonar operated by Nigel Kelland. The team finally located the midget submarine and having gained permission from the Ministry of Defence for recovery were able to raise her bow and middle sections. These were hauled on to the shore, where it became obvious that they were part of X7 not X5. The Germans had raised the aft section of X7 in early October 1943, using drag nets slung from the ocean tugs *Arngast* and *Bardenfelth*. This had contained at least one body, that of Bill Whittam, who was buried in Tromsø. They had also recovered the engine, hence the Germans' line of questioning of Godfrey Place in 1943. Among the material recovered by Peter Cornish from the bow section of X7 was a diving suit, three Luger pistols, a pair of binoculars and a sextant. The team were able to arrange for the salvaged sections of X7 to be shipped back to England and be displayed at the Imperial War Museum, Duxford.

With parts of X7 recovered, the two surviving members of her crew were interviewed by the expedition members. Robert Aitken visited the Imperial War Museum and demonstrated how he had made his escape through the hatch of X7; he pointed out that, compared with the last time he had executed this manoeuvre, 'It was much easier when someone gives you a hand from on top.' The sextant recovered from X7 was returned to the manufacturers, who cleaned away thirty years of accumulated material. It was then presented to Place, who noted that in fact it was not his own, since as he pointed out, 'That was too valuable to be taken on the mission.' The sextant recovered from X7 was one issued by the Admiralty. At the same time Place was asked what he thought had happened to X5 and he replied, 'I don't honestly know. I don't think I've ever tried to make an opinion about X5,' but he went on to add:

> Henty-Creer was a good friend, in fact a very good friend of mine, I knew him well … whatever happened then I can say he was a very 'press on' sort of character and I am sure that he pressed on as far as he possibly could.(3)

The expedition to Kaa fjord had been followed closely by Henty-Creer's sister, Pamela Mellor, who visited the area several times both before and during the expedition. The Henty-Creer family had always believed that Henty should have been awarded the Victoria Cross for his role in the attack, and in 1988 wrote a book, partly based upon Henty Henty-Creer's autobiography. (4) This raised awareness of the fact that in the original recommendations for the award of the Victoria Cross made by Admiral Barry in October 1943 Henty-Creer was one of the three officers recommended for the award, but that at some stage over the ensuing months his name was removed. (5) There appears to have been little communication between the Henty-Creer family and Godfrey Place after the war, perhaps due to a general feeling that he could have said more in support of his friend and colleague. But he could only give an opinion based on known facts, and his comments on the issue were always measured and consistent. The mystery of X5 remains, as do continued calls that Henty-Creer should have been awarded the Victoria Cross, despite there still being no tangible evidence that he did indeed make an attack on the *Tirpitz*.

Although retired from the Royal Navy, Place remained committed to service in his work with the Victoria Cross and George Cross Association. The Association had been founded (as the Victoria Cross Association) in June 1956, during the celebrations to commemorate the centenary of the Victoria Cross. Brigadier Sir John Smyth VC, MC, MP received suggestions that he should form a Victoria Cross Association and was about to turn this down when he was approached by Sir Ralph Raynor MP, Chairman of the Royal Society of St George, who invited him form a VC Association based on

St. George's House and 'under the umbrella' of the Royal Society of St George. When the Association was formed the Patron was HM Queen Elizabeth, the President Sir Winston Churchill KG, OM, and the Chairman Sir John Smyth. The objects of the Association were:

1. To establish a central focus and headquarters in London for Victoria Cross holders from all over the world and to provide a centre where holders could meet and communicate.
2. To cement the brotherhood of the holders of the Victoria Cross throughout the Commonwealth and thereby, through our own unity and strength make some contribution towards world peace.
3. To give such help and guidance to one another as might be possible and to give assistance to members who are in need, particularly those who have suffered injury during two Great Wars. (6)

At the second meeting, holders of the George Cross were invited to be associate members, and in May 1961 they became full members, at which point the name was changed to the Victoria Cross and George Cross Association. Place had been a strong supporter of the Association and attended all the reunions (held every two years) except for 1966, when he was serving in HMS *Albion* in Singapore. In 1962 he became a member of the Association's committee.

Sir John Smyth had served as both President and Chairman since Churchill's death in 1965. There was a need to appoint a new Chairman, and in July 1971 Godfrey Place assumed the position. This was not a job that Place would have rushed to do, involving as it did a considerable amount of liaising with the press. However, his sense of duty came to the fore; he realised that the job needed doing, and in the words of his late mother 'he will do it well.'

Soon after becoming Chairman, Place made the Association more of a 'family' by inviting widows of medal holders to the reunions, a move that was seen as very positive. But before long he was faced with a rather more difficult issue, namely the exchange of Albert Medals and Edward Medals for the George Cross.

The notion of an exchange of medals was not new; in 1940 holders of the Empire Gallantry Medal (established in 1922) were obliged to exchange their medals for the newly established George Cross. The Albert Medal was established in 1866 as an award for life-saving, and the Edward Medal was established in 1907, a civilian decoration that recognised acts of bravery by miners or quarrymen. The last awards of these medals had been made in

1948. In 1968 Prime Minister Harold Wilson advised that holders of either Medal would receive a tax-free annuity of £100, as of 14 December 1968; this followed the award of the same annuity to holders of the Victoria Cross in 1959 and holders of the George Cross in 1965. In October 1971 Prime Minister Edward Heath announced that, 'With the approval of Her Majesty the Queen, all holders [of Albert and Edward Medals] will be required forthwith to exchange their awards for the George Cross.' The vast majority of those who were eligible did exchange their medals, and they were invited to join the Victoria Cross and George Cross Association. There were, however, some reservations on the part of the membership, since both the Albert and Edward Medals had had different levels of award, namely Gold or Bronze for the Albert Medal and Silver or Bronze for the Edward Medal. It was felt by some that this devalued the award of the George Cross. Regardless of these objections, Place saw that the new members were welcomed to the Association and the reunions.

Place had strong views on the issue of money and awards for gallantry. He pointed out that the initial award of the Victoria Cross was one without any cash value. Personally he felt that holders of the Victoria Cross should not receive an annuity. His views, and those of the Association, on selling medals, for whatever reason, were made public in a letter in 1966. Responding to news of the possible sale of the Victoria Cross awarded to William Hall, he wrote:

> The policy of our association with respect to the sale of VCs is that we are firmly against it and indeed, it very rarely happens that a man sells his own Cross, but we do realise that there are circumstances where a VC is left to relatives who are in difficult circumstances and they realise what large sums can be obtained from the sale. We have to acknowledge that circumstances alter cases. When that happens we, as an association, try and get the Regimental Association, a Museum or HQ mess or similar reputable body to make an offer for the medal rather than it should fall into the hands of private speculators. (7)

In his time as Chairman, Godfrey Place became very much the 'voice and face' of the Association and was often quoted in the press; at one reunion he was described as 'hovering around the hotel lobby greeting old friends', and when asked about the membership of the Association stated, 'The thing about us is we have no axe to grind, no demonstration to make and no "common denominator."' A few years later, he spoke of the importance of the Association for its members:

Once in a lifetime you're first to meet the Monarch. You head the queue in front of all the KCB and that sort of thing, and the main purpose of our association is to ensure that those who have won the award should not feel that they never got to the front line of things again. When they come to our reunions they are important people and I think that does them good. (8)

In May 1973 he opened the newly created Victoria Cross and George Cross Room at the Imperial War Museum, and commented:

Although a museum necessarily displays things, this exhibition also recaptures something of the way of life and spirit and emotion of these people. I hope that it may be an influence on others in time of crisis to serve their fellow men in the tradition of the best in our civilization. (9)

Over the next thirty-five years the room became home to the medals and many associated items belonging to Victoria Cross and George Cross holders. It was closed when a new gallery (funded by a donation from Lord Ashcroft KCMG) was opened in 2010, and was then converted into part of the research department of the Imperial War Museum,

Amongst the many friends of the Victoria Cross and George Cross Association was Ross McWhirter, the sports journalist, publisher and broadcaster. He had been introduced to Godfrey Place by Odette Hallowes GC, and had provided media support and publicity to the Association. McWhirter had stood, unsuccessfully, as the Conservative candidate at Edmonton in the 1964 general election and had later co-founded the National Association for Freedom. In 1975 there were a number of terrorist attacks in London by members of the Provisional IRA, leading to the deaths of, amongst others, Captain Roger Goad, an explosives officer killed in August by a bomb he was attempting to defuse[1] and Professor Gordon Hamilton-Fairley who was assassinated in October. McWhirter proposed that Irish citizens in Britain should have to register at a local police station and also offered a reward of £50,000 for the arrest of those responsible for terrorist activities. He recognised that this made him a high-profile target, and in November 1975 he was killed outside his home in north London. Place was one of several signatories to a letter appealing for donations for a fund set up in memory of McWhirter; other signatories included the Leader of the Opposition, Margaret Thatcher, and Odette Hallowes GC. Place was

---

1. Captain Goad was awarded the George Cross posthumously in 1976.

one of the founding sponsors of the Ross McWhirter Foundation, which in 2004 was renamed the McWhirter Foundation. (10)

In 1976 the reunion of the Victoria Cross and George Cross Association coincided with the fiftieth birthday of the Association's Patron, the Queen. On her birthday, 21 April, Her Majesty did not undertake any official engagements, but was keen to meet members of the Association who were invited to Windsor Castle. Place, with the help of Sir John Smyth, presented the Queen with a gift, at which point the assembled members starting to sing 'Happy Birthday'; although much appreciated by the Queen, the spontaneous chorus caused some consternation amongst the attendant courtiers. In 1981 the reunion was held over for an extra year (the previous one had been 1978) and took place in May; this coincided with the Silver Jubilee of the Association and was marked by a reception hosted by the Queen, followed by a dinner at the Savoy Hotel, where the guest of honour was the Prince of Wales.

On 2 April 1982 the Falkland Islands were invaded by Argentinian troops, and in response a task force sailed from Britain to the South Atlantic. Seventy-four days later, the Commander Land Forces, Major General Jeremy Moore OBE, MC* was able to raise the Union Jack at Government House in the capital Stanley. There were countless examples of gallantry during the campaign, and in July 1982 there were rumours in the press of the possible award of a Victoria Cross to Lieutenant Colonel H. Jones OBE, who had been killed on 28 May 1982 when commanding 2nd Battalion The Parachute Regiment at the Battle of Darwin. Place was asked for his views on the possible award, to which he replied, 'There were as many VCs in the Indian Mutiny as in the Second World War. It is very hard to judge between deeds and over the years other bravery medals have been brought in.' (11) In the event, both Lieutenant Colonel Jones and Sergeant Ian MacKay (3rd Battalion The Parachute Regiment) were awarded the Victoria Cross for gallantry in the Falklands; both posthumous awards were announced in the *London Gazette* on 11 October 1982.

The Falklands War had struck a chord with Godfrey Place; in 1983 he visited RNAS Yeovilton with Melanie to hear of the exploits of members of the Fleet Air Arm operating both Sea Harriers and helicopters during the conflict. Having listened to an enthralling description of current naval aviation, they drove home to Corton Denham. On the way Place said, 'I would have loved to have gone to the South Atlantic'; although he had retired over ten years earlier, his passion for service and excitement with the Royal Navy remained.

Sir John Smyth died in 1983 and there was a need for a new President of the Association. Place suggested that they should invite Her Majesty Queen Elizabeth, the Queen Mother to be President, a decision seen by some members as being rather high-risk. He initially approached the Queen Mother's treasurer, Sir Ralph Anstruther, meeting him at Clarence House but returned more than a little frustrated, having been unable to get anywhere. He later returned with Mrs Didy Grahame, the Secretary of the Association, and this time the meeting was a huge success. In July 1984 the Queen Mother became the President of the Association, and the event was reported in *The Times* on 7 July, which carried a picture of the Queen Mother sitting with Place and members of the committee under the rather apt headline, 'A Place of Honour'. Place had first met the Queen Mother over forty years earlier, when she invested him with the Distinguished Service Cross at Buckingham Palace in June 1943, and they had met again on several occasions in 1945. He would meet her many times over the coming ten years and she came to admire his work with the Association. Six years later, a parade was held on Horse Guards Parade to mark the ninetieth birthday of the Queen Mother, and amongst the groups who took part were members of the Victoria Cross and George Cross Association. Place was there, but with typical modesty did not lead the members but instead walked in the middle of the group as they passed their President.

As Chairman, Place very much led the Association, and in committee meetings there was not a great deal of discussion. At one meeting a member took exception to Place's attitude and effectively offered his resignation, to which the Chairman replied that he was sorry to hear this, but accepted it. It would be some years before the member concerned attended reunions again.

By July 1991 Godfrey Place had served as Chairman of the Association for twenty years, and a luncheon was held to celebrate this. The Queen Mother sent a letter of congratulations on 'his splendid achievements during the years that he has filled a most demanding office.' The occasion took place just a month after Place had been appointed a Commander of the Royal Victorian Order on the occasion of the Queen's birthday in June. A number of letters of congratulations were received, including a telegram from Prince Philip: 'Many congratulations on your well deserved honour.'

During his retirement, Godfrey Place had more time to spend with his family, making up for those periods when he had been away for months with the Royal Navy. Andrea had moved to France to run a vineyard, and her father and mother purchased a small adjoining property. Place enjoyed spending time in France; the relaxed village lifestyle was very much to his liking and reminded him in many ways of life in West Camel some twenty-five years earlier. He also was able to spend time visiting his sister, who had moved to Ibiza following her husband's retirement from teaching. As children, Godfrey and Helen had been very close, but after they had both married their relationship had become more distant.

In the late 1980s Place was persuaded by the Imperial War Museum to contribute to their sound archive of personal experiences in war. He described in some detail both 'Operation Source' and his time as a prisoner of war. In retrospect, this was cathartic for him, especially about his time as a prisoner, and after this he did attend a few reunions of former prisoners at Marlag-O, something he had not felt able to do before. (12)

For Godfrey Place, who had been such an active person, a heart attack in 1977 was a cruel blow. He was at home when he started to feel unwell, but attempted to dismiss this. Althea was not convinced and called for an ambulance; it arrived to find Godfrey waiting in the drive, holding a suitable overnight bag. Treatment at the local hospital was complicated by the onset of an infection which spread through the blood and affected his heart. Ironically, having effectively walked into hospital, he very nearly failed to leave it; the infection caused his temperature to rise dramatically and he was extremely unwell. Typically, he survived, but the episode had taken its toll. Damage to the valves of the heart was such that the only treatment was their replacement. This took place a few years later at St Bartholomew's Hospital, London. It was a major affair, involving open-heart surgery, but he pulled through and the operation appeared to be a success. In 1993 Godfrey and Althea Place were able to celebrate their Golden Wedding in July, attended by their children, grandchildren and many friends they had known for fifty years or longer. At this time, however, his health was again failing, although he never complained or mentioned the subject. But aware of his limitations, he was unable to attend the unveiling of a cairn to men of the 12th Submarine Flotilla on the banks of Loch Cairnbawn.

The implanted heart valves had a finite life span, and by 1994 it was apparent that he would require further surgery. By now he was suffering from considerable shortness of breath and lack of energy. He requested the operation in a typically courageous bid to improve his condition – it was not in his nature to be content with anything other than an active life. (13) He retired as Chairman of the Victoria Cross and George Cross Association that year, after twenty-three years in the post, and in November was invited to luncheon by the Queen Mother. Place later confided that the invitation had kept him going. Soon after this he entered St Bartholomew's Hospital for further surgery; he knew that it would not be plain sailing and told Tony Kenber, 'This is going to be a bit of a battle.' He was right, and although he recovered briefly from the operation, complications set in and he remained in intensive care for almost two weeks, before passing away on 27 December 1994, aged seventy-three. Althea received many letters of condolence including messages from both the Queen and the Queen Mother.

Godfrey Place would have wanted his funeral to be a low-key affair, preferably held at St Andrew's Church Corton Denham, where he had worshipped for many years and served as a churchwarden. However, the church was too small for the expected congregation, and access via a sloping and uneven gravel path would have caused difficulty to many of those attending. Instead, the funeral was held at Sherborne Abbey on 2 January 1995. Special dispensation was granted from the Admiralty to allow his coffin to be draped in the White Ensign, normally reserved for serving naval officers. The address was given by Vice Admiral Sir Gerard Mansfield KCB, CVO, who had joined Hood term sixty years before on 1 January 1935 with Godfrey Place. He spoke of Place's 'very keen perception of anything pretentious or pompous' as well as his deceptively detached air:

> I remember in the early days being in a group with Godfrey – we were laughing at some joke, one of the group said, 'Why aren't you laughing too Godfrey, don't you think it is funny?' Godfrey said 'Yes I did, I was amused inside.' He had a most original mind and when sometimes he appeared pre-occupied he was probably thinking out some new scheme.

He described Godfrey Place's nature as 'unobtrusively extremely kind and caring,' told how he went out of his way to help anyone in difficulties, and said, 'If he felt something was not right he said so, irrespective of who it might offend.'

Godfrey Place was buried in St Andrew's Church graveyard at Corton Denham. His headstone carries the inscription:

> When I was born I took my life in trust
> An heirloom in the heritage of man
> For my enjoyment in my earthly span
> And others benefits when I am done

Fittingly, the poem was written by Place whilst in Marlag-O fifty years earlier, on 31 December 1944.

The final words of this remarkable life must rest with Godfrey Place himself who, when writing to Althea in March 1943, wondered:

> And then, when we're old and our children are starting to do well we'll walk out in the garden one night – calm, summer evening – and look at our star and ask him if the world has been a better place for our living?

Appendix I

Immediate Family Tree for
Basil Charles Godfrey Place

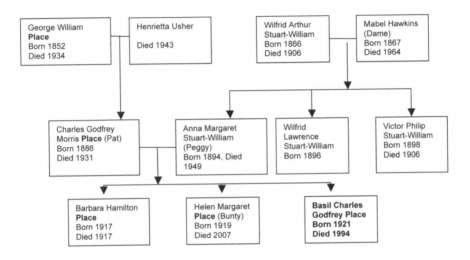

Appendix II

Time Line for Basil Charles Godfrey Place

1921
19 July: Born at Wintercott, Little Malvern, Worcestershire
November: Sailed to Mombasa, then on to Entebbe

1923
June: Returned to England, to live with Allen family, Kemerton, Gloucestershire

1926
September: Commenced schooling, Sandgate, Kent
December: Sailed with family to Cape Town and then to Livingstone, Northern Rhodesia (arrived January 1927)

1929
September: Returned to England, commenced schooling at The Grange, Folkestone

1931
September: Parents returned from Northern Rhodesia
December: Death of father, Charles Godfrey Morris Place

1934
November: Entrance examination for Royal Naval College, Dartmouth

1935
January: Entered Royal Naval College, Dartmouth as Cadet

1938
August: Passed out of Royal Naval College, Dartmouth
September: Appointed to HMS *Vindictive*

1939
April: Left HMS *Vindictive*
May: Promoted Midshipman, appointed to HMS *Newcastle*
November: Loss of AMC *Rawalpindi*

1940
November: Battle of Cape Spartivento
December: Left HMS *Newcastle* at Gibraltar for passage to England

1941
January: Acting Sub Lieutenant. Courses at Portsmouth
May: Promoted Sub Lieutenant
June: Appointed to HMS *Elfin*, submarine training
August: Appointed to 10th Submarine Flotilla, Malta
November: Appointed to ORP *Sokol*, Awarded Polish Cross of Valour
December: Appointed to HMS *Urge*

1942
February: Promoted Lieutenant, Joined HMS *Una*
March: Appointed to HMS *Unbeaten*
June: Returned to England
September: Appointed to X-craft training

1943
April: Announcement of engagement to Althea Tickler
June: Investiture of DSC, by H.M. Queen Elizabeth
July: Marriage to Althea Tickler
September: 'Operation Source', taken prisoner

1944
February: Award of Victoria Cross

1945
May: Returned home from Germany
June: Investiture of Victoria Cross, by H.M. George VI

1946
May: Birth of daughter, Andrea

1947
February: Appointed to HMS *Cardigan Bay*, Mediterranean Fleet

1948
October: Returned to England from HMS *Cardigan Bay*

1949
January: Death of mother, Anna Margaret Place
July: Commenced flying at Royal Naval Flying Club
August: To USA for training
September: Birth of son, Charles
December: Returned from USA

1950
January: Promoted Lieutenant Commander. Appointed to Staff of Flag Officer Air (Home), RNAS Lee-on-Solent

1951
May: Appointed to 23RN Course, RAF Syerston

1952
June: Promoted Commander
September: Appointed to 801 Squadron, HMS *Glory*, serves in Korean War

1953
February: Left 801 Squadron, return from Far East
April: Birth of daughter, Melanie
May: Appointed to Staff of Flag Officer Flying Training, RNAS Yeovilton

1955
July: Appointed in command HMS *Tumult*

1956
January: Appointed Executive Officer HMS *Theseus*
November: Suez, 'Operation Musketeer'

1957
February: Appointed in command HMS *Corunna*
May: Escort to HMY *Britannia* on State visit to Denmark

1958
January: Appointed to Joint Services command Course, Latimer
November: Appointed Chief Staff Officer, Flag Officer Aircraft Carriers, HMS *Eagle*.
December: Promoted Captain

1959
May: Transfer to HMS *Victorious*
July: Visit to USA

1960
February: Meets former Captain of *Tirpitz*
March: Transfer to HMS *Ark Royal*
April: Appointed to Admiralty, Deputy Director Naval Airwarfare

1961
April: Death of Commander Donald Cameron VC
August: Leaves Admiralty

1962
April: Appointed in command HMS *Yarmouth*
May: Transfer to HMS *Rothesay*

1963
October: Left HMS *Rothesay*
December: Appointed in command HMS *Ganges*

1965
October: Left HMS *Ganges*

1966
January: Appointed in command HMS *Albion* (at Hong Kong)

1967
June: Departed to West Africa, Nigerian Civil War
October: Withdrawal from Aden
December: Left HMS *Albion* at Singapore

1968
January: Promoted Rear Admiral
February: Assumes Admiral Commanding Reserves

1970
January: Appointed Commander of Bath
June: Retired from Royal Navy

1971
Assumed Chairmanship of VC & GC Association

1994
Retired as Chairman of VC & GC Association

27 December: Died at St Bartholomew's Hospital, London

1995
January: Funeral at Sherborne Abbey

Notes & Bibliography

Chapter 1

1. Cunningham A.B., *Sailor's Odyssey*, Hutchinson & Co, 1951
2. Greene J. & Massignani A., *The Black Prince and the Sea Devils. The Story of Valerio Borgese and the Elite Units of the Decima NAS*. Da Capio Press, 2004
3. Holloway A., *From Dartmouth to War*, Buckland Press Ltd, 1993
4. Ship's log HMS *Valiant*, December 1941. TNA ADM 53/115151
5. Ship's log HMS *Queen Elizabeth*, December 1941. TNA ADM 53/114911
6. Cunningham A.B., *Op. cit.*
7. Churchill W.S., *The Second World War*, Volume 4 , Cassell & Co Ltd, 1952

Chapter 2

1. Military records for C.G.M. Place. TNA WO339/11483
2. Nichols G.H.F., *The 18th Division in the Great War*, William Blackwood & Sons, 1922
3. *The Times*, 4 May 1916
4. Bramwell V., & Peck R.M., *All in the Bones: A Biography of Benjamin Waterhouse Hawkins*, The Academy of Natural Sciences of Philadelphia, 2008
5. Battalion Records for East Surrey Regiment, 1914–1919. http://qrrarchive.websds.net/menu3.aspx
6. *London Gazette*, 17 December 1917, p.13180
7. Treves F, *Uganda for a holiday*, E.P. Dutton & Co, 1910
8. *The Times*, 15 December 1931
9. *How to Become a Naval Officer and Life at the Royal Naval College, Dartmouth*, Gieves Ltd, 1937
10. Fetherston-Dilke C., Imperial War Museum, Sound Archive 19571
11. *How to Become A Naval Officer And Life At The Royal Naval College, Dartmouth, Op. cit.*
12. Mansfield G.E.D., Imperial War Museum, Sound Archive 14744
13. Holloway A., *Op. Cit.*
14. Harrold J., & Porter R., *Britannia Royal Naval College Dartmouth: An Illustrated History*, Richard Webb, 2005
15. Mansfield, G.E.D., Address at the funeral of Rear Admiral Godfrey Place, Sherborne Abbey, 2 January 1995
16. Kempson R., (Lady Redgrave), *A Family and Its Fortunes*, Gerald Duckworth & Co, 1986
17. Ship's log HMS *Iron Duke*, May 1937. TNA ADM53/104453
18. *The Times*, 30 July 1935

Chapter 3

1. Hayes J., *Face the Music*, Pentland Press Ltd, 1991
2. Ship's log HMS *Vindictive*, September 1938. TNA ADM53/106718

3. Examinations held in HMS *Vindictive*, Spring Cruise, March 1939. TNA ADM116/3962
4. Ship's log HMS *Newcastle*, May 1939. TNA ADM 53/109917
5. Ship's log HMS *Newcastle*, September 1939. TNA ADM 53/109921
6. Ship's log HMS *Newcastle*, November 1939. TNA ADM 53/109923
7. *Sinking of AMC Rawalpindi*. TNA ADM 1/19900
8. Ship's log HMS *Newcastle*, November 1940.TNA ADM 53/112890
9. Ship's log HMS *Newcastle*, December 1940.TNA ADM 53/112891
10. Somerville J.F., Despatch of Vice Admiral Sir James F Somerville KCB, DSO, Flag Officer Commanding Force H, *London Gazette* Supplement, 5 May 1948

Chapter 4
1. Churchill W.S., *The Second World War*, Volume 3, Cassell & Co Ltd, 1952
2. *The Times*, 21 January 1941
3. Patrol Report *ORP Sokol* March 1941–December 1944. TNA ADM 199/1854
4. Patrol Report *ORP Sokol, Op. cit.*
5. Wingate J., *The Fighting Tenth: The Tenth Submarine Flotilla and the Siege of Malta*, Leo Cooper, 1991
6. Simpson G.W.G., *Periscope View*, MacMillan, 1972.
7. Kryle-Pope S., *The Same Wife in Every Port*, The Memoir Club, 1998
8. Wingate J., *Op.cit.*
9. Karnicki B., *A Duffle Bag of Memories*, Marpress, Gdansk, Poland, 2001
10. Wingate J., *Op.cit.*
11. *Award of Cross of Valour*, November 1941–January 1942. TNA ADM 1/12328
12. Wingate J., *Op. cit.*
13. *Ibid.*
14. *History of ORP Sokol*, Sikorski Institute, London, MAR AV 28/7
15. Allen   P.R.H., *Wartime Correspondence,* Livadia Publishers Ltd, Auckland, New Zealand, 2007
16. Allaway J., *Hero of the Upholder,* Airlife Publishing Ltd, Shrewsbury, 1991
17. Jameson W.S., *Submariners VC*, Novello & Co, 1962
18. Simpson G.W.G., *Op. cit.*
19. Patrol Report HMS *Urge,* May 1941–July 1942. TNA ADM 236/50
20. Wingate J., *Op. cit.*
21. *Ibid.*
22. Simpson G.W.G., *Op. cit.*
23. Wingate J., *Op.cit.*
24. *Meeting of the War Cabinet,* 23 February, 1942. TNA: CAB/65/25/23
25. Wingate J., *Op.cit.*
26. Simpson G.W.G., *Op. cit.*
27. Patrol Report HMS *Unbeaten*, May 1941–April 1942. TNA ADM 236/43
28. Casemore J.R., Imperial War Museum Documents 04/2/1
29. Woods R., *Special Commando,* William Kimber, 1985
30. Simpson G.W.G., *Op. cit.*
31. War Diaries, Mediterranean and Home Fleet, 1942. TNA ADM 199/424
32. War Patrols in Mediterranean, HMS *Unbeaten*, March 1942. TNA ADM 1/14323

Chapter 5

1. Prime Minister's Office, Operational Correspondence and Papers. TNA PREM 3/191/1
2. Churchill W.S., *The Second World War*, Volume 4, Cassell & Co Ltd, 1952
3. *Ibid.*
4. Place B.C.G., Imperial War Museum Sound Archive 10431
5. Trials of Job 82. TNA ADM 179/213
6. Shean M., *Corvette and Submarine*, Max Shean, 1994
7. Gallagher T., *Against all Odds*, Macdonald & Co, 1971
8. Hezlet A.R., Imperial War Museum Sound Archive 12571
9. Lavery B., *Shield of Empire: The Royal Navy and Scotland*, Birlinn Ltd, Edinburgh, 2007
10. Maclagen I., 'Ships Bells', Transactions of the Buteshire Natural History Society, Volume XXVII, 2008
11. Alexander A.V., Correspondence to W.S. Churchill, 1942. TNA ADM 1/25845
12. Mitchell, P., *Tip of the Spear*, Richard Netherwood Ltd, 1993
13. Sinking and salvage of submarine X3, report by Commanding Officer HMS *Varbel*. TNA ADM 1/11758
14. Mitchell, P., *Op. cit.*
15. Barry C.B., Correspondence to J.S. Wilson, February 1943. TNA HS 2/206
16. Churchill W.S., *Op. cit.*
17. Fleming G., *Magennis VC*, History Ireland Ltd, 1998
18. Walker F., & Mellor P., *The Mystery of X5*, William Kimber & Co, 1988
19. Simulated attack by "X" craft on HMS *Bonaventure;* PBX4 trials, March 1943. TNA ADM 1/12929
20. HMS *Varbel*, formation of 12th Submarine Flotilla, February 1943. TNA ADM 1/12880
21. Place B.C.G., 'Off the Beaten Track, A Lecture for Cadets', Journal of Navigation 8:26-27, 1955
22. Shean M., *Op. cit.*
23. Hindmarsh R.X., *WW2 Peoples War, X-Craft diver 1943*, at: http://www.bbc.co.uk/ww2peopleswar/stories/41/a3945341.shtml
24. Winton J., *The Submariners: Life in British Submarines 1901-1999*, Constable, 1999
25. Barry C.B., Correspondence, July 1943. TNA HS 2/206
26. Ship's log HMS *Thrasher*, June 1943. TNA ADM 173/18226
27. Ship's log HMS *Malaya*, July 1943. TNA ADM 53/117882
28. Ship's log HMS *Bonaventure*, September 1943. TNA ADM 53/117081
29. Gallagher T., *Op. cit.*
30. Fell W.R., *The Sea our Shield*, Cassell & Co, 1966

Chapter 6

1. Jacobsen A.R., *X-Craft versus Tirpitz, Mystery of the Missing X5*, Sutton Publishing Ltd, Gloucestershire, 2006
2. Operation Source, Midget submarine attack on *Tirpitz*, 1943-45. TNA ADM 199/888. Final version published as Supplement to *London Gazette*, 10 February 1948
3. Fleming G., *Magennis VC*, History Ireland Ltd, 1998
4. *Ibid.*

5. Warren C.E.T. & Benson J., *Above Us the Waves*, Pen & Sword, 2006
6. Operation Source, Midget submarine attack on *Tirpitz*, 1943-45, *Op. cit.*
7. Winton J., *The Submariners, Life in British Submarines 1901-1999*, Constable, 1999
8. *Ibid.*
9. Shean, M., *Corvette and Submarine*. Max Shean, 1994
10. Place B.C.G., Imperial War Museum Sound Archive 10431
11. Mars A., *Submarines at War*, William Kimber & Co Ltd, 1971
12. Place B.C.G., *Op.cit.*
13. Aitken, R., *WW2 People's War, X-craft and Operation Source*, 2004, at: http://www.bbc.co.uk/ww2peopleswar/stories/77/a3237077.shtml
14. Gallagher T., *Against all Odds*, Macdonald & Co, 1971
15. Dabner E.C., Questionnaire on release from Prisoner of War. TNA WO 344/82/1
16. Obituary of R. Kendall, *The Times*, 9 February 2006
17. Bremecke, J., *The Tirpitz* (translated from German by Frederick Holt), Robert Hale Ltd, 1963
18. Aitken R, *Op. cit.*
19. Prime Minister's Office, Operational Correspondence and Papers. TNA PREM 3/191/1
20. Churchill W.S., *The Second World War*, Volume 5, Cassell & Co Ltd, 1952
21. Damage sustained by the German battleship *Tirpitz* during attack by midget submarines. TNA 1/16834
22. Prime Minister's Office, Operational Correspondence and Papers. TNA PREM 3/191/1

Chapter 7
1. Place B.C.G., Imperial War Museum Sound Archive 10431
2. Worsley J. & Giggal K., *John Worsley's War*, Airlife Publishing Ltd, 1993
3. Thomas G, *Milag-Captives of the Kriegsmarine*, The Milag Prisoner of War Association, 1995
4. Camp History of Marlag und Milag Nord. TNA WO 208/3270
5. Report by Captain G. F. Wilson RN on the RN prisoners at Sandbostel and Marlag und Milag Nord. 1945. TNA WO 224/101
6. James D., *A Prisoner's Progress*, Hills &Carter, 1954
7. Buckley P.N., Imperial War Museum Sound Archive 4759
8. Lambert G.R., Imperial War Museum Documents 476 90/19/1
9. Operation Source, Midget submarine attack on *Tirpitz*, 1943-45. TNA ADM 199/888
10. Prisoner of War Questionnaire, Lieutenant B.C.G. Place VC, DSC, RN, 28 April 1945. TNA WO 344/254/1
11. Prisoner of War Questionnaire, Lieutenant W.P. Mewes, RNVR, 3 May 1945. TNA WO 344/217/2
12. Escape of Lieutenant James RNVR from Germany. TNA ADM1/16847
13. Escape of Lieutenants Campbell and Kelleher from Marlag (O), March 1944. TNA ADM 1/16842
14. Operation Source, Midget submarine attack on *Tirpitz*, 1943-45. TNA ADM 199/888
15. Place B.C.G., in *Lost Voices of the Royal Navy*, (ed. M. Arthur), Hodder & Stoughton Ltd, 2005

16. Wilson G.F.W., Imperial War Museum Documents 4531
17. Letters to Prisoners of War in Malag, (with embedded messages). TNA WO 208/3501
18. Paterson K.G., 'Travels without a Donkey', Imperial War Museum Documents 7766
19. Wilson G.F.W., Imperial War Museum Documents 4531
20. Shooting of Flight Lieutenant C.L. Bryson, April 1945, Marlag. TNA WO 311/135
21. Worsley J. & Giggal K., *Op.cit.*
22. Report by Captain G. F. Wilson RN on the RN prisoners at Sandbostel and Marlag und Milag Nord,1945. TNA WO 224/101
23. Langley J.M., *Fight Another Day*, Magnum Books, 1980

Chapter 8
1. Morel P., 'Memories of Cardigan Bay, 1945-62', Imperial War Museum Document K10/577
2. Stewart N., *The Royal Navy and the Palestine Patrol*, Frank Cass, 2002
3. Report of proceedings on Mediterranean Station, 1945-1948. TNA ADM 116/5638
4. Interception of illegal immigrant ships *Pan York* and *Pan Crescent*. TNA ADM 1/20793
5. Morel P., *Op cit*
6. Ship's log HMS *Boxer*, January 1949.TNA ADM 53/125622
7. Future of Royal Naval Flying Club. TNA ADM 1/26235

Chapter 9
1. Operations Record Book, RAF Syerston, January 1951–February 1953. TNA AIR 29/2159
2. Ship's log HMS *Illustrious*, July 1952. TNA ADM 53/132636
3. Place B.C.G. in *HMS Glory*, Barrett P., Parapress Ltd, 1996
4. Thomas W.G., Imperial War Museum Documents 4032
5. Report of Proceedings of HMS *Glory*, 1951-1953. TNA ADM 116/5944
6. Lansdown J.R.P., *With the Carriers in Korea*, Crecy Publishing, 1997
7. Report of Proceedings of HMS *Glory*, 1951-1953, *Op. cit.*
8. Thomas W.G., *Op. cit.*
9. Ship's log HMS *Glory*, November 1952. TNA ADM 53/132579
10. McCart N., *HMS Glory 1945-1961*, Maritime Books, Cornwall, 1992
11. Report of Proceedings of HMS *Glory*, January 1953. TNA ADM 116/5946
12. Thomas G., *Furies and Fireflies over Korea. The Story of the Men of the Fleet Air Arm, RAF and Commonwealth who Defended South Korea, 1950-1953*, Biddles Ltd, Kings Lynn, 2004
13. Ship's log HMS *Glory*, January 1953. TNA ADM 53/135290
14. Ship's log HMS *Illustrious*, March 1954. TNA ADM 53/138420

Chapter 10
1. Ship's log HMS *Tumult*, July 1955. TNA ADM 53/142534
2. Izzard B., *Gamp VC*, Haynes Publishing, 2009
3. The Victoria Cross Centenary Exhibition, 1856-1956. TNA PREM 11/1590
4. Ship's log HMS *Theseus*, June 1956. TNA ADM 53/145353
5. Swainson A., *Smelling of Roses*, GB Publications Ltd, 2000
6. Ship's log HMS *Theseus*, July 1956.TNA ADM 53/145354

7. Sayer G.B., Imperial War Museum Documents 11510
8. *Ibid.*
9. *Ibid.*
10. Ship's log HMS *Theseus,* November 1956. TNA ADM 53/145358
11. Ship's log HMS *Corunna,* February 1957. TNA ADM 53/146336
12. Hill J.R., *Lewin of Greenwich*, Cassell & Co, 2000
13. *Ibid.*

Chapter 11

1. Fetherston-Dilke C., Imperial War Museum Sound Archive 19571
2. Ship's log HMS *Eagle,* December 1958. TNA ADM 53/149086
3. Pakenham W., *Sometimes at Sea*, Better Book Co, Chichester, 2007
4. *Ibid.*
5. *The Times*, 14 April 1959
6. Ship's log HMS *Eagle,* April 1959. TNA ADM 53/151390
7. Ship's log HMS *Victorious,* July 1959. TNA ADM 53/152540
8. Ship's log HMS *Victorious,* January 1960. TNA ADM 53/154686
9. Ship's log HMS *Victorious,* February 1960. TNA ADM 53/154687
10. Ship's log HMS *Ark Royal,* April 1960. TNA ADM 53/152819
11. Smyth J., *The Story of The Victoria Cross 1856-63*, Fredrick Muller Ltd
12. Operations Record Book RAF Linton-on-Ouse,1961-1964. TNA AIR 29/3498

Chapter 12

1. Ship's log HMS *Yarmouth,* April 1962. TNA ADM 53/159126
2. Ship's log HMS *Rothesay,* May 1962. TNA ADM 53/158587
3. Ship's log HMS *Rothesay,* November 1962. TNA ADM 53/158593
4. Ship's log HMS *Rothesay,* December 1962. TNA ADM 53/158594
5. *The Times*, 19 February 1963
6. *Herald Express (*Brixham*)*, 12 September 1963
7. Gibson D.F.E.C., *Haut Taut and Belay: Memoirs of a Flying Sailor*, Spellmount Ltd, Tunbridge Wells,1992

Chapter 13

1. Douglas J., *HMS Ganges, Tales of the Trogs*, Second City Publishers, Cornwall, 1995
2. Purchase of Erwarton Hall for Captain, HMS *Ganges.* TNA ADM 1/29342

Chapter 14

1. McCart N., *HMS Albion 1944-1973: The Old Grey Ghost*, Amadeus Press Ltd, Huddersfield, 1995
2. Ship's log HMS *Albion,* January 1966. TNA ADM 53/165007
3. Ship's log HMS *Albion,* April 1967. TNA ADM 53/166828
4. *Liverpool Echo*, 6 May 1967
5. Prime Minister's Office; Nigeria, Situation in Nigeria 1966-1967. TNA PREM 13/1661
6. Ship's log HMS *Albion,* May 1967. TNA ADM 53/166829
7. Ship's log HMS *Albion,* June 1967. TNA ADM 53/166830
8. Nigeria, emergency planning on evacuation of mission. TNA FCO 38/274
9. *Navy News*, August 1967

10. *The Times* ,17 October 1967
11. Treves F, *Uganda for a holiday*, E.P. Dutton & Co, New York, 1910
12. Aden; Naval Task Force 1967. FCO 46/64.
13. Mitchell C.C., *Having Been a Soldier*, Mayflower, 1970
14. Aden: Participation of Task Force 318 in withdrawal operations 1967-1968. TNA DEFE 24/296
15. *Ibid.*
16. Ashmore E. & Grove E., *The Battle and the Breeze*, Sutton Publishing Ltd, Gloucestershire, 1997
17. Ship's log HMS *Fearless*, November 1967. TNA ADM 53/167430
18. Ship's log HMS *Albion*, November 1967. TNA ADM 53/166835
19. Ministry of Defence, Chiefs of Staff committee, Aden October 1967. TNA DEFE 11/535
20. Aden: Participation of Task Force 318 in withdrawal operations 1967-1968. *Op. cit.*
21. Ship's log, HMS *Albion*, November 1967. *Op. cit.*
22. Aden: Participation of Task Force 318 in withdrawal operations 1967-1968. *Op. cit.*
23. Ship's log HMS *Albion* December 1967. TNA ADM 53/166836
24. *Ibid.*
25. HMS *Albion* Commission Book, 1967-68

Chapter 16
1. *The Times*, 4 February 1975
2. Place G., 'Third Report of Lay Observer to Law Society, to the Lord Chancellor', 7 March 1978
3. *The Hunt for X5*, Undersea Productions, Wexford Films Ltd, Poole UK, 1976
4. Walker, F., & Mellor, P., *The Mystery of X5*, William Kimber & Co, 1988
5. Operation Source, Midget submarine attack on *Tirpitz*, 1943-45. TNA ADM 199/888
6. Smyth J., *The Story of the George Cross*, Trinity Press, 1962
7. Place B.C.G., Letter to Commander R.B. de M. Leather, Commander, Royal Naval Barracks, Portsmouth, 8 December 1966. Imperial War Museum Document 2875
8. Percival J., *For Valour*, James Methuen, 1985
9. *The Times*, 4 May 1973
10. *The Times*, 5 December 1975
11. *The Times*, 8 July 1982
12. Place B.C.G., Imperial War Museum Sound Archive 10431
13. Mansfield G.E.D., Address at the funeral of Rear Admiral Godfrey Place VC, CB, CVO, DSC, Sherborne Abbey, 2 January, 1995

Index